William "Whistler" Monk invites you to ride on his shoulders, reading his thoughts, simply by turning the pages of *Whistler's Way … A Thru-Hiker's Adventure on the Pacific Crest Trail*. This is Monk's second long trail book. The first chronicled his 2017 eastern adventure, *Whistler's Walk: the Appalachian Trail in 142 Days*. In *Whistler's Way*, Monk ran headlong into a big snow year on the PCT. So many hikers "flipped, skipping the Sierra Nevada, re-starting further north, with the hope to return later to John Muir's "Range of Light." Monk, too, made that hard decision, testing his philosophy: "I've never had a bad day in my life." That philosophy was sorely tested again on the slopes of Mt. Jefferson when he careened down an icy bank, breaking ribs. Still, 37 days later, Monk was back on trail. That this book exists at all is the result of Monk's promise made to himself; "[A]s difficult as it was, I committed to myself that I would never miss a day of writing in my journal." Monk's trail companion of over 2,000 miles reported in the Foreword that Monk was "excited and giddy" whenever he stopped to jot journal notes. *Whistler's Way* certainly covers the trail sights and stunning landscapes, but Monk makes sure to focus on what was most important to him–the people, repeatedly the people, how good-spirited and kind Monk found them as he thru-hiked the Pacific Crest Trail. Just as for Monk, readers of *Whistler's Way* may find their faith in people renewed and restored.

— Barney "Scout" Mann, author of *Journeys North*

WHISTLER'S WAY

WHISTLER'S WAY

A THRU-HIKERS ADVENTURE
ON THE PACIFIC CREST TRAIL

WILLIAM MONK

PUBLISHING

Charleston, SC

Whistler's Way
Copyright © 2020 by William Monk
All rights reserved

First Edition

Printed in the United States

ISBN-13: 978-1-952019-02-9
ISBN-10: 1-952019-02-8

THWUP-THWUP-THWUP-THWUP...

How did I ever become "That guy?" That guy who'd been laid out on the trail on his back for over twelve hours, and now looking skyward at the hovering Air National Guard Blackhawk helicopter preparing for his rescue. As the medic repelled down to check my vitals and current physical condition, I found myself in complete disbelief that there were people moving heaven and earth to aid this crazy hiker who took just one misstep.

Was this it?

Was my PCT thru-hike over?

Contents

A Foreword by Scooby

I first met Bill Monk, aka Whistler, in early May of 2017, just outside Waynesboro, Virginia. Our shared dream was to complete a thru-hike of the Appalachian Trail, and at that point we were both about 850 miles into the 2,200-mile attempt. I was sitting on the edge of a bridge on an isolated forest road having my second breakfast when Whistler came along the trail, introduced himself, and sat down next to me. We ended up completing our thru-hike of the Appalachian Trail together, ascending Mt. Katahdin on July 24th, 2017. Bill wrote a book about that adventure titled *Whistler's Walk: the Appalachian Trail in 142 Days*.

You learn a lot about a person spending 24/7 with them for almost three months. I often think about Whistler's response when passing fellow hikers. The usual question was, "How are you doing?" My own usual response was, "Fine." Whistler's response, however, was always, "I've never had a bad day in my life." Completing a thru-hike takes great physical effort, and many a thru-hike is ended because of injury. But far more are ended from mental exhaustion. It takes a positive attitude and a real commitment to completing the goal, to endure all that time away from family and the comforts of home. Whistler's positive outlook on life helped get me through many tough stretches along the trail.

So, when Whistler called me in the spring of 2018, asking whether I would join him on his attempt to thru-hike the Pacific Crest Trail in 2019, I said, "Sure!"

The PCT is a great American asset, and indescribably beautiful. The only way to really feel its beauty is to hike the trail. But the next best thing is to read as much about it as you can. Whistler wrote constantly while hiking the trail, posting entries daily to the blog site trailjournals.com. It was fun to watch him get excited or even absolutely giddy when stopping to jot a note down on something interesting we'd encountered along the trail. I often wondered why most of his inspirational thoughts occurred while hiking *up* mountains and never on the way *down*.

Whistler is committed to his readers. He knows most will never get the opportunity to experience a thru-hike, and he wants his descriptions of the trail to be inspirational even to them. I believe his AT blog had around 200,000 regular readers, and nearly the same for the PCT. I would be exhausted and collapsed in my tent after a long day's hike, committed to examining the backs of my eyelids. But after setting up camp, Whistler would nearly always be writing his daily blog post, and next morning he would be hunting for a spot along the trail with cell phone reception until he could upload the blog. Technology follows us in today's world, and some don't like it in the wilderness, feeling it's a distraction. I always thought it amazing that you could be on top of a mountain in the middle of the Sierras and be speaking with a family member in Germany or New Zealand.

Everyone deserves to be passionate about something. Whistler and I have both been fortunate to have lasting marriages, wonderful children, and successful careers. It has been my pleasure to share the passion for long-distance hiking with Whistler. I am writing this foreword during the height of the Corona-19 virus pandemic in the United States. People from around the world are drawn to hike the PCT, but have had to give up or postpone their dream of completing a thru-hike in 2020. I hope they can adjust their plans and maintain their passion for the trail.

Having picked up this book, you no doubt want to learn more about the Pacific Crest Trail, and may even be thinking about hiking all or part of it. I can't give away the stories in the book—not my job. I won't even tell you if Whistler finishes or not. Okay, fine, he finishes, and I don't. I will, however, provide a little foreshadowing. At least at one point in this book you will say to yourself, "Wow...*that* must have been a bad day." Knowing Whistler as I do, I can assure you that he would look you in the eye and tell you, "I have never had a bad day in my life."

Read on, fellow adventurers. You will thoroughly enjoy *Whistler's Way* by Bill Monk.

Mark "Scooby" Skouby
Spring 2020

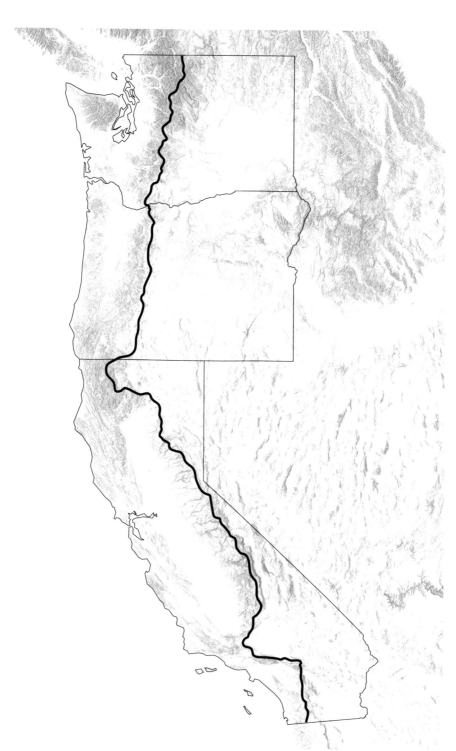

Image provided by: Pacific Crest Trail Association

Introduction

I wouldn't refer to it as a calling. No, it was more like a tug. How does one go from a successful thru-hike on the Appalachian Trail in 2017, convinced that one wasn't really interested in hiking another long trail, to where I found myself now, preparing for a thru-hike of the Pacific Crest Trail?

To step back for a moment, I once said the following words, "No, I don't think I would hike another long trail—been there, done that." Was it the hurt and pain I had experienced during and after that 2,189-mile hike, along with a highly emotional summit of Mt. Katahdin on those final days of my hike, that had me utter the words I would later enthusiastically take back? I honestly can't answer that question.

I do know there had not been a single day since my July 24th, 2017 summit that I had not thought about my thru-hike of the Appalachian Trail. I also know that I continuously found the need to stop myself from talking about my hike with perfect strangers who politely nodded as they casually stepped away from me. Sure, my friends and family listened with what appeared to be genuine interest, but of course, they loved me.

It was just a few months after I returned home from being away on that 142 day "walk" that I started to feel that all consuming tug of the trail. But I also started feeling a high level of guilt. Not guilt for considering leaving behind my wife of 39 years for up to six months. No, Annie is too giving and kind to allow for that. Instead, it was almost like a betrayal of my first love—a betrayal of the AT. Annie put an immediate end to those thoughts when she compared my feelings to those of a mother. Her words of wisdom reverberated within me and gave me permission. She told me, "A mother can love all her children equally while also loving them differently."

I had permission to hike another day.

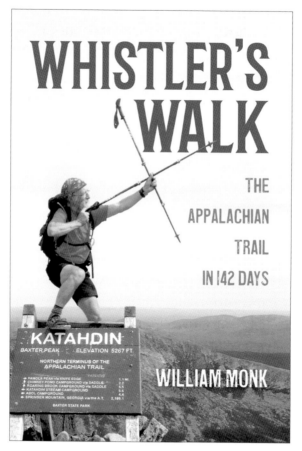

The cover of my first book

So, I once again found myself sitting at a keyboard making an honest attempt to capture and express that need within to hike another day. I'd utilized Trailjournals.com for my AT hike, with the intended purpose of sharing my experience with friends and family. Little did I know that my journal on that public forum would garner well over 200,000 hits, along with a hugely positive response and high moral support from perfect strangers. Their following of my 2017 AT journal prompted my publishing *Whistler's Walk: the Appalachian Trail in 142 Days*, which has enjoyed success beyond my wildest expectations. To write another book was not necessarily my intent. It wasn't until I had hiked several hundred miles through the desert of southern California that I realized there was content there. I had another story to tell, I just didn't know how that story would develop. But it soon became apparent as the story revealed itself—the story of a 2,650 mile thru-hike on the Pacific Crest Trail.

This, then, is the story of my journey.

SECTION ONE

PRE-HIKE

"A journey of a thousand miles begins with a single step".

The old Chinese proverb seems so literally perfect and appropriate for me. Of course, this journey is a bit longer than a thousand miles, but fitting just the same.

The crucial first step for me was applying for my PCT hiking permit. The process the Pacific Crest Trail Association—the PCTA—has in place was a bit nerve-racking for me, and I'm certain also for all those who found themselves in the same position. After hiking the Appalachian Trail the year before where all I had to do was show up, this PCT permit process was a major hurdle.

November 14th, 10:30 a.m. PST was when the permit process opened up, which was actually 1:30 p.m. EST, because my wife and I were travelling south for the holidays. There I was in our motor home at the KOA campground at Natural Bridge, Virginia, waiting for 10:30 a.m. with fingers crossed that the Wi-Fi at the campground wouldn't fail. I had my command post set up, while at the same time communicating with Scooby, who was at his home in Cleveland, Ohio, at the ready to simultaneously apply for his permit.

Scooby and I met while hiking the Appalachian Trail the year before. It was a fateful meeting and the start of a friendship that will likely last a lifetime. How could it not? We shared too many experiences for the bond not to have us permanently connected. While on my thru-hike in 2017, I found I was in need of a break from the trail due to a serious medical issue with my feet. I'd been off the trail for eight days to heal, and on my very first day back I met this guy when I was crossing a dirt road. He was sitting on a stone wall eating a bag of chocolate doughnuts. Enter Scooby.

This chance meeting took place at mile 669, just after I had entered the Shenandoah National Park. Scooby and I then leapfrogged for the next two days, at which time we realized that we were starting and ending at the same places. We decided that we would hike out together, and as it happened, we hiked the next 1,300-plus miles together and had the absolute pleasure of sharing our Mt. Katahdin summit on July 24th.

Scooby and I missed Trail Days that year as we were too far north to consider heading back south for the iconic and much-coveted trail celebration. We instead committed to each other that we would attend the following year as class of 2017 alumni. I had already started making plans for a 2019 PCT hike prior to our meeting at Trail Days, and that was when I started working on my good friend to join me. Well, I got him to agree to start with me, but not a firm commitment for a complete thru-hike.

At that point, I began to diligently work at my negotiation skills to see how I might convince him to stay on the trail with me for our next grand adventure. We had selected April 9th as our planned start date, and now all we had to do was wait in the virtual queue that would randomly allow us to enter the online permit room to apply. The random number assigned to me was 1,565, which meant that there were 1,564 people ahead of me. Scooby was number 1,377 which would allow him to view the dates available before me and thus pass on that information. Naturally, the allotted permits for April 9th were gone by the time my number came up. Not to worry though, because April 11th was still available. It was a timely reminder that a thru-hiker must be flexible.

The next step on the journey? Wait about three weeks to see if our applications are approved.

Imagine my elation when I opened the email from the PCTA and found that my permit application had been approved. The following statement in the email put a huge smile on my face. "It looks great! Your trip is scheduled." Well, Merry Christmas to me! Scooby received his email the day after I received mine, and our actual permits would be issued starting January 16.

Happy New Year, Whistler!

I'd taken the trail name "Whistler" when I hiked the AT, and it has become synonymous with friends, family, neighbors, and followers of my journal and book. Hikers are known to, and somewhat expected to take a trail name. It's generally a fitting name—I whistle a lot—and the name you will be known by as you hike. After all, you aren't the same person on the trail as you are in the life you knew prior to being on the trail. A hiker's identity and how they identify is completely different from everyday life, and their name should be, too.

Planning the logistics of how to get to San Diego with my backpack and gear in tow was to be the next step. My wife and I had already booked a cabin in the North Carolina mountains in late March for ourselves, our two sons, and their families. We would spend three precious days together as a way of seeing me off on my next adventure. From there, we would drive down to see my sister and brother-in-law in Mississippi, and from there I would fly out to San Diego.

Prior to planning on flying, I had come up with a full array of possible travel plans. First, I thought, wouldn't it be neat to take a train? I researched this and quickly changed my mind once I saw how long it would take, and found that the price was prohibitive. My next idea involved driving with my wife in our motor home. Again, the time, the cost, and my wife not liking the idea of having to drive the motor home back by herself nixed that idea. Then I thought I would rent a car one way. Again, the cost was ridiculous. So, just for the heck of it I checked on flights, and found that it was stupidly inexpensive. Ninety-two dollars for a one-way ticket was far less than I had ever expected. I jumped all over that ticket as soon as I could get my credit card out of my wallet, and before Priceline realized their mistake and increased the price.

What ended up being all-consuming was the reading and planning. I read pretty much every book I could lay my hands on, with the objective of gleaning tidbits of information that I might one day pull from my arsenal or little bag of tricks. While reading I would pick up that a hiker did this, that, or another thing, that might later be of use to me once I found myself in the same predicament as they had.

To expound a bit, I had found myself in the unique position of watching the calendar and ticking off the days to my start date at the excruciatingly, mind-numbingly slowest rate imaginable. Had there been additional hours added to each day leading to my hike, unbeknownst to me? I'd started to believe that daylight savings time was actually sneaking in additional hours along with that annoying time change. Slowly the hours crawled by and the endless days passed like tortoise years.

So, what to do while time basically stood still? Read, and read some more. Read book after book about someone *else* and *their* thru-hike. With my head on my pillow I found myself swiping my finger across the screen of my Kindle as quickly as I could while my face was aglow from the screen's backlight. Was I really trying to gain knowledge, or was I just vicariously hiking along with them...? Reading the trail journals of those who had blazed this trail before me had become increasingly prevalent in my daily routine, and was truly one of my guilty pleasures.

To change things up a bit, I researched equipment. I'd read reviews on the latest and greatest equipment choices until my head was ready to explode. I remember once actually pulling out my sun-brella and showing it to my son Richard. He held it for a moment, handed it back to me, and with a serious look of concern asked if I was going to be the only person hiking with an umbrella. Admittedly, if anyone had told me that one day I would be hiking through the desert looking like Mary Poppins carrying an umbrella, I too would have had a dazed and confused look on my face, just like Richard.

My response was, "No Richard, most people use an umbrella while hiking through the heat of the desert. At least that's what my research tells me."

As this hike slowly became a reality, I internalized the burning question that I knew must be answered. Where does the desire come from to walk away and abandon the comfortable life I loved so much? Why would anyone think it was a good idea to pack meagre supplies in a backpack, throw it on their back, and walk away from life as they knew it? I was happy and I felt completely fulfilled; but, was I really? I did at times ask myself what my purpose in life was. Doesn't everyone? It was easy to answer that question when I'd worked at a high-pressure job that kept me running and at the top of my game. I'd worked stupid hours, was highly successful, and compensated fairly for my efforts. I'd woken up each morning knowing what my purpose in life was. My heart pounding with excitement and the adrenaline that rushed through my veins was what drove me and gave me purpose. Providing for my family and watching my two sons prepare for their own lives was all the motivation I'd needed to drive me through a successful career.

But then I had an awakening. I lost my sister just before her fiftieth birthday. After a long and admirable fight, Joanne lost her battle with breast cancer. I remember thinking, how long can I do this and when is enough, enough? I could continue working, which translated into fighting the good fight, being in that daily grind, until it robbed me of what life I had left. Or I could retire and add years to my life. That choice, my friends, was easy.

But then what? I remember someone once asked me what I'd done prior to retirement, and I recall responding, "I used to be important." Really? Is that what happens to people once they retire?

There had to be something else for me. I still needed a purpose!

Thru-hiking the Appalachian Trail in 2017 served as another awakening. It changed me, and I discovered something—I discovered that I like people. Sounds a bit crazy but it's true. I found what makes people good, kind, and compassionate. I found that I enjoy hiking with today's youth, and that they enjoy hiking with me. I found that on the trail, we are all truly equal. We each have the same goal—or purpose—with a definitive target in our sights. We know where we come from, and we know where we must go in order to discover the enlightenment we each seek as we complete the task at hand. We know it's not easy, and in fact it is difficult—as it should be. After all, if it were easy, everyone would do it.

So, will this unquenchable quest for personal fulfilment ever be achieved? Can a person ever be satisfied with who they are, or where they are in life? I could not begin to answer that question, but what I did know was that I needed to try to walk there to find out. Perhaps you know the song sung by Doris Day. The fourth verse says it all.

Never thought my heart could be so yearny, why did I decide to roam? Gotta take that sentimental journey, sentimental journey home.

I am pretty sure I am able to speak for those who, like me, have a good number of decades behind us, in that I started contemplating all those sentimental miles travelled. No, I'm not talking about physical miles. I'm talking about time.

It's normal, I'm told, to have these melancholy thoughts as a new year makes its approach. I've always been an old soul with sentimental tendencies, but at nearly 60 years of age, I believed I was starting to tip the scale toward mushy. I found that I spent a healthy amount of time thinking about my blessings. My family is first and paramount on that very long list of God's given blessings for which I am so grateful. It might just be me, but I sometimes get these thoughts in my head with regard to my visions, and the expectations that I need to play out according to my visions.

I had one of these thoughts recently, where I wanted to spend some time with my two sons. Nothing too serious, just to be able to head out to a local brew pub and enjoy a beer or two with them. Why such a big deal? Right? I don't know why...it just was. At that particular time, I was just 103 days away from the start of my hike and thoughts of family were swirling around in my head. I'd be leaving my wife for another extended "leave of absence" like when I thru-hiked the Appalachian Trail. Some of us—myself included—leave our families, spouse, and loved ones behind who must then take on what amounts to an unfair burden. This selfless acceptance of who we are and what we do to fulfil our selfish need to hike is unfathomable. That scale is definitely out of balance. I know it, and you do, too. Yet, those who love us don't judge us, and they definitely would never make us feel guilty. We do that all on our own. Still, we lace up our hiking shoes, throw on our packs, and we walk away.

As the new year approached, I committed to being forever cognisant and appreciative of my many blessings as I took my sentimental journey home.

As those months slowly ticked off, I remembered looking at the calendar and realizing that I was just 91 days from my start date of April 11th, and my head started spinning. I had so much to do at home before I took those first steps...but I admitted to myself that I was just not feeling any of it.

This was the time of year Annie and I would take on winter projects at our Nova Scotia bed and breakfast. I had a relatively long list of things I knew had to get done, but my mind and spirit were just not cooperating. I was way too busy thinking about what lay ahead on the trail to be bothered with being a responsible person right now. Here was the real kicker—I have always been a responsible person. It was not like me to be unable to focus on the here and now.

That same day I suggested to Annie that we should walk into town for coffee. It was beautiful outside with a light dusting of snow covering the entire landscape, which made it the perfect day for a walk. While crossing over the river causeway, we saw a group of people protesting Nova Scotia Power's tidal generation facility. This group was carrying large signs letting those driving past know their feelings about the fish that were being killed through the use of the tidal power turbines. I appreciated that they felt so passionately about their cause, their purpose, but I walked on toward my coffee reward that awaited me.

While at the coffee shop, I ran into the editor of our small local newspaper. Larry was in town to get the scoop on the protesters, and had stopped in for coffee. I asked him if he'd gotten his story. I guess my question opened the door to some of his deep, innermost thoughts. Larry shared a story about a time he sat down to interview an indigenous elder in the small local village of Bear River. This elder held his people's belief that the only thing separating us humans from the animals of the earth are our tears and our ability to communicate. We humans cry sad tears when we witness an injustice and we cry happy tears when we witness something beautiful. We have the ability to speak up for those who cannot speak for themselves—which was precisely what those picketers were doing.

Now, you may ask what could this possibly have to do with hiking the PCT? I guess what I'm saying is we all need to, or at least probably should, pick a cause or have a purpose.

I'm not a preachy person, but I have always believed in the importance of service and of giving back, especially if you take. My conversation with Larry quickly reminded me that I had not yet made a donation to the Pacific Crest Trail Association, and now was the time I needed to give back for that which I would soon be taking. After all, I knew I'd soon be crying happy tears for all that is beautiful.

How does one train for a 2,650-mile hike, and how would that training differ from the training I did for the Appalachian Trail? Those were pretty much the first questions asked of me by friends and family when they found out I was planning on hiking the Pacific Crest Trail. The PCT starts with gradual ascents compared to the AT's immediate and relentless climbs, which might lead one to rethink a training approach. Yes, it's true, these iconic trails are two entirely different animals, but much of my training would remain pretty much the same. What the two trails do have in common is distance, and that was why my training remained the same. Lower body strengthening, including feet, ankles, knees, and legs was paramount.

While training for the AT, I started my serious training a couple of months prior to my start date. With my pack loaded and on my back, I did hundreds and hundreds of ascents and descents of flights of stairs. Long hikes and snowshoe treks outside when the Nova Scotia winters allowed were also part of my regimen. One thing my thru-hike of the AT did teach me was that your body will take what it needs in the way of nutrition. Burning between 5,000 and 6,000 calories each day is impossible to replace while hiking. That being said, it was shocking for me to see how strong my legs became while at the same time having lost so much of my upper body muscle. My body had pretty much decided it needed all that nutrition for my legs to help me climb all those mountains. So much so, that when I looked at myself in a mirror, I saw the chest of an adolescent and not that of a grown man.

With this experience and knowledge, upper body strengthening also became a major part of my training for the PCT. Now, if all this could assure a successful thru-hike, I would be pleased with my physical preparation. The problems come with all of the variables and unknowns that are completely out of a thru-hiker's control. With this understanding and acceptance, my training plan included all that I could manage, and that which I could control.

So, I was able to control my start date by getting a permit to start on April 11th. I was able to control my training, my choices regarding equipment and mail drops. I was also able to control and manage my transportation to California with a plane ticket already in hand. What I was not able to control was the record amounts of snowfall the Sierra Nevada was experiencing.

Keeping up with the snowfall and snow pack along the entire PCT had become a regrettable and depressing bi-weekly task. As of February 19th, the snowfall from Kennedy Meadows to Echo Lake was at 180%, or what the snow reports described as well above average. The generally recommended entry date into the Sierras is typically June 15th, but it was now recommended to be closer to June 25th. What to do, what to do, what to do?

There was nothing to do! Nothing to do but wait and see what the rest of the winter had up its figurative sleeve. No one could control the weather. It would be whatever it would be. For all I knew, a heat wave could hit the west coast and take this concern completely out of the equation. The good news was, there would be plenty of water for the hiking class of 2019.

The 2019 class of PCT hikers now had their permits with designated start dates. Some hikers had selected better than I did, with what in hindsight would prove to be comparatively ideal start dates. But none of that was relevant, because it truly was out of my control. Instead, I would dutifully take my first step, followed by the next, and then the next, on April 11th. With God's help, and if it was His will, I would reach the Sierras healthy and prepared to make the best decision on how to safely move forward.

The average person has a stride of 2.3 feet. That equates to about 2,296 steps per mile. Multiply 2,296 steps per mile times the 2,650 miles of the PCT and you would have taken more than six million steps on that trek. But those steps we take are seldom taken alone. It's our physical and literal steps that start us on that trek, but it's the support from family, neighbors, friends, and most certainly a spouse that provides the steam for driving us forward. Attempting to explain the concept of living out in the wild for five to six months can be as daunting as the actual challenge of a thru-hike.

"You're going to do *what*?"

"*How* many miles?"

"You'll be gone for *how* long?"

"Are you *crazy*?"

Those who are closest to us get it, and they not only support us, but they support us unconditionally. Blessed are those who receive the support of a spouse to take on the monumental challenge of a 2,650-mile hike. I know no other way to describe it other than to say, I know I am ridiculously blessed to be married to one of the most selfless people on the planet, while at the same time knowing that I must be one of the most selfish people on that very same planet.

While hiking the Appalachian Trail in 2017, Annie found a certain level of comfort in following my footsteps by tracking my forward progress on a wall map of the AT. I journaled every day while on the Appalachian Trail, and was able to speak with her on almost a daily basis, thanks to Verizon and their almost perfect coverage of the Appalachians. Annie would plot my northerly migration, which she said allowed her to remain engaged and an integral part of my quest. Those weekly plottings, which appeared as small gains of inches on a map, would eventually translate to huge gains of miles in reality. That map, and now a new map representing the Pacific Crest Trail which I ordered from the PCTA, hung on the wall of the stairwell to our bedroom suite. This new map told of a future story, but not the whole story, which is aligned with the topography of the 2,650-mile journey, with a starting point and an ending point, but it doesn't give the "how to" points. It was basically a blank page, a story without substance, a story requiring abundant filling in of the countless gaps.

That said, the names of towns and geographical locations were almost as familiar to Annie as they were to me, as we had both spent countless hours watching documentaries about the PCT on YouTube together. What my story would end up being was unknown, but this much I did know—those steps we take are seldom taken alone.

The last few weeks before the start of my thru-hike passed at sonic speed. It had once seemed as though time was at a crawl, but now it was speeding by. I was at that place in time when I knew I had to say goodbye to dear friends, neighbors, and of course, family.

I recall a day where I found myself in our front room staring at a roaring fire in the wood stove. The flames licked and struck at an invisible target while my mind was transfixed, and I realized that I was absent. I wasn't actually even there—I might as well have been on another planet. I tried to read a book, but why did I even bother? There was zero comprehension of the simple text, and I found myself rereading the same sentences over and over again. Earlier that same day, Annie and I had listened to some old 70's music which eventually had us hugging one another. We both cried as we held each other in that tight, never-let-me-go embrace. Old familiar music that had always been fun and uplifting, on that day was extremely nostalgic and difficult to listen to, reminders of our youth, growing up, and our growing old together. We were just a week from leaving for our trip south to spend time with family before my big send-off...and more goodbyes.

It was at times like that I had to force myself to remember why I was doing this. Why I had decided to leave my wife of 39 years for a five to six-month, 2,650-mile hike. I questioned myself as to why I had volunteered to abandon my wonderful life. Why had I made this choice? It wasn't because of second thoughts or a desire to back away from that choice—no, it was simply a part of the required process of mentally preparing for what lay ahead.

I had trained for this, I was physically strong and prepared, but it was time to get into the required head space for what awaited me. My immediate future included a journey few get to experience, an opportunity afforded to few, and certainly abundant blessings. I knew this because I know I am truly blessed.

Spending time with family prior to starting a long trail journey had become a welcome tradition. It was just two years earlier that Annie had planned a weekend retreat at a cabin close to Amicalola Falls and Springer Mountain with our family to help see me off on my AT thru-hike. In similar fashion, Annie arranged a beautiful and secluded cabin at Lake Lure in the North Carolina mountains for my PCT send-off.

Annie and I started our southern migration from Nova Scotia and took our time as we meandered along, seeing some beautiful sights and mostly enjoying our time together. We eventually made our way to the agreed-upon rendezvous where we, our two sons, and their families descended on the cabin in the woods for a quiet and peaceful respite. Six adults and four very special grandchildren, a beautiful mountain setting, great food, and amazing memories—again, a true blessing. And why not throw in a huge hot tub with some quiet serenity for good measure? The walk down to a mountain creek, exploration of the Lake Lure Flowering Bridge, time at the community playground, a picnic lunch, and a huge family dinner made for a full and memorable week-end. It had been terrific to spend this precious and truly peaceful time together, and I am forever grateful for how everyone coordinated and planned to make it happen.

The Grandchildren

Unfortunately, as always, time slipped away and so did our time together. The kids all headed back to South Carolina while Annie and I made our way south to Florida, to see Annie's mother for a quick visit and another goodbye. From there it was on to Mississippi where we would visit my sister Susan and brother-in-law Top.

Let's not call what I am about to share "paranoia", let's call it what I like to describe as a healthy abundance of caution. I found that I was starting to approach everything I did with thoughtful consider-ation...as opposed to my previous pervasive reputation as a guy who jumps in with both feet. Imagine that! I now found myself planning tasks and considering consequences for what might and might not go wrong based on lack of planning. Some would call it wisdom; I pre-ferred to regard it as simply being tired of self-induced physical harm.

This newfound approach toward self preservation had been heightened with the knowledge that I'd planned for this thru-hike for a very long time, and the very last thing I needed was to injure myself before I even started.

For example, while visiting my sister Susan and her husband Top on their 30-acre hobby farm, I wanted to assist with some of the daily chores. Allow me to preface this with what might be an obvious observation to most—farms are ridiculously dangerous. I'm a relatively handy guy, and generally approach tasks with a high level of energy and prideful vigor. While helping Top swap out a tractor tiller for a bush hog I found myself taking digit—finger—inventory, watching to keep stupidly heavy equipment from crushing my piggies—toes—and cautiously observing the very real danger of my melon—head—getting whacked off my shoulders.

This newfound wisdom could, and likely was, based on the fact that I'd invested a lot of time, training, and capital into this venture, and I was not about to allow an act of careless foolishness to interfere with bringing my master plan to fruition. Sure, hiking 2,650 miles from Southern California to Canada is in itself a dangerous undertaking, and I certainly accept that, but getting to the trailhead in one piece is a requirement before I could even take that first northbound step. Then, and only then, would I throw caution to the wind. After all, a tiger really can't change his stripes.

Leaving my sister and brother-in-law's home put Annie and me onto the next leg of *our* pre-hike journey, heading down to New Orleans where I would catch my flight to San Diego on April 9th. I recall thinking back to when there were just 100 days until the start of my long anticipated PCT adventure. Where had all that time gone? Proof I believe, that we all need to cherish our time, and do everything we can not to let too much of it slip away, for then it will be forever lost.

New Orleans was just a short two-hour drive away, and home to the Louis Armstrong New Orleans International Airport where United Airlines had agreed to fly me to San Francisco and then on to San Diego for that ridiculously inexpensive ticket price. We were up at 4:15 a.m., checked out by 4:45, and driving the short five-minute route to the airport where Annie and I would part. Not being bashful, I asked a perfect stranger to take our photo as we hugged and said our goodbyes. Yep, saying farewell was hard—it's always difficult to leave my sweet Ann Marie. I have to admit it felt awful telling my wife that I hoped *not* to see her for five-plus months. So many miles between us, too much time apart.

Saying goodbye to Annie

Seat 23c was an aisle seat. I always select an aisle seat. I have convinced myself that the aisle provides more leg room. I sat in the painfully confining space of 23c on flight number 1013, and while at 35,000 feet I finally had the time to reflect on what it had taken for me to get there. Months of planning, preparation, and training were obviously major contributors, but more important was the support and love of my wife, family, and friends. I find myself in constant awe of the people in my life who are so kind and thoughtful. I'm not sure why, but it always amazes me how thoughtful people can be, and I find myself as a constant benefactor. Text messages and emails from those close to me—and at times from those I hardly know—with well wishes caused me to pause and wonder why I should be so worthy of their kindness. Perhaps it's the constant exposure to negative world views from the ever-present 24/7 cable news cycle that most of us pay way too much attention to that has us more surprised than not by what is good in this world. Or, perhaps it's those rare and infrequent evil human specimens we encounter in our lives that we allow to tip the scales and weigh heavily on us and darken our hearts. They can sometimes cloud our faith and distort our trust, and do so like it's their job. I, for one, am thankful for those acts of kindness and the pleasant nudge toward my timely and sometimes desperately needed attitude adjustment. It's those frequently received acts that remind me it's not always doom and gloom.

The disparity between darkness and light presents a choice of direction for us all. With help, I've chosen my path, my direction. People for the most part are good, life is good—very good. Thank you, kind people.

One of my deepest regrets from my time hiking the Appalachian Trail was that I had not taken the time to collect stories from all those I had the absolute pleasure to meet and hike with. I spent much time with my trail family, and we obviously had the trail in common, but I didn't delve into what made them tick. I really hoped to attempt to understand why they—we—hike at all. I also hoped to collect and tell the stories of trail angels and volunteers. Trail angels Scout and Frodo—their trail names—thru-hiked the PCT in 2007 and quickly realized there was a need that was not being met. That need was the logistics of providing aid to hikers once they arrived from distant locations to San

Diego—specifically help to get rest and have time to gather gear and food for the journey. Hikers come from all over North America and, believe it or not, every other continent on the globe. Well, perhaps not Antarctica. How will they all get to the trailhead? Who would be there to pick them up from the airport, train, or bus station?

Enter Scout and Frodo. This couple opened their home to strangers each hiking season. They and their merry band of volunteers would pick you up, take you to their home, provide a safe place to sleep, feed you, provide rides to local outfitters, provide shipping materials, accept mailed packages, provide shower facilities, give you a ride to the southern terminus, and lastly, a big hug for your safe travels. Oh, and they offered this service for up to forty hikers every night, and they refused to accept payment.

Scout and Frodo started welcoming hikers into their home in 2006, the year before they too thru-hiked the PCT. Scout shared with me that he had heard many hikers say their first day on the trail was their worst. He and Frodo wanted to make it their best. He also told me that they knew opening their home to hikers would fan the flame of their own interest and excitement over the trail. Finally, they do this, as Scout would tell you, "Because we can."

Hikers from previous years often step up and give back as their way of paying it forward. So many, in fact, that Scout and Frodo have to schedule them on a calendar. These volunteers spend a couple of days and up to two weeks assisting thru-hiker hopefuls.

Here are some of their stories.

Giggles, age 26, received her trail name while on her 2017 PCT hike. She tells the story this way. "While hiking the PCT, I and two others found refuge from the heat of the desert in the form of a small patch of shade. The three of us were cramped in the little shade provided, and the other two stretched out. I ended up with their butts in my face and I couldn't stop laughing." Giggles has hiked the PCT, the Southern Sierra high route, and was currently preparing to hike the Continental Divide Trail—the CDT—starting April 18th. This high energy hiker owns and operates her own company called "With the Wild Things." As the sole proprietor, she teaches outdoor skills and thru-hike coaching. Giggles found her love for hiking when she was guiding sections of the AT while attending school, and she never looked back. She volunteers at Scout and Frodo's to give back to the trail and because they were such a big part of her own hike.

Diggy, age 36 and an interior designer, got her trail name while on her 2018 PCT thru-hike. She shared with me that she had purchased a green cotton T-shirt with an image of a Pokémon character called Diglett from a thrift store for 50 cents. The caption above it said, "Can you diglett?" A play on words. Other hikers tried to give her the trail name Diglett, but she didn't like or accept the name—a hiker's prerogative. Instead, while practicing yoga, she found herself in the dirt and she looked like she had been digging in it. Diggy was born. This capable hiker has the Colorado, John Muir, and Patagonia trails under her belt, to name a few. Why give up her free time to help others? Diggy told me, "Because I stayed here and absolutely loved what they—Scout and Frodo—stood for." After her PCT hike, she recalled the many people who helped her, and just knew she wanted to give back.

Joker, age 34, has hiked the PCT 3 times—in 2008, 2009, and 2012, and the CDT in 2010 and 2017. He has worked as a chef, served in the US Army, does some writing, and is currently a project manager. Why the trail name Joker? Telling jokes has lightened his attitude, and his one-liners help with discomfort in certain situations. He says he will make jokes if things are not going well, and that they keep him centered. Joker volunteers because he connected well with Scout and Frodo, and he too wanted to give back. He has volunteered at least five times, from a couple of days up to two weeks.

Whistler, Diggy, Frodo, Scout, Joker and Giggles

As with most things in life, all good things must eventually come to an end. After fifteen years of serving the hiking community, Scout and Frodo announced their retirement from hosting PCT hikers in their home. The class of 2020 would be the last to receive the Scout and Frodo mega blessings. I know I join the multitudes of hiking alumni when I give praise and thanks to this wonderful couple for their kindness and generosity.

Scooby arrived in San Diego the following day, April 10th, the day before our hike was to start. It was a great reunion, and it just felt that all was right with the world. My goal for the night before the start of the hike was to be under my sleeping quilt by nine o'clock, which I achieved. Unfortunately, my tent mates had different plans. It's understandable though. Everyone—myself included—was obviously excited about what the morning would bring. Earlier, immediately following dinner, Frodo had issued our marching orders, which gave us purpose and proved that we all still had some work to do. After all the years she and Scout had hosted hikers, they knew how to keep the system moving like a well-oiled machine. We were informed that our packs needed to be on the front deck by 5:00 a.m. with breakfast scheduled to be served at 5:30. I was up at 3:00 a.m. after spending most of my evening doing all I could to ignore the sawing of logs by my tent mates. At one point, I carried my sleep pad and quilt out to the lawn and tried to sleep under the stars. I finally gave up and packed my backpack early.

Frodo and her volunteers started breakfast at 4:30 a.m. while I stayed out of the way and patiently waited for the coffee to be ready. I estimate that I might have slept two to three hours, but it really didn't matter. I was too excited about how my long-anticipated start of this coveted trail would unfold. The cars lined up in front of the house while we finished our breakfast. With our nourishment needs met, we loaded up and made the hour drive to the Mexico-California border and home of the southern terminus PCT monument for pictures and a great send-off.

The day had finally arrived!

Whistler and Scooby at the Southern PCT monument

Section Two

Campo, California to Walker Pass, California
Miles 0 to 652

First Steps...

Taking those first steps was surreal. Those months upon months of research, planning and training had finally brought me to where I was destined and desperate to be—back on the trail.

The weather was perfect, hovering at 58 degrees that first morning, with afternoon temps in the low 70s. It really was a perfect day to hike. The trail itself was mostly sandy and easy to negotiate. I have to admit that my thoughts of hiking through a desert created mental pictures of tall sand dunes and waterless, thirst-induced mirages. Instead, I found a gentle meandering trail, and the heavy rains in recent weeks had filled the streams that now flowed freely and abundantly. So, on our first day, accessible water meant that our water carries never required more than two liters, thus allowing for a lighter pack. Both Scooby's and my pack now weighed in at 25 pounds each.

Those higher than usual rains in the high desert, in addition to the heavy snows during the past winter, had set the stage for a spectacular wildflower show. Most dry years leave seeds in a dormant state, but not this year. This year presented a rare occasion event called a super bloom. It was just too beautiful to describe. Scooby and I stopped frequently to take breaks when some of the climbs were steep and long. My legs felt great, but my lung capacity was lacking. Our highest elevation on that first day was just 3,400 feet, but I was feeling lung fatigue—not from the altitude but from the lack of lung capacity. On the first night there were twelve other hikers at our campsite, with every one of them just as excited as I was. Everyone set up their tents and prepared their dinners in a rush of frenzied activity, and finally we all crawled into our private abodes by seven o'clock so we'd get the much-needed rest to do it all again the following day. As I awaited slumber to over take me, I found myself listening to the frogs croaking, the owls hooting, and other mysterious calls that were unfamiliar to me. With limited sleep the night before, and today's 15.4-mile hike, I knew nothing would keep me awake that first night.

Mile one

As one might expect, I found myself doing a full comparison between the Appalachian Trail and what I had briefly experienced on the Pacific Crest Trail. If the Appalachian Trail was an apple, then the Pacific Crest Trail was a cantaloupe. Thus far, the PCT had lived up to, and actually far exceeded, what I had been expecting. The elevations were gradual and gentle, where the AT was a bit more abrupt and harsh. The AT—or as it is un-affectionately called, "The Green Tunnel"—keeps secrets from you. What was coming up ahead was always a mystery. By comparison, the PCT was wide open with expansive views of the trail and rewarding landscapes that offered hikers views for as far as they could see. Don't get me wrong, the two trails were both challenging, while at the same time so different. This trail was absolutely beautiful, and not what I'd envisioned prior to seeing it for myself.

I guess at the end of the day there is beauty everywhere. You simply need to keep your eyes open while you take it all in. It was just my second day on this trail, but I was already in love with it. Okay, let's call it infatuation for now.

Scooby and I were on the trail by 6:15 a.m. with a modest climb of about 1,200 feet over 2.5 miles, not all that difficult. We made a stop for our second breakfast at the Oak Shores Malt Shop, located at mile twenty. Their breakfast burrito is legendary and highly recommended. After that early break, it was time to burn off that burrito fuel. We hiked just over 22 miles on the second day, stopping frequently for pictures and to speak with some of the other hikers we had been leap-frogging since the day before.

That night the temperature fell below freezing, which called for gloves, sleeping bag liner, toque, and my down jacket to keep warm overnight, not anything that unusual. I awoke at five-thirty, and prepared my oatmeal and coffee. Still a typical day. Scooby and I started hiking at seven, with the trail taking us through a beautiful conifer forest. The trail tread was covered in pine needles, which was easy on the feet and so welcome. We came across a group of over 60 hikers who were doing a 15-mile training hike that weekend. They were training for a 28-mile hike as a fundraiser for Make a Wish Foundation. We chatted with them as we stepped off the trail to allow this motivated and enthusiastic group to pass. This was their third year conducting this fundraiser, and at the time of our meeting they had already raised $365,000.00 of their goal of $500,000.00. Incredible! They call the event Trail Blaze Challenge and there would be over 160 hikers participating.

We hiked on and eventually found our way to the Laguna Mountain Lodge where Scooby and I had our first mail drop delivered—still a typical day. And then it all started to change. We started seeing things we had never seen before. It was as though we had been abducted, plucked from this earth, and transported to another planet. The landscape was unrecognizable and foreign to us. We gazed in awe at the most spectacular mountains. I stopped to take photos, but realized I'd have to quit before using all my camera's memory. We looked at our Guthook guides— a phone app that provides maps and hiker information along with satellite GPS—and discovered that, no, we had not been abducted by extraterrestrial beings, but we were for the first time getting a glimpse of what was soon to come.

The heavily snow-capped San Jacinto Mountain standing at 10,834 feet was still 181 miles away, and Mount Baden-Powell with a peak of 9,407 feet was 377 miles away, yet there they were, so incredibly majestic, seemingly close enough to touch but still so far away.

I was excited for this experience and for the future secrets that our third rock from the sun would reveal.

Pioneer Mail Trailhead Park was a perfect place to stake our claim for the night...except of course for the NO CAMPING signs. The park had a water source, shade trees, beautiful green grass, a trash can, and best of all, a pit privy. But, no camping! It really wasn't a problem, though, because there were plenty of perfect sites directly outside the boundary fence. Problem solved. We got a great campsite along with all the amenities of a park.

The hiking on day four was also perfect, with a beautiful clear sky and ideal temperatures. Scooby and I agreed that we hit the lottery with regard to the weather. But back to the skies... I've never in my life seen such big, open skies. They seemed to have no end. This virtually tree-less trail provides views that are difficult to imagine or comprehend. Coincidentally, while taking a break, Scooby was on his back looking at the beautiful sky when he saw a huge glider. This glider pilot was doing small, tight circles in a limitless sky, with an almost full moon as his backdrop. It looked like this glider could have stayed up there forever. I couldn't help but wonder if that pilot's view of the sky could possibly have been any better than mine. I'm pretty sure not.

So, about rattlesnakes. As I was hiking along—because that was now my job—I heard the warning of what had to be a huge rattler. It sounded like it was only a couple feet from me on the side of the trail in some brush, but I never saw it. That rattle did have my heart skip a beat, or two...maybe even three. Unbeknownst to us, it wouldn't be too long before rattlesnakes became an almost daily occurrence, as we would cross the paths of countless rattlesnakes in the weeks to come.

With sixteen miles hiked on day four, we stopped and made camp near a water cistern which on a typical day would be somewhat suspect. But here in the desert, it was an oasis. I recall thinking that I seriously hoped my water filter was doing its job.

And now a poem.

SKY

It starts at the beginning yet has no end.
Its presence is silent, save for the wind.
Eyes wide open to the hue,
a sky so deep, so clear and blue.
The clouds are wispy, big, and light,
with the room they need to take flight.
It constantly changes, never the same.
One day it's clear, the next day it rains.
Amazing though, is when it's night,
how can it hold all those stars and all their light?

To wake up at 5:10 a.m. when my plan had been to get up at 4:30 got me started on the wrong foot—pun intended. Scooby and I had agreed on an early departure of six o'clock, to take advantage of the early cool temperatures. Not wanting to hold us up, I skipped my coffee and oatmeal. Definitely not a good start. I got everything packed, filtered some water, and put a protein bar in my backpack waist-belt pocket for easy access while hiking. Thankfully, the day went perfectly after that rough start. The hiking was a pleasure, with gradual climbs and descents, and beautiful cool breezes pretty much all day. I'll never say no to a cool breeze while hiking in the desert of Southern California.

The scenery continued to amaze me. I had watched countless YouTube videos of others hiking this trail, but those videos couldn't come close to seeing it live and in person. While hiking, we did come across a few of the usual suspects with whom we'd been leapfrogging since the start of this epic journey. I learned from my AT hike that as common as it was to meet up with hikers you met at the start of your hike, it was just as possible that you would never see some of those hikers ever again. Even still, I was starting to see this year's PCT hiking class beginning to bond. They all wanted to know if Scooby and I were planning to hitch into Julian for some free pie at Mom's Pie House. Mom's is a traditional stop for PCT hikers, but until we were asked, we had thought we might skip it. Julian is twelve miles off the trail, which would require a hitch. Scooby and I now agreed that we should go if for no other reason than to get the whole PCT hiker experience. Our good fortune was that we met up with Marie—no trail name yet—and Wiki. Good fortune because female hikers tend to get a hitch much faster than stinky male hikers. This is where the clever hiker term "ride bride" comes from. Ten minutes is all it took before trail angel Jen pulled over to give Scooby, Marie—our ride bride—and me a ride to Julian. Wiki and another hiker, Mark, got picked up immediately after. Jen told us some interesting historical facts about Julian, and some great stories about other hikers she had picked up over the years. Our repeated attempts to give her some money—the proper etiquette for a thru-hiker—was refused. I almost don't know what else to say about Jen except that I hope and pray she receives that same generosity in return one day.

Once at Mom's, we simply showed our hiking permits and we were invited to order a slice of pie with ice cream and coffee, all for free. There was a tip jar that was rightfully filling up because hikers are cool and they always show their appreciation—a subliminal message to hikers that are not cool or do not show their appreciation.

Enjoying our pie at Mom's

So, now that our bellies were full, how did a stinky hiker get back to the trail which, as you remember, was twelve miles away? Well, you stand on the side of the road, stick your thumb out, try not to look dangerous or like a hobo. In about ten minutes, a van pulls over and the driver opens the back for your backpack, you get in, and the driver takes you all the way back to the trailhead. This trail angel went by the trail name Ghost. He makes it a habit to serve the hiking community by picking hikers up whenever he can, and entertains them for the twelve miles back to the trail. It had been a long time since I'd laughed so hard. When Ghost dropped us off, he would not accept payment either. There were three hikers hitching in to Julian and Ghost loaded them up and made the return trip back. There are so many gracious, selfless, and kind people in this world and I always feel so blessed to be witness to their giving spirits. So, my day went from a not so good start to a really great finish.

Scooby and I had carefully selected a campsite that overlooked the expansive valley 3,500 feet below us while also being perfect for watching the sunset. It was pretty windy, so we assisted each other in pitching our tents, as the wind attempted to turn them into kites ready for takeoff. It was at about 4:30 a.m. when I received an abrupt wakeup call from intense audible winds that tried to take my tent for another flight, this time with me in it. Having good cell and data service, I checked the weather reports and radar. The severe wind warnings we now found ourselves in the midst of included current wind speeds at 25 to 35 mph with gusts recorded at 45 mph, and some isolated locations experiencing 55 to 60 mph winds. I decided to start packing up. But first I followed my now mechanical routine, which included getting into my hiking clothes—day six for those, not pretty. I then set up my stove in the vestibule and boiled water for coffee and oatmeal, and finally I took care of the personal stuff too, which required the use of a large rock to keep my Ziploc bag of toilet paper from being sucked into the wind vortex. At this point I'd packed everything up except for my tent. As soon as there was a lull in the wind I jumped out, pulled the tent stakes and trekking poles, and rolled my tent into its stuff sack. Meanwhile, Scooby slept through the entire event.

I never thought I would ever be hiking the Southern California desert wearing a down jacket. The temperatures remained in the high forties and low fifties all day. We came across a couple taking a coffee break—a very good idea. When it was time to break for lunch, I pulled out my cook stove and made my second cup of coffee of the day.

The major highlight on day six was when we passed the hundred-mile mark. We knew it was coming, but when we came across the stones spelling out "PCT 100" on the trail, it felt incredibly gratifying. We also received the unexpected but always welcome trail magic in the form of fresh fruit, candy, cookies, and soda. Trail angels Randy and Louie were set up at a road crossing and took exceptionally good care of all passing hikers.

With the day coming to a close, we camped just past the cow pasture that we hiked through in the latter part of the day. Not just any cow pasture. No, we hiked for three miles to get from one end to the other...all the while watching our steps to avoid the ubiquitous cow patties.

The next day would take us to Warner Springs Community Resource Center, where a much-needed shower could be found as well as an opportunity to do laundry, and where we would accept delivery of our next resupply boxes.

Scooby and I were hiking by 6:00 a.m., excited at the prospect of getting to Warner Springs as early as possible. But first, we were about half a mile into our hike when we arrived at Eagle Rock. This natural rock formation has been one of the iconic points of interest on the PCT that I'd been looking forward to seeing. We arrived just as the sun was rising, which cast a light with a golden glow on the eagle. This was truly a magical time.

Eagle Rock

Interestingly, when Scooby and I were leaving Eagle Rock, we met a lone hiker with some serious personal issues. As we continued on, Scooby and I got into a conversation about the baggage some people carry with them, and how some people are never happy. This made me think of an analogy that I shared with Scooby. While hiking, some people carry too much in their backpack. They bring along items they don't need and that consequently weigh them down, which in turn slows their forward progress. They know this, but refuse to unload the useless stuff from their packs, all while complaining about how heavy their packs are. Isn't it time we all lighten our packs?

We continued our trek, heading for the extremely hiker-friendly town of Warner Springs. But first, while hiking along, Scooby had me stop as he pointed out what he had observed and I had failed to notice—all of the singing birds. We were walking through a huge cow pasture, and a countless variety of birds were talking about this and that, so we stopped to have a listen.

And then it was onward to Warner Springs. This small town opens up their community center to hikers during the hiking season, and provides a variety of services. Pretty much anything a hiker would need is made available, such as the much-coveted bucket shower.

What's a bucket shower, you ask? This is how it works: you get a towel and a five-gallon bucket. Now you take your bucket to a big sink and fill it with warm water, then you take it to an outdoor stall. You strip down and attempt to wash six days of grunge off your body. I half expected to see men in hazmat suits at the ready to clean up the toxic waste. The next step after you are somewhat clean is to take the same bucket back to the sink, get fresh water, and start washing your clothes in the bucket. This requires several goes, because the black, filthy water needs to be replaced numerous times. Clothes are then hung on a line to dry. Ta-da! Semi-clean body and clothes.

The center also has a resupply store, cold drinks, charging stations for electronics, a clean restroom, and a huge field if you want to pitch your tent and spend the night. The local post office is just a short walk away, and that was where Scooby and I went to pick up our resupply packages which we had previously mailed to ourselves.

We were there for about five hours to accomplish everything I described, and then hit the trail by one in the heat of the afternoon to hike another ten miles. That additional ten miles brought us to a high mountain campsite where we observed the most spectacular sunset.

A full moon lit up my tent overnight and gave the appearance that I had a streetlamp directly over my tent. Ordinarily this would have kept me awake, but you could have shot a cannon through my tent and I wouldn't have woken up. That's how tired I was. By the time Scooby and I were ready to start hiking in the morning, the moon was setting at just about the same place the sun had set the night before.

Something that had long since become apparent over the many miles we were hiking buddies was the efficiency with which Scooby and I hiked together. With me out front and Scooby on my heels, we communicated effectively and planned our hike while we were on the go. Things such as where to get our next water, where and when to stop for a break, and where to end our day to set ourselves up for the next day's hike, all made for a well-oiled machine. We managed to be efficient and work our plan as we hiked. Most of the time this method was flawless.

Well, except for the minor error we made on that day. More about that in a bit.

The weather had started to warm up, which quickly reminded us that we were in the high desert, and how fortunate we had been thus far with extraordinarily hiker-friendly conditions. Now the water sources became less frequent, which required that we carry more. One of our planned stops was the famed and iconic stop along the PCT called

Mike's Place. We had planned on stopping at Mike's Place only to fill up on water and to take a midday break. I'm not going to get into it too much so as not to impose my opinions on others, but both Scooby and I agreed that we should move on after a very brief time there. I should have been a bit suspicious when we saw the caretaker walking around with a tail attached to his clothing. As this caretaker was holding court, he shared that he wears a tail because, in his words, it gives him balance. The visit was an interesting experience, to say the least.

So, about that minor error in our planning...

While on a short break, I called and made hotel reservations for Saturday and Sunday in Idyllwild. When we stopped at about 4:30 p.m. for what we thought was the end of our day, we reviewed our plans for the next couple of days and realized that we were off by about twelve miles. We had already made camp when we discovered this error. We needed to make up those twelve miles or we'd get into Idyllwild very late on Saturday. The goal of getting into a town was to maximize your time there. So, we decided to break camp and keep hiking. We hiked an additional five-plus miles. Those additional miles included a lot of ascents, which after an already exhausting day was tough. What was rewarding, though, was that we pushed ourselves and our bodies closer to our limits, and that we achieved what was required at the time. We would wake up the next morning after just enough rest for our bodies to recover, and we would prepare ourselves to do it again, because that was what this hike and this dream mandated.

While hiking the Appalachian trail, I never really recalled seeing a moon that was this full, probably because on the AT we were usually under a tree canopy. In the high desert there are no trees, and absolutely zero light pollution to take away from the ability to appreciate that lunar sphere as it floated high above one's tent. It pleased me to once again witness the moon set in the cloudless sky just as the sun made its glorious morning announcement.

The previous day had been a difficult one for me and my hiking partner. We awoke this morning, and with rested and clear heads, discussed several options for the coming days. We both agreed that we needed to take a bit of a break. We altered our original plans and decided to hike the 9.1 miles to the Paradise Valley Cafe for breakfast, then hitch to Idyllwild. The original plan had been to hike to the Paradise Valley Cafe, hike back to the trail, then hike the remaining day and a half to Idyllwild. This new plan would get us into Idyllwild a half day early on Friday, where we would camp at the local state campground for the evening and then take a double zero on Saturday and Sunday at our hotel instead of the previously planned nero and zero. A short day of hiking is called a nero—as in a near zero day of hiking. A zero is a day of no hiking. This new plan would require us to hitch back to the Paradise Valley Cafe on Monday morning to make up the missed miles. The plan received a unanimous vote because we both knew our tired bodies needed a break.

The Paradise Valley Cafe definitely lived up to its well-known reputation amongst the thru-hiker community. I ordered a breakfast burrito that was nearly impossible to finish. The new plan also allowed us to sit, relax, and socialize with the numerous hikers taking advantage of this desert oasis.

While we were sitting at our table another hiker came over, stood over us, and said, "Hello Whistler. Hello Scooby." I felt terrible because I couldn't place how we might have known him, even though he looked familiar. We had already met so many people on the trail and it was difficult to remember everyone, especially by their trail names. That was when he told us his trail name was Lone Wanderer.

Scooby and I looked at each other in complete disbelief. We had met Lone Wanderer at the summit of Mt. Katahdin when we hiked the AT two years earlier! After that epic summit, Lone Wanderer, Scooby, and I hiked back down to Baxter State Park together, and we had not seen him since. And yet, he remembered us.

When it was time to leave and attempt a hitch for the fourteen-mile trip into Idyllwild, we went and stood on the shoulder of the highway with thumbs out. After about five minutes a produce delivery truck pulled over to give us a ride. We threw our packs in the back of the refrigerated truck and sat in the cab with the newest trail angel to enter our lives. Again, we tried to offer some money for the ride, but our new friend unsurprisingly refused. We made our way to Jacinta State Park where we pitched tents to spend the night. With much needed showers taken and laundry done, it was time to find some pizza and beer for dinner. On our way to get dinner, we had the distinct honor of meeting the mayor of Idyllwild. Mayor Max of Idyllwild is an American Golden Retriever, and has been mayor since his birth on May 6th, 2013. Mayor Max works with his deputy mayors, Mikey and Mitzi—also Golden Retrievers—and two chiefs of staff, Phyllis Mueller and Glenn Warren—humans. According to their website, their goal is to "Make the world a better place by conveying unconditional love and doing as many good deeds for others as possible."

Whistler and Mayor Max

It turns out, you can't keep two crazy and motivated hikers idle for very long. Scooby and I met at the picnic table for breakfast and a planning session the following morning. Although two full days off had seemed like a good idea at the time, it looked like we were going to go with plan C. Enough of this soft living. We needed and wanted to get on the move. Idyllwild is a wonderful town and extremely hiker friendly, but we'd achieved all we needed to on Saturday, and were ready to get back to trail living.

I had retrieved my resupply boxes from the local post office, which kept Saturday hours for package pickups from 1:30 till 3:00 p.m. One of my packages was one I had forwarded on from Mt. Laguna. It was awaiting my arrival along with a package from my sister, and a third package which was a perfect and thoughtful Easter gift from my wife. So, after a day of work and leisure, Scooby and I completed all our remaining tasks and prepared for departure on Easter Sunday morning instead of Monday. But we did find time for adding some culture to our lives by working a movie into our busy schedule. Not just any movie. No, we made it to the three o'clock showing of Captain Marvel. Not exactly Academy Award-winning material, but it was still a fun escape. Finally, we grabbed dinner and a beer at a local brew pub, and that was the end of our perfect zero in the beautiful town of Idyllwild.

We were itching to return to the trail, so we were up and ready to grab an early breakfast. The management at the Silver Pines Motel was very kind to accept our request to check out a day early, saying they would have no problem re-booking for that Sunday night. We made our way back to the Red Kettle restaurant for a big hiker breakfast and to speak with the waitress, Cathy, who the day before while we enjoyed lunch had offered to drive us the fourteen miles back to the trailhead. As kind and generous as her offer was, she wouldn't get off work until noon. So, Scooby and I finished our breakfast, picked up our packs, and stuck out our thumbs. As had been our previous good fortune, we got a hitch in about three minutes.

That ride was in the back of a pickup truck, which added another bit of fun to our entire hiking experience. There is something so freeing about having the wind whip through your hair while riding in the back of a pickup truck. Our trail angel was only able to take us about five miles closer to our destination, but we soon caught another ride back to the Paradise Cafe. Once again, neither of our trail angel drivers would accept gas money. Hiking out of town always means additional weight and the burden of a full, food-laden pack. In fact, we were carrying out six days of food for the next section of trail, which equated to about twelve additional pounds. By 9:30 a.m. we were on the trail and hiking right where we'd left off two days earlier.

Our hike that day brought us through a portion of the trail in the San Bernardino Mountains that had been closed since the fires of 2013, but had just recently been reopened for the first time since those fires. Hikers from the 2013 class and up till our year had been forced to skip this section of the trail. During that six-year period, the PCTA had strongly discouraged roadwalking the highly travelled and dangerous California State Route 74 into Idyllwild. Most hikers would simply hitch, with the understanding that the miles they were unable to hike due to a fire closure would not count against a thru-hike because it was out of their control.

It was tough hiking through this newly reopened section, witnessing all the devastation left behind by those fires. It was extremely difficult to imagine how this and other burned-out forests could ever recover. It was pretty apparent that little to no trail maintenance had been performed in the area during that whole six-year period, either. A huge number of burned and downed trees crossed over the trail which required a lot of rerouting around, over, and at times under those trees. In one place we needed to hike down a very steep side-trail to retrieve water. This side-trail was a full mile long, meaning a two-mile round-trip. Because we knew there would not be any more water available for about 17 miles, we each carried out four liters, which added another eight pounds of weight to our already heavily-laden packs. But we now had enough water for the rest of that day's hiking, dinner, and breakfast in the morning.

The following day would be a big day for us. Our plan was to start at 6:00 a.m. on our ascent of Mount San Jacinto. The trail would take us through snow-covered trails and fields, and a climb to over 9,000 feet in elevation.

We started our biggest climb of the day in the early morning, with hopes of reaching the anticipated snow before the sun softened and melted it causing postholing conditions. Postholing, as the name implies, is when your foot punches through the top crust of snow and you sink through it risking injury from unseen dangers such as jagged boulders and fallen trees. On this day, the first three miles were steep, with countless switchbacks making our progress very slow. We eventually came to a high ridge which we hiked along for just over a mile. On one side of the ridge we saw the expansive desert in all its beautiful glory. Meanwhile, on the other side all we saw were the skeletal and charred remains of the 2013 fires. It was an unattractive sight, difficult to look at, and I found myself averting my eyes. My thoughts, my hopes, were that this devastation was caused naturally by lightening, and not by a careless hiker.

We finally came to where the snow started covering the trail at mile 169.5 and around 7,000 feet of elevation. It was time to break out those micro-spikes whose additional weight had been a burden up until now. It was time they repaid me for that free ride deep in the bottom of my pack. We came across a hiker we hadn't seen since first meeting him back when we'd all enjoyed pie and coffee in Julian. We found Bodega packing a plastic bag full of snow to apply to his sore shin splints, a common injury of hikers who put on too many early miles instead of working up to it. That was how the trail worked. You never knew if, when, or where you might see one another again.

The little bit of snow that day was brief and quickly conquered. It wasn't until we were close to about 8,000 feet in elevation and on the northern exposed side that we found enough snow to keep us busy for hours upon hours. Following the trail was tricky, as it had obviously been for those who came before us. Footprints went in every direction as the history of earlier hikers told their stories. A great deal of time was used up trying to establish where the trail was. If not for the marvel of GPS and the trail guide applications such as Guthook on our phones, we might still be in search of that elusive trail. With tired, worn out, and exhausted bodies, we found water, a camp site, had dinner, and retired to our tents for some much-needed rest.

That night was one I would not soon forget. Our campsite was unfortunately on an exposed ridge with high winds that were gusting at well over 40 miles per hour. Those winds had me exiting my tent twice during the night to re-secure tent stakes and add the weight of several heavy rocks to help the stakes stay put. In addition to the overnight winds, we also got hit hard with hail and sleet. I must have been pretty tired to have fallen asleep with that storm howling and doing its best to interrupt my sleep. When morning arrived and I eventually awoke, it was once again peacefully still and quiet outside.

As I was packing up and preparing for the brand-new day, I noticed that the screw holding one of my eyeglass lenses in its frame had come loose. Not having my glasses on the trail would not have been good for me. Not at all. I had visions of myself walking into trees, rocks, or even walking off a cliff. I shared my dilemma with Scooby, who fortunately had a Swiss Army knife with a small screwdriver attachment. Disaster averted.

Once on the trail, we hiked a three-mile steep ascent which took us past many beautiful water sources from the snow that was melting higher up that mountain. The highest elevation that day took us up to just over 9,000 feet as we continued our hike of Mt. San Jacinto. This mountain had had its way with us the day before, and it still wasn't finished with us. That day was some of the toughest hiking I had ever taken on. Micro-spikes were helpful in the early morning while the snow was still hard-packed and frozen, but less of an aid once the sun rose higher, softening and melting the snow. I wouldn't characterize any of this part of the trail as dangerous, but I did slip and fall more times than I could count. Postholing in the soft snow caused me to twist a knee, bruise a rib, and twist an ankle while also receiving a couple gashes on a shin. In one place it took us a full hour to advance three tenths of one mile. For reference, we typically hiked two and a half to three miles per hour. It was exhausting. The reports we had read earlier stated there would be deep snow up to mile 191. Those reports were accurate.

Once out of the snow, we had an easy descent down to 3,500 feet, at our average speed of three miles per hour. It was a task made more difficult because of our battered bodies. But we had a goal, and nothing was going to stop us—including a 9,000-foot, snow-covered mountain. We were highly motivated to reach the 200-mile mark. We finished the day having reached our goal, and at mile 201.2 we made camp.

I woke up the next morning and gathered everything I needed for my breakfast, then found a patch of desert to sit on while watching the sunrise. I enjoyed my oatmeal and black coffee as I watched the sun's morning glow cast its brilliance on the snow-capped Mt. San Jacinto. The added bonus to my private show was that the waning moon was hanging just above that 10,834-foot peak while I observed as a mere mortal from 3,304 feet.

With bodies nearly healed after a good night's rest, it was time to take on today's adversary—the sun. The advantage to hiking at 9,000 feet is the cooler temperatures. On this day we would find ourselves hiking down to the desert floor at 1,200 feet, home to extreme desert heat. The forecast called for temperatures in the mid eighties. The thermometer hanging off my backpack actually registered 103 degrees. Scooby said that was only because it was in the direct sun. I quickly pointed out that we were also in the direct sun. Our early morning hike was a nice gradual descent with countless switchbacks. While hiking, our conversation turned to how varied this trail was. It's pretty diverse when one day you're trekking through six feet of snow and the next day you're hiking the blazing desert.

As we continued our trek, I mentioned that we had not experienced as much trail magic as we had when hiking the AT. It wasn't much later that we met Andrew, who was working on a photo project while also providing trail magic. The trail does provide. It couldn't have been more than five minutes after we left Andrew when we met trail angel Waltzing Matilda. A 2018 thru-hiker, he was now our host, serving barbecue chicken, potato salad, watermelon, and cold drinks. As we thanked him profusely, he simply and quite humbly said that he gets more out of giving.

As I said, the trail does provide. At mile 213.4 we came across a huge wind farm which was also very hiker-friendly. The staff invites hikers to come into their air-conditioned office—which is out in the middle of the desert—to have their fill of cold drinks and ice cream, for just a small donation.

Yep, the trail definitely provides.

We left that wind farm oasis and started a huge, steep climb. We finally gave up and sat in some shade we were lucky to find. We rested in that shade for about an hour while the sun did its best to melt our shoes on the hot desert sand. We eventually got moving again and hiked the last six miles to Whitewater River, where we happily lounged in the rushing water to cool our overheated bodies. I set up my tent beside the river, which provided me with the sound of rushing water to sleep by. The trail does provide!

I had told myself that if I was going to tell my story, it had to be real, and it had to be honest. This was day fifteen of my thru-hike, and not exactly one of my best. In fact, at that time I could say with one hundred percent confidence that it was my very worst day hiking. Of course, little did I know that later on I would have a day that was far worse.

This one started just fine at 6:00 a.m. as we left what was certainly one of the nicest campsites in the history of all campsites. Soft white sand was the foundation, making for a flat even, cushy base upon which to erect my humble abode. The swift-running Whitewater River close by provided the perfect background noise to fall asleep to. When morning arrived, I was fully rested from the difficult hike the day before. Everything was just perfect, with the minor exception of the heat. It wasn't until we approached Mission Creek that the wheels just seemed to fall off. Mission Creek runs down the mountain we happened to be hiking up. We knew in advance from news reports and prior research that the creek had washed out the trail in what could only be defined as total devastation...but we had never imagined what we would find.

It was almost comical at first, but got old real fast. We were literally bushwhacking our way up the mountain, constantly looking for what remained of the trail. Progress was slow, with an average speed of just over one mile per hour. We would cross the creek going in one direction, only to discover minutes later that we had to cross it yet again in the opposite direction. We crossed Mission Creek so many times that my shoes, socks, and feet never had a chance to dry. My feet turned into prunes, which in turn developed blisters. Painful, bottom-of-my-foot-pad blisters. With me in the lead and Scooby taking on navigation via Guthook, we progressed at a crawl, along with every other hiker we came across. Being in the lead, I was also the first to come across the three rattlesnakes we clearly startled, as indicated by their audible warnings. Their warnings were greatly appreciated, though, because I nearly stepped on one of them. Two were approximately four feet long, while the third, which was attempting to swim across the creek, was only about three feet long. Only…

Later that day I started feeling weak, and my breathing was labored from what I guessed was due to dehydration from the triple-digit temperatures. I've read about heat-related illnesses, but never expected that I would fall victim to heat exhaustion. I have always been one of those guys who is like a camel, needing less water than most. But it soon became pretty obvious that I had allowed myself to become dehydrated. Scooby and I took numerous breaks in shade when we were able to find that rare desert commodity. When we found a suitable tent site at about six that evening, it took all I had in me to set up my tent and crawl in. The sun had set behind the mountain where we now found ourselves, which fortunately supplied cool breezes to which I quickly fell asleep. I woke up at 9:30 p.m., drank a full liter of water, made myself some dinner, and took some time to write down the day's events in my journal. Writing each evening, especially after a day like that day, could be a challenging chore. But I knew if I allowed a single day to go by without writing, it would give me permission to skip other days. So, as difficult as it was, I committed to myself that I would never miss a day of writing in my journal. With my self-imposed commitment met, it was now time to get back under my quilt for some more much-needed sleep.

My sleep was deep and restorative, but as with most good things, it came to an abrupt conclusion. At four o'clock, it was time to prepare for our agreed-upon departure of 5:30 a.m. We had decided on the earlier start to beat the heat and get some cooler miles in. I knew that before hitting the trail I would have to perform some foot surgery on myself. The pad of my right foot had developed a nasty blister from walking through the waters of Mission Creek for hours the day before. I put a flame from my disposable lighter to my knife, made a small cut in the center of the blister, and extracted the fluid that had collected there. With some antiseptic cream and KT tape, I was good to go.

The goal that morning was to get in as many early miles as possible. We were in a battle with the sun. As we ascended the mountain, the sun was also on the rise. The sun's rays started at the top of the mountain as we were marching up, up, to where we would eventually meet. The sun won. It always wins. But we marched on. We wove up and around by way of those countless switchbacks, taking us into glorious shade at times while the sun was still low in the sky.

I felt fantastic at first, but it wasn't long before I started feeling the same symptoms as I had yesterday. Nausea made it difficult for me to drink even a sip of water, though I knew I needed much more. Eating is something I rarely have trouble with, but the thought of eating made me more nauseous—a perpetual problem that only rest could cure. We were able to take a couple of hour-long breaks in much-coveted shade when we could find it. Scooby was fine and pretty much unaffected, so it was my problem, but he stuck with me and was patient.

We had miles to make up because of our lack of advancement the day before due to those time-consuming washouts of Mission Creek. We had previously made reservations for a room in the town of Big Bear Lake for Saturday and Sunday, so we knew we had to make up some lost time. So, we hiked on, and then we hiked some more. We got to our planned campsite at almost seven o'clock. We made camp, ate dinner, and then were off to our tents. The next day would be a short ten-mile hike to the highway for a hitch into Big Bear Lake. Our plan was to take both a nero and a zero.

The morning's hike from where we had camped the previous evening was just a short 9.8 miles to the highway, California State Route 18. I was up early again to write in my journal, as I had once again been in no condition to do anything but sleep the night before. I awoke and felt really good, which told me that I wasn't sick. Based on my symptoms, my sister, who is a family practitioner, agreed that I wasn't getting enough electrolytes. Once we got to town, I would find powdered Gatorade to pack out as Scooby had done since the start of our hike, which probably explained why he was doing just fine.

When we arrived at Hwy 18, we received some greatly appreciated trail magic. A trail angel had left a cooler of cold soda at the trailhead along with a nice note congratulating us for having hiked one tenth of the PCT and welcoming us to Big Bear Lake. Meanwhile, Lone Wanderer was already standing on the side of the highway trying to hitch a ride. The three of us put our good luck thumbs out in hopes of getting to town, which was six miles away. Car after car passed us by with some obvious efforts from those drivers to avert their eyes. We were a ragtag outfit of hikers with a week's worth of grime, sweat, and stench they could probably smell a mile away. A few moments later, Milo came walking down the trail with her big beautiful smile. She stood next to us and stuck out her thumb. A van going in the opposite direction turned around and picked up all four of us. Our driver was a gracious host and trail angel who dropped us off in town, but first he gave us the drive-through tour.

The little town of Big Bear Lake has much to offer: two grocery stores, plenty of dining options, laundromat, brewery, and of course, overnight accommodations. Scooby and I stayed at the Vintage Lakeside Inn which was neat, clean, reasonably priced, and had a very friendly and especially hiker-friendly staff. Shuttle rides to and from the grocery store for no additional cost was a major plus since the stores were a couple of miles away. Breakfast was only offered on Saturday and Sunday during spring, a slow time of year. The town is set up to serve tourists and snow skiers in the winter, and mountain biking in the summer on those very same ski slopes. In fact, the ski slope operators rig the ski lifts with special attachments to accommodate lifting mountain bikes to the top.

After our brief tour, we went to the local brewery for a hiker hamburger and beer for lunch, then Scooby and I checked into our motel room. I took a much-needed shower, with the dirt and grime coming off me like it was a mudslide—so sorry housekeeping! I got most of it off, but was pretty sure a second and third go at it would be required. While in the bathroom, my reflected image showed that I had already lost a considerable amount of weight. My caloric intake had clearly not been sufficient, and I would need to remedy that immediately. With lunch already taken care of, it was time to plan my next meal. The dinner menu was decided—pizza. Lots and lots of pizza. And beer—strictly for the caloric benefit, of course.

Please don't think that a day off the trail—a zero—translated to a day of leisure and relaxation. Long-distance hiking requires carefully planned activities to ensure success for future miles. So, the next day, it was off to breakfast first, and then a trip to the local and well-appointed Von's supermarket. Once our purchases were made, it was time to head back to our motel where we packed our bags with enough food to take us through the next five days and hundred-plus miles of the Southern California desert. We found the local laundromat and went through the motions of trying to wash our clothes.

With our chores completed, it was time for a bit of entertainment and leisure. Scooby and I made our way to the local theater for the matinee showing of *The Avengers: End Game*. For dinner, we were off to Taco Bell for burritos and tacos.

I also used the weekend off the trail to journal and answer the frequently asked question from family, friends, and fellow hikers.

How would I compare the Appalachian Trail to the Pacific Crest Trail?

This is my opinion based on my 2017 AT thru-hike experience when compared to those first 250 miles of the PCT. My first observation was that on the AT, I would crawl into my tent each night and take off my sweaty and soaked clothes. In the morning I put those same sweaty and soaking wet clothes back on. Whereas on the PCT, I'd crawl into my tent, take off my somewhat damp clothes, wake up in the morning and, thanks to the dry desert air, put on my now very dry—albeit, still stinky—clothes. The AT required you to climb high and steep ascents, while the ascents on the PCT were more gradual, following long, laborious switchbacks. You carried little water on the AT because of how abundantly available it is. By comparison, a hiker on the PCT will carry between four and six liters of water, weighing two pounds per liter, because of fewer water sources. Although this particular year there were more water sources than usual because of excessive snowfall in the high desert.

Next, the AT crosses close to local communities on a regular basis, while the PCT requires you to hitch longer distances into a town for resupply. On the PCT you battle dry heat and at times cold temperatures. On the AT you battle heat with high humidity, plus some cold temperatures at night and at high elevations. On the AT you experience numerous trail angel opportunities, while on the PCT there are not quite as many, though they are just as kind, generous, and appreciated.

On the AT, also known as the Green Tunnel, you really never know what is coming up regarding views. On the PCT, you can usually see for miles ahead. On the AT you see very little of the sky. On the PCT you see nothing but beautiful wide-open skies. The AT is a foot trail that is well-blazed and easily followed, while the PCT is far less marked or visible, and requires careful attention to ensure that you are, in fact, on the trail. The AT has shelters approximately every ten miles, while the PCT has virtually no shelters. The AT has limited or required camp locations, while the PCT is not nearly as restrictive. The AT has easy accessibility for section and day hiking, while the PCT is far more remote, thus rarely do you see section or day hikers.

These were some of my early observations, and they held true for most of my hike.

At the end of the weekend, we checked out of the motel where we were staying, and they provided shuttle service that morning to the trailhead.

Time to get back to the daily grind.

It was a great day to be back on the trail. It's not often you leave a town with a full pack, heavy with resupply, and not have a huge climb up. Well, that was what we were blessed with on this day—just gradual and easy ascents and descents all day. The temperatures never got above the high forties, and while it threatened to rain, it never did. We wore our rain jackets mostly for the added thermal layer and as a safeguard in case the sky actually did open up. Because we were above 7,000 feet for portions of the day, we saw snow again but, fortunately for us, there was no snow on the trail itself.

As uneventful as this day of trail life appeared, there was an eerie feeling that went mostly unspoken. There were no real views, and not just because we found ourselves hiking in a heavy mist and a low ceiling of cold clouds. It was primarily because we were hiking through a badly burned mountainside, and were forced to see it in detail since there was nothing else to look at. We have all seen TV news stories about huge fires over the years, and hear of people losing their homes and the tragic loss of life. Walking through the burned-out areas, as I've also done while hiking the Appalachian Trail, truly hurts my heart. In an effort to place a positive spin on it, I kept reminding myself that sometimes you have to hike through these off-putting sections so you can sincerely appreciate the extremely beautiful sections. I would usually take photos throughout the day, but today there was really nothing worthy of recording. I finally forced myself to pull my camera out and take several photos of that horrific place just so I would never forget what I had witnessed. Those photos will forever serve as my reminder of just how precious and sensitive our natural resources are.

While sleeping in a single wall tent you run the risk of condensation forming on the inside of the material from your breathing and exhaling all night. This is exacerbated if you camp close to a water source, as we had done the night before. Add in some below-freezing temperatures and you'll wake up to a thick layer of frost and ice on the interior walls and ceiling of your tent. A bit inconvenient as you pack up the much heavier wet tent. Thankfully, airing it out later during my lunch break was a quick remedy. We were on the trail by six o'clock, and it soon became abundantly clear that this was a brand-new day. Clear skies and a beautiful mountainside to traverse provided a fresh and healthy outlook for us. When it was time for our second breakfast, I decided I would add to that magnificent day by having a second cup of coffee. Yep, it was a terrific start to a great day!

While hiking along that day I had an interesting thought. I bet there were some people who would be interested in what a thru-hiker's diet might look like. Who doesn't love sharing a few recipes, right? In that spirit, here are a couple of examples.

Yesterday, Scooby prepared himself a lunch that any of us would envy. Starting with a tortilla, he added Nutella, a can of Vienna sausages, and topped it with cheese. Mmm. For his Easter dinner he had spam chunks which he blended with instant loaded mashed potatoes. Another holiday classic! My lunch today consisted of a tortilla wrapped around string cheese and a fat slab of spam and spiced with mild Taco Bell sauce packets I had left over from our dinner in Big Bear Lake.

These shared recipes might be the highlight of your day, but ours was that we passed our 300-mile mark. Another monumental milestone! I had only 2,350 miles to go...

An amazing end to our day was arriving at our planned destination of Deep Creek Hot Springs. It's not just a name, there really are hot springs. These geothermal-fed pools varied in temperature from warm to hot, and were the perfect way to relax after a long mile day. Clothing was optional, but I maintained my long-standing tradition of pervasive modesty and went in with my hiking shorts as my chosen attire.

Meanwhile, others were quite comfortable in their birthday suits. Ah, the life of a thru-hiker…

The campsite at the Deep Creek Hot Springs had the added bonus of being directly on Deep Creek, which provided the ideal background noise for a great night's sleep. We had hiked most of yesterday and for a long period today on the trail high above Deep Creek as it made its way through the deep caverns far below us. Expansive and elaborate bridges aided our crossing several times, and with each crossing the rushing, cascading water kept us mesmerized with its thundering and echoing sounds. The excessive and unusually high water level served as a constant reminder of their source—the snowmelt from higher elevations. Mount Baden-Powell lurked in the not-so-far distance, looking down at us from its still snow-laden peaks. This 9,400-foot monster was the topic of every conversation within the hiking community. With Mount San Jacinto still fresh on our minds, there was a healthy fear of Mount Baden-Powell. Word had been that many earlier hikers took the road-walk around Baden-Powell. We would be in Wrightwood in a couple of days and made plans to ask the folks at the local outfitters what their opinion was. I didn't want to skip Baden-Powell as I was committed to hiking every PCT mile that was open…but I'm not an idiot either.

Another observation while hiking out that morning was the huge amount of graffiti on the rocks. The Hot Springs are a very popular gathering site for locals and is accessible from a roadside parking area with just a few miles hike required. Hundreds of spray-painted rocks with an insurmountable amount of garbage sprayed all over them can really take away from your outdoor experience. I can promise that the people that defaced all that rock were not thru-hikers. Thru-hikers have way too much respect for nature to do anything so stupid and destructive.

Later while fording a creek, we met a hiker who called himself Ketchup. He told us that he, too, had thru-hiked the AT in 2017. His summit of Mount Katahdin was just six days after ours.

We also met Sailor at that same crossing. I asked how she had gotten the trail name Sailor. My first thought was that she must have served in the Navy or lived on a sailboat. Nope, her response was that she says f**k a lot, and was told she curses like a sailor. Well there you have it.

The next morning, I was wide awake at 4:00 a.m., and I knew there was no way I would ever get back to sleep. It's okay, I had planned on getting up at 4:30 anyway. I'd crawled into my tent the evening before, thinking about it while repeating the number that was now imprinted on my brain: 341.9...341.9...341.9. I'd quickly fallen into a deep sleep. Who wouldn't, after having hiked 21.6 miles?

The funny thing was, I would ordinarily avoid that place like the plague. But it was the very place that now tugged me along...341.9. I raced up the mountains, and allowed gravity to aid in pulling me back down the other side, until it was time to race up the next one.

Scooby was in tow and directly on my heels. It was then I realized that I was a fool. He wasn't in tow; he had been drafting me! Just like a professional stock car racer, he was far cleverer than I'd given him credit for. He was just waiting for the perfect moment to pass me...341.9. He couldn't though, because the trail was only eighteen inches wide. Would he have pushed me off the mountain we were now racing up?

Twelve miles passed at an alarmingly rapid pace. We were almost there, mile marker 341.9. A right turn and four-tenths of a mile more. and we arrived—at *McDonalds*! Yes, the pull of McDonalds was our motivation on this day to hike like our stomachs depended on it. Scooby enjoyed a Big Mac, large fries, and a large drink followed with two Quarter Pounders and a chocolate shake. I had two sausage Egg McMuffins, large fries, and large drink followed by two more sausage egg McMuffins. The large drinks were on special for one dollar with free refills included, I filled my large cup four times. Hiker hunger had struck! We were there for two and a half hours, for our second breakfast followed by lunch, arriving at 10:30 a.m. with a departure of 1:00 p.m. Then it was time to add another ten miles to our day, to burn off that newly acquired high-calorie fuel.

The next 30-mile section had no reliable water source, which meant the longest water carry thus far. Scooby and I both left McDonalds with six liters, or twelve pounds, of water on our backs, which would last us till the following afternoon. Six miles later, we found that trail angels had left a water cache with about 50 gallons. Oh well, you can't count on a water cache. It's always best not to depend on that, but to carry your own needs.

Camping on a dirt road that night wouldn't have been our first choice, but it was our only choice. Mind you, it was a dirt road at 5,200 feet, so we weren't expecting a lot of traffic. Even so, a pickup truck came by at 9:30 p.m. and the driver let us know that we were camped on a road. He pulled up to each of our four tents and yelled out his window, "Hey, camper in the tent. Can you hear me?" Hmm, not sure about everyone else, but I left my soundproof tent at home and was able to hear him loud and clear. In the hiking world, 9:30 p.m. is "sound to sleep" late and his waking me up was not entirely appreciated. Anyway, we all made it through the night without getting run over by someone who might have been crisscrossing the mountaintops in the middle of the night. In fact, at last count he was the only person commuting on that 5,200-foot-high dirt road.

Scooby and I agreed that we wanted to get an early start, so we were on the trail by 5:30 a.m. This early a departure not only allowed us to beat the rush hour traffic on the dirt road at 5,200 feet, but it would get us to Wrightwood early as well. When we made it to the trailhead at Hwy 2 and stepped from the trail onto the pavement, a car pulled up to us. The driver rolled down her window and asked if we were PCT hikers. At our affirmative reply, she asked a few more questions about the trail. When the time seemed appropriate, I asked if she might consider giving us a ride to Wrightwood. She and her two passengers were quick to agree, but I'm sure the poor passenger in the back was probably sorry after we'd climbed in next to her. It had been a week without a shower. I did apologize.

Once in town we checked into our room, took showers, and did laundry. As I was standing out front on the sidewalk, a gentleman dropped off Daddy-O and Snake Charmer—a father daughter hiking duo. I asked Rubin, the driver, if he often gave rides to hikers. He said that after being married for 60 years he would often tell his wife he needed to go for a drive. He said it made him feel free. So, I asked if he would consider giving Scooby and me a ride back to the trail on Sunday morning. Rubin asked what time we would like to be picked up, so I asked if 6:00 a.m. would be okay. He told me he's normally up at 4:30, anyway, and that he'd see us at six.

As zero days went, this day was very productive, starting with a great breakfast at the Evergreen Cafe. Next, I went to the grocery store to buy postage stamps for mailing postcards, the local hardware store to see if they had new tips for my hiking poles—struck out—and finally, back to the grocery store to finish up my resupply. After shopping, we sat outside under an open-air tent that the grocery store provided for hikers as a meeting spot and lounge of sorts.

Just then a gentleman named Hal stopped by to ask if we needed a ride back to the trail. Since we were not leaving until the next morning, we thanked him and invited him to sit with us. He mentioned that he had recently driven a hiker to REI, the recreational equipment co-op. That quickly got my attention, as I still had to get new tips for my hiking poles. In addition, I had been thinking about how I would feel far more secure going up Mount Baden-Powell if I had an ice ax. I asked Hal if he might give me a ride, too, and he was quick to agree. Hal understandably asked for gas money, which I was happy to provide. Unfortunately, REI did not carry the tips I needed so I ended up having to purchase new trekking poles. The next item on my to-do list was to pull out a needle and thread to repair a pocket on my hiking pants.

The time for rest and relaxation had now come to an end. It was time to get back to trail life. One and a half days off was exactly what was required to take care of our hiker duties, and the time off gave us the time we needed to recoup and recover from a tough week on the trail.

Our early departure of 6:00 a.m. with the assistance of trail angel Rubin worked out perfectly. Rubin had us back to the trailhead by 6:15, at which time we started our steep ascent. Mount Baden-Powell peaks at 9,400 feet and Mr. Powell didn't want to make it easy. Previously known as North Baldy, this mountain was dedicated and renamed Mount Baden-Powell at a ceremony on Memorial Day weekend in 1931.

As Scooby and I hiked on, it became apparent that we were both noticeably quiet. I asked him if he, like myself, was experiencing some anxiety. As I suspected, we were both a bit nervous about this big climb, but we were also very excited for what lay ahead. The first 4.6 miles brought us to the base of the mountain at 6,600 feet. We hit our first bit of snow at about 7,000 feet, and it was slow in the snow the rest of the way. Hiking the actual trail became virtually impossible once we hit five to six feet of the white stuff. Instead, we simply hiked straight up, bypassing all the switchbacks. Under normal circumstances, I would never hike off the trail, knowing it can cause damage to nature and to the integrity of a trail. These were not normal circumstances though, and there really was no safer way to go. I used my micro-spikes and shortened my trekking poles, turned my attention to the top of the mountain, and started climbing. It was exhausting! My pack weight after leaving town with my resupply was tipping the scales at about 32 lbs., and gravity is not your friend when you are making a near vertical climb. Postholing became hazardous, since the late morning sun did all it could to add to the already challenging hike before us. We finally reached the peak of this spectacular mountain at just past eleven o'clock, which was the perfect time for taking photos and enjoying our lunch with a million-dollar view.

Whistler at the summit of Mt. Baden-Powell

The Baden-Powell monument which was erected in 1957 was a nice tribute to the father of Boy Scouting, and worth the hike there. Another anticipated attraction was the 1,500-year-old limber pine tree that I had read so much about. I now found myself standing next to it for a once in a lifetime photo opportunity. A 1,500-year-old tree. Incredible!

Lunch was eaten just as slowly as the climb up. We didn't want to or really need to leave, so we took our time dining above the clouds. When it was finally time to bid farewell to our biggest challenge yet, we did so with the vigor required to make the big descent. We ended our day camped at 7,500 feet, where it was ridiculously cold. I dug deep into my pack and put on every stitch of clothing I had with me in an effort to stay warm. The positive bright side was, there were no bugs.

Poodle-dog bush—*eriodictyon parryi*—was the plant to avoid the next day. This invasive plant is one of the first to make its presence known in those areas that have experienced fires, and this puppy doesn't play. It's easy to identify with leaves that plume like a poodle's hair. It also has a distinct scent which is similar to marijuana. In fact, I've read that some unsuspecting hikers have actually tried to smoke it. Merely touching this plant will have you breaking out in intense blisters that will likely put you in the hospital. This was the first day we saw countless examples of this plant, but fortunately, efforts to remove it from hanging over the trail had been successful. From poodle-dog bush to butterflies—thousands upon thousands of these winged beauties flew all about as we hiked along.

As a general rule, I never have trouble getting to sleep, especially when hiking twenty-plus miles every day. This night was a difficult one though. I found myself lying in my tent staring up at the ceiling mere inches from my face for hours. I had a number of issues on my mind that I just couldn't shake, so instead I'd check my watch every 30 minutes or so while willing myself to sleep. One such issue was the high snow levels in the Sierra Nevada Mountains. The most recent PCT snow report showed very little improvement north of Kennedy Meadows. Entry into the Sierras was now recommended to be July 6th. On a normal snowfall year, the recommendation for entry would be June 1st through the 15th. Simply put, like many other hikers, we were too early. Decisions would have to be made, with numerous approaches as to how to plan the rest of the thru-hike. That was weighing heavily on my mind.

It was starting to look as though jumping ahead would be the first option, then returning to the Sierras to complete the thru-hike later when the snow levels were less dangerous. There were some limited low-lying snowless areas in Oregon and Washington, while there were still huge areas of deep snow north of the Sierra Nevadas. Had I just picked the wrong year?

Next on my list of concerns was that I would have to change my resupply strategy.

And finally, Scooby would be leaving me and the trail in about two more weeks. His plan had always been to hike with me to mile 652, Walker Pass, where he could catch a bus to the airport for his flight home. Scooby had been the perfect trail mate and an invaluable friend, but I knew from the start that his departure was inevitable.

As I lay there in my tent, I just wanted and needed to get sleep. Sleep finally came, but not the restorative sleep my body needed. Our planned departure time was 7:00 a.m. I must have fallen asleep after 10:00 p.m., as that was the last time I could recall looking at my watch. I awoke again at four o'clock, and I couldn't get back to sleep. Well, I guess it was time to get up and have coffee anyway. I pulled Scooby's and my food bags down from the bear hang which was reminiscent of our thru-hike on the AT. I'd always pull down our bags and place his at the vestibule of his tent. While on the AT, I would hear him still sawing logs. Not today. He was up and lacing his shoes. With another big-miles day ahead, we did what all good hikers do—we hiked on.

I learned a long time ago that a requirement for being a thru-hiker was to accept that the plans you make must be flexible. Our plan the previous night was to hike 24 miles into Agua Dulce. The hiking was spectacular with regard to weather, trail conditions, and views. Once we reached Soledad Canyon Road, we were just four-tenths of a mile from the KOA campground at Acton. It happened to be lunchtime, so why not stop in for a cold Coke? I could tell that Scooby wasn't quite as keen on this detour as I was, but he finally gave in to my high-pressure tactics and agreed.

Once we arrived at the KOA it became clear that we would be changing our plans. Fifteen dollars for a tent site and two dollars for a towel rental, shampoo and soap was tempting, but it was the laundry facilities that sealed the deal. I spent a stupidly long time in the shower and managed to exit relatively cleansed, making that the best two bucks I had ever spent. There was a terrific lounge area where all the hikers congregated to catch up with one another, but more important, to charge all electronic devices. Just about everyone was ordering in pizza, but Scooby and I abstained since we agreed that we needed to lighten our food bags. We planned on hitting the trail at six-thirty the next morning, and we'd hike the ten miles into Agua Dulce and Hiker Heaven to pick up our next drop boxes. My sister Susan had mailed my box, which I anticipated would likely have a few of her surprises—always a welcome treat.

As I previously mentioned, I was having to change my resupply strategy. My sister is a serious kayaker and was currently in training for the Missouri 340, which is a 340-mile race on the Missouri River. Unfortunately, with that training, her busy work schedule and her hobby farm, she was having difficulty keeping up with mailing my drop boxes. I was so greatly appreciative of the support she had been able to provide as it had been absolutely invaluable. But as said, a thru-hiker needs to be flexible. So, my new plan was to self-support, which would add a few kinks into the works. I'd already met many hikers who were self-supporting, especially those who had traveled from every other continent on the planet. One surprising finding was that I believe there were actually more foreigners hiking the PCT than there were North Americans.

The next two weeks would require some intense planning as to how to continue this hike. The Sierras had just received an additional two feet of snow, and the snow pack was currently at close to two hundred percent above the yearly average. The recommended entry had been moved from June 15th to July 7th, but I was currently on pace to arrive there somewhere around May 23rd—about six weeks too early. Talk on the trail had most thru-hikers planning on skipping the Sierra Nevada for now, with others planning on taking side trips, others taking a month off the trail, while some were just going to quit their thru-hikes altogether.

Quitting was something I had not even begun to consider. It's just not what I do. Remember, a thru-hiker's plans need to be flexible. My current plan was to skip ahead past the Sierras to where conditions were a bit better and continue hiking north, hopefully following the snowmelt. Once I got to Manning Park and the northern terminus, I would return and complete the Sierras.

That was the current plan.

Then again, a thru hiker's plans...

Staying at the KOA campground the previous night had seemed like a good idea, but it proved to be somewhat of a mistake. The tent area filled up as the day wore on, and it wasn't long before it looked like a refugee tent city. I'll admit I am a light sleeper, but the snoring was unbearable. I knew I was in real trouble when the trains traveling close by also sounded their bells and blasted their horns every half hour or so. There was actually one point that I hoped the trains would wake the snorers so I might get back to sleep before they did. The problem being that not even a train going directly through their tents would have woken them up. Then there were the barking and fighting dogs doing their part to keep me up, as well. And of course, there were all the young hikers who were planning on taking a zero the next day, with no real reason to get to bed early. After all, they did have all that beer, wine, and vodka to drink like it was their job. Honestly, if I were their age, I would probably have been right there with them. Truth be told, they didn't really stay up too late either. They had all hiked just as hard and as far as I had, so they must have been just as tired as I was. And they really were great people. In all, I got about four hours of sleep.

Now, a bit more about the next day's hike. We got off to an early start and hiked through Vasquez Rocks Park early that morning. Vasquez Rocks is a popular park with some highly unusual rock formations which are the result of past volcanic activity and millions of years of erosion. This site is a favorite location for Hollywood productions, having been used as the backdrop and set for numerous Westerns, for Planet of the Apes, the Flintstones Movie, and the TV series Star Trek, to name just a few. In fact, there was a production company there doing a shoot while we were passing by. We might have been unsuspecting extras.

Rock outcropping at Vasquez Rocks

Our continuing miles brought us to the iconic Hiker Heaven at mile 454.4, which was a true treat. Trail angels Donna and Jeff Saufley open their beautiful property to PCT hikers, provide services a hiker can only dream about, and have been doing it for 22 years. How about the fact that they will do your laundry? You can have your mail drop sent there, camp on their property for up to two days, and longer if you have an injury. They have a tent with a common use computer to check email and charge your electronics, a hiker lounge tent, a boxing and mailing tent if you need to mail anything, as well as showers, a first aid station, shuttles to grocery stores, restaurants, and the list goes on and on. Scooby and I stayed a short time while we sorted our drop boxes, took showers, and later took them up on a shuttle to a local restaurant for some town food. They operate on donations with no set fees for all the services they provide. Donna, Jeff, and their volunteers are truly amazing trail angels.

A couple of quick comments on the subject of equipment. I was really pleased with the selection of my Altra Timps hiking shoes. They had really worked well for me and held up pretty well for having over 450 miles, but it was now time to start thinking about the future. I got with Annie to ask her to order a new pair from REI. She got on it and had them shipped ahead for me to pick up in about ten more days. I had also taken the opportunity to donate my Sun-Brella to the hiker box back at the KOA campground, in hopes someone else would get better use out of it. A hiker box is where hikers put things they don't need, so a future hiker can use them. I had researched the Sun-Brella prior to my hike, and used it a couple times, but just didn't care for it. I also didn't see the value in carrying that additional 8 ounces of weight. Into the box it went.

When Scooby and I arrived at our camp that night, it was under the heaviest fog or mist I'd ever seen. We were soaked, as though we'd been hiking in a rainstorm all day. One thing about me—without getting too graphic—is that my feet don't do well when they stay wet all day. Once in my tent, I quickly took off my shoes and socks in an attempt to allow them to dry out. We were camped on another dirt road which intersected with the trail at about 4,500 feet. These roads are common occurrences which serve as fire roads used by the US Forest Service for their work in fighting fires in these difficult to access locations. If there are no dedicated tent sites available, hikers will pitch their tents anywhere there is a flat spot, including, as a last resort, a dirt road.

It continued to rain all night and into the morning up until our planned departure time, which we delayed until the rain stopped. When we eventually got going, the trail was an easy and gentle trail with minor ascents and descents. We saw very few hikers, as most must have stayed at Hiker Heaven during the rain—easy to understand when you consider how welcoming the Saufleys were.

One young hiking couple we did meet. Air Bud and Fit Bit, like Scooby and myself, were both class of 2017 AT thru-hikers. In fact, they had met in the Smoky Mountains and have been together ever since. It was around two o'clock when we arrived at the Green Valley Fire Station, a USFS station that allows hikers to draw water from their hose bib. This stop on San Francisquito Valley Road is where you would walk or hitch one and a half miles to the Casa de Luna. Casa de Luna is another iconic hiker hostel. It's operated by the Andersons, who have been hosting hikers for years. When you first arrive at Casa de Luna, you will be invited to pick a Hawaiian shirt from their large collection, as has been their long tradition. Next, you would pitch your tent and prepare yourself to relax, do arts and crafts—really—enjoy a taco salad for dinner and pancakes for breakfast.

Scooby and I got water from the firehouse and kept hiking. Boring right?

Well, unfortunately, we were now on a strict timeline and really needed to keep to it. Scooby had just purchased his plane ticket and it was non-refundable. So, we both agreed that we would put in a few additional miles. Naturally, as we hiked on it began to rain again. And they call this a desert? We literally started running in an attempt to get to our planned campsite. So once again we were camped at yet another intersection of where the trail meets a Forest Service dirt road.

Early the next day we hiked past three caves we had previously read about on Guthook. They varied in size, with the largest being roomy enough for up to five people. I took a couple of photos, but I wasn't too interested in going inside. It was still early and I didn't wish to wake a sleeping bear or mountain lion.

We had a long water carry the night before, so we were looking forward to an anticipated spring that was described in our hiking guides. When we arrived, it was the most beautiful, fresh, cold mountain spring I could ever have imagined. Cool water just bubbled out from the side of the mountain as though someone had drilled a hole and struck water. I have always filtered every drop from every source I have ever taken along the trail—as I did here—but I was pretty sure filtering this pure gift from the mountain wasn't required.

Later, we hiked an eight-mile section that looked and felt reminiscent of the Appalachian Trail. We hiked through the most beautiful forest, which provided us with cool shade that surrounded us for all those miles, leaving us to question if we were still in the desert. Those miles rolled off easily and helped make the day's hike the best since the start one month earlier. Water was once again a challenge, though. We stopped at a cistern listed in our guides, but thought better of it when we found a dead bear in it. Somehow, this bear had crawled in for a drink and couldn't get out. Pretty sad. Sad that he had died, but also sad that we couldn't get water from that source. Once we made camp, we quickly got into our tents because a storm was brewing. Rain and hail pounded my tent like the percussion section of a junior high school band, but thankfully passed quickly and moved on as though it had never occurred.

As I hiked each day, I would often think back to some of the sights I had been blessed to see, and sometimes my mind would get stuck on something that I wouldn't be able to stop thinking about. That day I got stuck on that 1,500-year-old limber pine at the top of Mount Baden-Powell. I thought about what that tree had seen over all those years, and if the tree could speak, what it might have to say. If you recall, Mount Baden-Powell was named after the founder of the Boy Scouts, Lord Baden-Powell who died in 1941. But it wasn't until 1957 that a group of Scouts carried all the materials up the four miles to the crest to build his memorial. They carried all the cement, wood for forms, water, and railings used to build the memorial that still stands today. This is what I believe that 1,500-year-old tree would say.

THE LIMBER PINE

A seedling was I fifteen hundred years ago,
and what I've seen you'll never know.
I've dug in deep upon this crest,
it's where I live, it's where I rest.
From my perch at nine thousand feet,
I cast my shadow over those I meet.
Perhaps the greatest I did not know,
was a leader who helped young men grow.
Lord Baden-Powell's monument lives here with me,
no finer man could there be.
His oath, Scouts pledge to this day,
the foundation many live by today.

The next day I made an entry in my journal that we had hiked just 15.2 miles. When had 15.2 miles hiked become "just"? Along the way we came across a paved road, and after we crossed, we found an unusual arrangement of rocks and sticks. The rocks spelled out H20 with an arrow made from sticks pointing up the road. Reading it, I told Scooby that I guessed the road must be Highway 20. He laughed and pointed to the water cache siting under a tree, reminding me that H-2-0 might also mean two atoms of hydrogen and one atom of oxygen. Duh. I guess the desert sun was having an effect on my brain.

Our goal was to get into Hikertown, where Scooby had a resupply package waiting for him, and where I could shop for my resupply as well. We also looked forward to being able to grab some town food. The term town food means anything other than pepperoni, peanut butter, tortillas—you get the idea I'm sure. When we arrived, Bob the caretaker located Scooby's box, then kindly asked if we wanted to borrow his van to go get lunch. Hmm, let me think for a second. Yes! We would like to borrow the van to get lunch. Let me attempt to best describe Bob's van. First of all, it actually and surprisingly started. Next, I was pretty certain it was leaking an equal amount of fuel as the engine was combusting. As the designated driver, I was pleased to find that the windows worked, so I quickly stuck my head out the driver's side window in an effort to avoid passing out from the fuel fumes. I drove as fast as the vehicle would go, but the vehicles behind us passed at any opportunity, including crossing over double solid yellow lines. I guess that's legal in California? Luckily, none of those passing vehicles tossed a lit cigarette out the window, as I'm certain the van and passengers alike would have gone up in flames. Anyway, after hiking at about three miles per hour for these past four weeks, I felt I was driving more than fast enough. We made it to our destination, where I ordered a cheeseburger with fries. I'd always tell myself I would order a salad instead of fries, but that just never seemed to happen. When that burger arrived at our table, I took a nice big bite and proceeded to break a tooth. That first bite made for one expensive hamburger, since a future visit to the dentist would soon be required.

Hikertown is another hostel open to hikers that allows camping on their grounds for free—with a donation recommended. I pitched my tent in what appeared to be an animal holding pen. It had a gate that could close, so I felt pretty secure knowing a bear wouldn't get my food...or me. Next on my to-do list was to take a shower and do my laundry. I waited patiently while Bob the caretaker attempted to repair the outdoor shower. After an extended period of time, and with some obvious frustration, he looked up and invited me to use the indoor shower located in the garage. It was an amazing hot and welcome shower, except for the fact that there was no soap or shampoo. I eventually found and happily used a tube of Disney *Frozen* Winter Berry scented body wash. I was now Winter Berry clean.

The following day would be a big one for us. We would be hiking 20 miles along the Los Angeles aqueduct. The aqueduct moves water from the Owens River in the eastern Sierra Nevada for 419 miles through a system of concrete canals and a 12-foot diameter pipe. It is a true marvel of engineering. Construction originally started in 1908, bringing its fair share of controversy along with it. Unfortunately, the water that runs through the aqueduct is only for the residents of Los Angeles and not for thirsty hikers. That water runs through the desert where we will walk on and over it, but won't be able to access a single drop. In other words, there was a long, hot hike and a long water carry in our future.

Our stay at Hikertown was what I would call adequate at best. They were very friendly and extremely accommodating, but the place was a bit run down compared to Hiker Heaven or Scout and Frodo's. Still, it did meet our minimalist needs while adding to the hiker experience.

A common practice among the hiking community is to recognize and respect "hiker midnight." It is understood that there are hikers who will head out early and need to get to sleep. With no actual time assigned to hiker midnight, it's usually around sunset. Hikers this evening were up and very vocal to all hours. The late-night yelling, screaming, and overall partying reminded me why I'm not a big fan of staying at hiker hostels, especially if there are no guidelines to adhere to posted by the hosts. This was a real problem since we had planned on getting up at 3:00 a.m. and hiking out at four o'clock. I know everything is not all about me, but I was lucky if I got four hours of sleep, which, when there is a planned 24-mile hike ahead, just falls flat.

We had agreed on the extra early start to our day in an attempt to beat the heat on the long, flat hike of the Los Angeles Aqueduct. It had been the best decision and approach to this section, and we had successfully hiked 10.5 miles by 7:00 a.m., and 17 miles by 9:30 a.m. This required a long water carry, but the cool morning made the hike tolerable. The hike itself was without question the most boring miles thus far—17 miles on the pipe, and later the concrete aqueduct. Walking above it was interesting—we could hear the water under our feet as it rushed toward its destination.

These miles of the trail were relatively flat, but still uniquely beautiful. We hiked the cool, calm, and windless morning with headlamps focused on the aqueduct below our feet. Kangaroo mice hopped before our light beams as we interrupted their nocturnal escapades. Coyotes howling and their pups barking contributed to the eeriness of the black sky with its crescent moon.

As the sun rose in the east, the sky made for a beautiful backdrop for the Joshua trees that now revealed themselves in the morning light. At first, they were merely black silhouettes against a daybreak sky, which soon became full, wide, and cloudless, with the sun's full force pounding us. We took regular breaks when we could find shade, and cautiously rehydrated ourselves with the water it took to last this long, waterless section. Leapfrogging a couple from the Netherlands, The

Flying Dutchman, and his girlfriend, The Duchess, along with Xena, made the hike a bit more fun. We turned the section into a race. We eventually made it to what was listed as an unreliable water source, but which proved to be an oasis with water flowing abundantly from a tap. We found shade behind a pumping station and enjoyed a break before moving on. We spent the rest of the day hiking through five miles of wind farms. There were windmills for miles upon miles. There had to be a thousand windmills for as far as the eye could see.

Waking up the next morning after a peaceful night's sleep was easy. I jumped up at 4:00 a.m. after getting a full eight hours, got dressed, and made a simple breakfast of a tortilla, peanut butter, and Nutella, with a cup of steaming hot coffee. I heard Scooby stirring around in his tent at 4:30 as I started packing up for a new day of hiking with a 5:30 departure. A couple of hours into our hike, Scooby pointed up ahead at a coyote that had just crossed the trail. We were pretty close, but he or she—I didn't get close enough to be able to say for certainty—didn't seem too interested in us. Which told me that being a stinky hiker had at least one advantage—not even a coyote would touch us. A short time later we came across a little oasis out in the middle of nowhere. Some trail angels had erected lawn chairs, patio umbrellas, and a huge cache of water in the most obscure place on the planet. It was so unexpected, and a huge lift to our morale. How those people were able to get all that up this mountain we would never know, but what we did know was that they were true trail angels.

Just the day before, I had seen the largest wind farm in my life, but today's wind farm was the granddaddy of them all. We hiked mile upon mile through thousands of windmills. A short time after hiking through the wind farm we reached Willow Spring Road, which was our exit point off the trail to get to the town of Tehachapi. Getting to Tehachapi would require a ten-plus mile hitch. Once we got to the road, we had to wait about a whole three minutes for a ride. A gentleman—Ian—who happened to work for the wind farms picked us up in a company truck. Ian shared with us that the owner of the company had instructed all associates who drive company vehicles to pick up any hiker trying to get a hitch into town. Not only that, they are also instructed to give hikers bottled water if they are in need. Once again, trail angels where and when you need them. Amazing. Ian also told us the wind farms are the largest employer in Tehachapi, and that there are about 5,000 windmills in the area. Historically, the Tehachapi Valley was home to the Native American tribe of the Kawaiisu people for thousands of years. It is possible the name Tehachapi comes from the Kawaiisu word *tihachipia* which means "hard climb." How perfectly appropriate.

Miles upon miles of windmills

Once we checked into our motel, we called someone on a list of local trail angels that was posted at the trailhead. We phoned Patty, who was actually in Colorado at the time, but her husband was still back in Tehachapi. Patty called her husband, Ron, and asked him to come get us and deliver us to the local Albertsons supermarket so we could shop for our resupply. Incredible. While in line at the grocery store, Scooby started joking around with another customer, and after a few minutes he asked the guy if he might drive us back to our motel. He told us his truck was too full of his tools. No problem, we said. A couple minutes into our walk across the parking lot, he pulled up to tell us that he could move the tools and had us hop in. Again, another trail angel to the rescue.

I don't believe it would be possible to hike this trail without trail angels and their kindness and generosity. The only thing left for us to do at that point was to find a ride back to the trail in the morning. Funny thing, I was not the least bit worried about it, because I knew there were angels among us.

Probably not surprising, but we were up at 5:00 a.m. and ready to take full advantage of the free motel breakfast. The Sure Stay Motel in Tehachapi offers a full breakfast of eggs, sausage, toast, muffins, waffles, cereal, fruit, and more. I believe I drank eight glasses of orange juice—OJ tends to be one of my cravings while hiking. Once we ate our fill, we made our way back to our room to see what we could do about getting a ride for those ten miles back to the trail. Getting back to the trailhead proved to be as simple as making two phone calls. That list of trail angels willing to provide help to hikers made this town a top hiker-friendly town. My first call failed to go through. My second call was answered by Tim on the second ring. I introduced myself as a PCT hiker, explained I'd found his number on a list of trail angels, and wondered if he might be available to take me and my hiking partner back to the trail. Tim's response was, "Sure!" Tim's trail name was Tim-Bob. He picked us up at 8:00 a.m. and had us hiking by 8:20. Tim shared that he offers rides to hikers because he also hikes and knows how helpful and important trail angels have been to him.

The next section we would be hiking was about 100 miles long, and would take us to Walker Pass. That section is known to be extremely dry, so there would be some long water carries, with the longest being 33 miles. The good news was there was a cold front forecast for that week. The expected day temperatures might get into the 50s, and colder overnight. The colder the temperatures, the less water needed. The bad news was, there was also snow in the forecast at elevations above 5000 feet. Yes, we would be well above 5000 feet. It was now the middle of May and we were looking at a forecast calling for snow. In California. I was praying for the meteorologist to be wrong.

You might not believe it, but once again we hiked through even more windmills. After three days of hiking through those darned things, I couldn't care less if I ever saw another stinking windmill for the rest of my life. And here's the thing—they place them there because it's *windy*. High winds had us taking three steps forward, one step back. The winds were so strong it felt like I was hiking as though I was intoxicated. But there were also times the wind was at our backs, and then we had no complaints since it helped blow us up the mountains.

The previous day, I had taken a pretty big fall on a part of the trail that had been washed out. Heavy rains and snow along the high desert mountains often take out parts of the trail. One minute your walking on a trail, the next minute the trail is gone. Trail maintenance crews must have their hands full along these desert miles where there are no trees with roots to limit soil erosion. Anyway, I carelessly slipped, slid, and twisted my left knee and left ankle. When I got back up, I was a bit nervous at the thought that I might have just ended my hike. Scary, but it really can take just one misstep to end a hike—a lesson I would relearn further up the trail. It hurt pretty badly, but I was able to walk on it so I decided to walk it off, and we hiked an additional sixteen miles. When I woke up the next morning, I hardly felt a twinge. I guess the five hundred-plus miles I had already hiked must have strengthened those muscles enough to take a big fall and manage to bounce back unscathed.

As we crawled into our tents the night before, we'd decided we would start our day at 7:00 a.m. Rain or not, we were hiking. Of course, we also agreed to text one another in the morning if it was raining too hard. The night sky was ominously dark, with raging clouds curling, twisting, and changing shape into monstrous formations. It was about 3:00 a.m. when the first drops made their unwanted appearance and started to thump my tent. I was so tired that I simply and easily ignored the storm's arrival, rolled over, and slept some more. At five o'clock, I realized I was safe, warm, and dry, but I needed to get moving. A cup of hot coffee was my motivation. A light rain continued to fall when Scooby sent a text.

SCOOBY: STILL ON FOR 7:00 A.M.?

ME: WHY NOT? NOTHING ELSE PLANNED FOR THE DAY.

We started with our rain jackets on, and they never came off the entire day. It wasn't just the rain, either. We could hear the *whomp, whomp, whomp* of the windmills—yep, more windmills—but could only trust in their presence as we couldn't see them for the fog. We were pelted all day long with rain, sleeting rain, and snow. The winds were so intense it was all I could do to remain upright on my feet. The whole time I was hiking I kept thinking about those poor thru-hikers who had already entered the Sierras. We had received word via the very reliable trail network that several hikers were trapped at high elevation with tents as their only shelter against what was certainly far worse conditions than what we were experiencing. We later found out that an additional two feet of snow had fallen in the Sierra Nevada Mountains just 100 miles north of us during this freak May storm, and that several hikers had to be rescued because of the dangerous weather. The radar application on my phone told a dismal story—this weather system would keep coming all day. Scooby and I hiked our miles with barely a break. We took a six-minute lunch break because we were starving, but knew if we stopped for much longer, we would start to freeze from the unseasonably cold temperatures. My hands were numb as it was. Who would have thought that winter gloves would be needed in the desert?

We made it to our planned campsite that day at 2:45 p.m. and quickly pitched our tents and climbed in. I told myself that even if the wind stopped, the rain stopped, and the sun came out, I still wouldn't get out of my tent. No worries though, because the wind and rain continued.

What would the following day bring?

Early that next day, I received a text from my wife asking me to give her a call. Annie had just learned of the tragic attack on two hikers on the Appalachian Trail. This attack had been the topic of conversation amongst the entire hiking community. One week earlier, on May 10th, 2019, a man and woman who were hiking the Appalachian Trail were attacked by a man with either a large knife or machete—news reports differed. The man died from his injuries while the woman who was brutally attacked played dead, and later escaped with critical wounds.

This terrible murder hit close to home for a couple of reasons. First, because I'd hiked the AT in 2017 and had nothing but fond memories of my time on that special trail. Unfortunately, now this horrific crime would be imprinted in the memories of the class of 2019 AT thru-hikers and the families of the victims for the rest of their lives. Second, the woman who survived the attack came from my home province of Nova Scotia, which brought this monstrous act even closer to home. People hike the AT and other long trails to challenge themselves, and for the opportunity to walk with nature in what can only be described as an awe-inspiring experience. We achieve what we do thanks to the random and selfless acts of kindness from entire nearby communities and trail angels. One evil person should never be allowed to define trail life, and hopefully won't change the outpouring of compassion and support we hikers receive from those communities and trail angels.

Hamp Williams Pass would never have been my first choice to camp that night. But more freezing rain, sleet, and snow helped convince me that it was really the only choice. I knew we were coming up on it in about eight tenths of a mile. As usual, I was up front taking lead with Scooby in his comfortable position a bit behind. I came across a section of the forest that I recall saying to myself, but out loud, "What an ugly part of the forest." Downed trees littered the forest floor. Rotting trees that had fallen years earlier made for an unsightly and sad presentation. I kept hiking, and a short time later I noticed Scooby was no longer behind me. I waited a moment or two and suddenly realized I had hiked too far. I checked my GPS and found I'd hiked two tenths of a mile past our agreed-upon camp. I backtracked and found Scooby having a good laugh. He had already pitched his tent, knowing I'd eventually figure out my mistake. It turned out that ugly part of the forest was Hamp Williams Pass, and exactly where we were camping.

By the time morning arrived, I had received ten hours of sleep. It was much needed sleep as our hike the day before had been exhausting. The first couple of hours hiking that morning was like a repeat of the prior day's hike, but it quickly changed into one of the most perfect days I had ever seen. It proved to be the calm after the storm. The weather and the trail conditions could not have been any better.

It was now time I faced the subject I'd done so well avoiding, a harsh reality that continued to weigh heavy on my heart. May 10th, 2017, was exactly two years and one week ago—the day I met my good friend and hiking partner, Mark, a.k.a. Scooby. I knew the date because as I was doing now, I had journaled each day I was on the Appalachian Trail, and was easily able to look it up. When I'd caught the hiking bug again and decided I wanted to hike the Pacific Crest Trail, I reached out to Scooby to see if he would be interested. He told me he would hike a part of the trail, but he didn't feel the desire to do a thru-hike again. I was thrilled to know he would start this journey with me, while also knowing there would be a defined departure date. That day was coming and it was approaching all too soon.

I woke up this morning to the blowing winds on this mountain pass where we were camping, and looked down at the remaining 55.6 miles

Scooby and I would hike together over the next three days. Scooby has been a great friend and companion for nearly 2000 miles of hiking together. What happens when two people hike that many miles together? There's a connection, a mutual understanding, patience, and acceptance of and for one another. There is honesty and trust. There are common goals and objectives that are met collectively and cohesively. There is good humor and, in most cases, humor that only the two of us could understand and appreciate. But most important is the ability to share and appreciate our achievements as friends, and to do that together with Mark has been a gift.

What does the future look like for this hiking duo? My hopes and prayers are for more miles hiked with my good friend.

I woke up early at 4:00 a.m. to a full moon illuminating my whole tent in a bright yellow hue. I thought to myself, "Where did that come from?" I realized we had not seen the moon for several days due to the intense weather conditions. I recalled the first full moon I had seen while hiking this trail, and the second. Two full moons already—how many more would I see? Three? Four? I was so accustomed to measuring time and distance in miles, I believed I would now look at the moon a lot differently. Each cycle of the moon would bring me closer to home.

While hiking the AT there was hardly a minute that I didn't have full cell and data service from my service provider, Verizon. The isolation and extreme terrain of the PCT was a different story. There had been many occasions when we camped in a deep valley or canyon and couldn't get cell or data service. When this occurred, as it did on this particular morning, I would hike out thirty minutes before Scooby in an attempt to reach a higher elevation so I could upload my journal. It took hiking four miles ahead before I was able to find a spot where I got even one bar of cell service. I climbed further up, off the trail, to a spot where I finally received data service for my upload. On those occasional days when there was no service at all, I would send a text to my wife via my Garmin inReach to assure her that all was well. It is my belief that it would be irresponsible for anyone to hike the PCT without a GPS satellite device such as a Garmin or SPOT. It was apparent that most hikers I came across agreed, as I was more likely than not to see a GPS device clipped to their backpack. For the record, the Garmin Mini inReach was by far the most popular on the trail. Depending on the subscription plan you have, two-way communication via satellite text messaging allows you always to be in touch with your loved ones. These devices also allow friends and family to follow you via the GPS tracking option.

When Scooby caught up to me, we continued on for another eight miles, and then we came upon some of the best trail magic imaginable. Two groups of trail angels had unbeknownst to each other planned on offering of trail magic. When they unsuspectingly met up at the same time, they joined forces and set up at a place where a dirt road crossed the trail, making a lot of hikers pretty happy. We were served pancakes and bacon, coffee, soda, fruit, snacks, and so much more. Scooby and I spent a full hour there with these amazing trail angels. With bellies full, we thanked our hosts and hiked on. We had a big climb out that took us from 5,500 feet to 7,000 feet. The summit was 3.5 miles up the trail, and we made the climb in just one hour fifteen minutes. We had only achieved that impressive climb with the added help of the pancakes and bacon from our trail angels. The true prize, though, was that once we reached the summit, we got our first glimpse of the Sierra Nevada—the huge, beautiful, snow-covered mountains due north.

Scooby and I made our plans to hike to Walker Pass and hitch into Ridgecrest the following day, which was a Sunday. Those new shoes Annie had ordered for me were waiting at the post office, but I would not be able to pick them up until Monday morning. We'd booked a cheap motel room that was centrally located in Ridgecrest, where we could do our laundry. I also needed to shop for my next resupply, including a few pieces of equipment—i.e. winter gloves, fuel, and socks. Like most others, I had decided to skip the Sierras due to the unusually high levels of snow this year, including the two additional feet they had just received this week.

Scooby rented a car and kindly offered to drive me to Chester, California, which was 689 trail miles north. My plan was to continue my hike to the northern terminus. Once there I would flip back south to Walker Pass, at which time I would hope to complete my hike through the Sierras. There were two important reasons I decided to take this approach. First, I wanted to live. The amount of snow in the High Sierras was at record levels, and in my opinion just too dangerous. Second, I wanted to see and enjoy the Sierra Nevada for what it is known for. I would still hike every one of the 2,650 miles possible, and my plan would still be recognized as a thru-hike. I and many others were just being prudent in how we approached the highly unusual snowfall that 2019 brought to the entire west coast.

Sometimes while mindlessly hiking, I'd have random thoughts come to me, two of which I'd like to share now. The first was how toward the end of each day, after hiking miles upon miles, we always knew which of those miles would be the last of the day. You're tired, and quite honestly ready to pitch your tent, eat, clean up, and ready yourself for much needed rest and sleep. The observation being that the last mile of the day was always the longest mile of the day.

My next observation was that while hiking the desert of Southern California, placing one foot down and then repeating with the other, I would often pause and take a look around me. Quite often I felt like a guileless child in absolute wonder at what was before me. Could what I was looking at really be this beautiful? How could a dry, dusty, and parched desert be so magnificently beautiful?

While enjoying the pancakes and bacon the previous day, one of our kind trail angels shared a printed copy of the upcoming weather report. This report told yet another dismal story. Another major storm was coming our way. We would once again face freezing temperatures along with rain, sleet, and snow. Knowing the forecast in advance helped us to decide to hike a few additional miles that day. That had been a good decision, as later we could feel the air changing and it was obvious the meteorologist had once again miraculously gotten it right. That morning I was awakened by the sound of ice pellets attempting to find a rhythmic beat on the tent fabric, inches from where I had laid my head. I wasn't cold though, as my 20-degree quilt, sleeping bag liner, glove liners, and toque performed well, wrapping me in a cocoon of warmth. The drum beat was actually calming, and I quickly returned to dreams of sunny days with cool breezes while hiking the PCT.

When it was time to get up I did so as usual, without the need of an alarm, and it was time to go work. It was cold and wet, but it was also time to prepare to hike those last eleven miles to Walker Pass—the last eleven PCT miles I would hike with my dear friend Scooby.

The trail was good to us, although we did get hit with a snow blizzard, white out conditions, and high winds that made walking a straight line impossible. If an officer of the law asked me to perform a sobriety test, I would have failed. Once we made it to Walkers Pass, I spotted two-day hikers preparing to get in their car. I walked up to them and asked if they might give us a ride to the town of Ridgecrest, which was 25 miles away at the foot of the eastern slope of the Sierras. Two minutes later we were on our way thanks to Vanessa and Alfred.

The following day would be a travel day with a nine-hour drive to Chester, a small lakeside town high in the mountains, right at the transition between the Sierra Nevadas and the Cascade Range, about equidistant from the eastern and western foothills.

As we left the desert of Southern California, I wrote the following poem.

DESERT CACTUS

I try so hard to understand
why you're here upon this land.
In this desert I do not know,
how you flourish, how you grow.
I do my best not to touch,
rub against, or even brush,
your pretty flowers that you flirt,
and those pointy things that really hurt.
I've traveled far and I'm pleased to say
your beauty added to my hike each day.

Ridgecrest was a much bigger town than I had expected, being on the sparsely populated eastern side of the Sierras. One would think that having to do a 25-mile hitch from the trailhead at Walker Pass to get there would make it a somewhat unlikely stop for a thru-hiker. But getting an easy hitch or even using the bus service that runs into Ridgecrest each Monday, Wednesday, and Friday makes it a thru-hikers destination.

In Ridgecrest it was now time to hit the ground running. We started the morning with an early breakfast at a local diner. After breakfast, I made my way to the post office for my shoes while Scooby was off to grab the rental car. Before leaving town, I did my resupply shop at the local Wal-Mart and also picked up a few equipment needs at a small outfitter. After that, we were off on our road trip.

Driving U.S. Route 395 with the High Sierras stretched out to our left was beautiful. The complete mountain range was covered in a deep blanket of snow that I was very happy to see from a distance, from the comfort of a heated passenger seat going 70 miles per hour.

We made a stop for an off trail feeding at the McDonald's in Lone Pine. While there, we talked to three hikers who had attempted going through the snowy Sierras. They told us of the difficulties and shared a few videos and pictures. They had been hiking above 10,000 feet with white out conditions while another two feet was falling on top of the deep snow already there. They also said they had been camping in Lone Pine for the past three days and were trying to decide if they would go back up. These guys were in their early twenties, strong and fit, but unsure what they were going to do. I could also tell they were in no real hurry to leave the safety of that McDonald's where any size drink was just a dollar with free refills. Meeting and speaking with them had me knowing I had made the best decision for myself.

The nine-hour drive from Ridgecrest to Chester was bittersweet for me. Those miles hiked with Scooby had been miles we shared. Every step, every view, and every experience had been shared. I've hiked many miles by myself over the years, and I've been fine with that. I've found peace and solitude in hiking by myself, which isn't a bad thing, it's just different. I've mentioned before how difficult it can be to hike with another person. Varied styles, speeds, and personalities are obvious reasons for the difficulty, but it goes deeper than that. Hiking with another person or persons requires a commitment. It's not always a perfect utopia. As an example, there were days when I wanted to do more or fewer miles than what Scooby had in mind, and I know he would say the same. But accepting that challenge to put on a few more miles, or accepting that your hiking partner was tired and wanted to stop for the day makes for a strong partnership. I would also have to say that we are probably an oddity. We saw others who said they were hiking together, but one was usually hours ahead or even days ahead of the other. To that point, I've even seen married couples that can't hike together. I can honestly say that I never felt as though I lost out or missed anything along the way when hiking with Scooby, but I do know the gains were immeasurable by hiking with this friend.

With the vehicle being rented under Scooby's name, he did all of the driving while I attempted to entertain, but I mostly looked out the windshield at the snow-covered Sierra Nevada Mountains. To be honest, I was feeling a high level of anxiety. I knew I was making the right decision to skip ahead, but was I skipping ahead to the right place along the trail? I guess I'd find out soon enough.

When we eventually arrived in Chester, we made our way to the trailhead at California State Route 36...mostly out of curiosity. We parked the car and took a few minutes to walk into the deep forest, again out of nothing more than curing our curiosity. I had booked a room for Scooby and myself in Susanville which was about 30 miles away, so we climbed back into the car and made our way there.

Scooby would drive me back to this same spot in the morning...and that's when we would say our goodbyes.

Section Three

Chester, California to Mount Jefferson, Oregon
miles 1,331 to 2,015

On My Own

When Scooby and I got to our hotel in Susanville, we checked in, and then went to the local pub where we could enjoy dinner and a couple of goodbye beers together. The next morning arrived, and we grabbed breakfast then drove back to the trailhead where I would begin the next chapter of my hike.

At the place where Hwy 36 intersected with the PCT, we climbed out of the car and said the goodbyes that I wasn't the least bit interested in saying. I didn't want to say goodbye. What I wanted was for Scooby to pull his pack out of the trunk, throw it on his back, and step into that forest with me. But you don't always get what you want. So, we said our goodbyes, and Scooby got back into his rental car to drive off to L.A., where he would catch his flight home.

And I stepped into the forest *on my own.*

Well, it started off great. The first couple of miles were hanging at about 5000 feet, and I was really enjoying it. I had left Southern California where the desert meets the Sierra Nevada just one day earlier, and now I was hiking through a beautiful forest. The trees here were the biggest and tallest I had ever seen. I was loving it…right up until it started raining…and then snowing once I got above 5000 feet heading toward Mount Lassen. It was miserably wet and cold. I was wearing my rain jacket, but I didn't have rain pants so I got soaking wet and cold. There was nothing to do but hike through it. By lunchtime, I was starving and wanted to stop, but the winter mix was really coming down now. A short time later I came across the North Fork Feather River where there was a nice bridge. I decided to sit on a boulder under that bridge, and was able to have a quick lunch. Quick because I was cold, wet, and shivering from the rain and snow falling through the bridge above me. Sitting under the bridge also wasn't getting me any farther up the trail, either, so I picked up my pack and hiked on. The higher I went, the colder it got, and the snow came down as a wet, heavy mess. I took a couple of photos and a video that I was able to send to Scooby while letting him know that he'd probably made the right decision by going home.

I ended up hiking through deep snow for the rest of the day. When I say deep, I mean deep. I was postholing all day long. At times I would posthole and end up in snow up to my waist. Snowshoes sure would have been helpful. Following the trail would have been impossible if not for the Guthook GPS app on my phone. I used this app so much that my phone battery was down to three percent when I finally made it to camp, where I was able to recharge using my battery bank. I camped at Warner Valley Campground, a seasonal campground just south of Lassen Peak that was closed at this time of year, elevation 5,600 feet. I had not seen another person or hiker all day. I was truly *on my own*. I pitched my lonesome tent and climbed in.

There was a report of bear activity in the area, according to comments on my Guthook app. The campground was supposed to have bear boxes for safe, bear-proof food storage. If there were any bear boxes, I never saw them. No doubt they were buried in the deep snow.

Out of sheer desperation, the campground pit privy served as my bear box instead. While working my way to the privy I came across fresh bear tracks in the snow. *Big* bear tracks. My final thought before falling asleep was that bears probably knew how to open the privy door. But I guess it's true that bears do poop in the woods because that bear never used the privy, and thankfully didn't eat my food, either.

When I woke up in the morning I put on my wet clothes from the night before. It reminded me of the Appalachian trail, because putting wet clothes on in the morning was the norm on that trail. After my oatmeal and coffee, I packed up and prepared for another long and extra difficult hike. I didn't mention this before, but I had pulled a muscle in a sensitive place during one of my postholing episodes the previous day. So I popped a couple of Ibuprofen and Tylenol tablets and hiked on. I knew I'd be above 6000 feet, which meant there would be deep snow waiting to challenge me again. I had no idea of the hours upon hours of slogging through the deep snow that awaited this naive hiker. I'm usually a pretty fast hiker, but this was pure torture. I could normally hike two and a half to three miles per hour, but I was now lucky to do one mile in an hour. There was no trail, since it lay somewhere under the six to eight feet of snow. Under normal conditions you would follow the defined trail and the occasional diamond-shaped tin blazes nailed to trees or posts. Those blazes are usually placed at a height of six to seven feet, but I never saw them because they were now below snow level. I also wasn't sure if I was actually even on the trail.

I made my way slowly with my micro-spikes on all day. I'd hike 100 feet or so and check my location to my GPS. Rinse and repeat. This was the most tedious and frustrating hiking I had ever done. I recall looking at my watch once and seeing that I had been hiking for nearly four hours, but I'd only advanced three miles. I wanted to scream, but I didn't have time for that. I had to keep moving or I'd end up spending the night on top of that Godforsaken mountain.

I eventually came upon some faint footprints that I could tell had been made by a hiker sometime earlier; they were almost filled with new snow. They seemed to be following the trail pretty closely, so I followed along somewhat trustfully while still verifying on Guthook from time to time. After eleven miles and eight hours of exhaustive trekking, the trail started to descend below the snow line where I was able to pick up the actual trail as well as my speed. As I hiked on, I would lose the trail when vast areas were covered with water from the melting snow. There were areas that looked like shallow rivers that I had to trek through until I came to slightly higher ground where I could follow the trail again. I considered myself extremely fortunate that it didn't rain, sleet, or snow that day. That would really have messed with my sensibilities. It did, however, rain like crazy later, after I was safe, warm, and dry in my tent. I must have been living right.

I had managed to hike 16.9 miles, which, based on the conditions, I considered a very productive day. I never felt I was in any type of danger, but I was feeling very alone. This was the second day I hadn't seen a single person, other than those footprints. It was also the second day with no cell or data service. The next one hundred-plus miles were going to be below 5,500 feet, which I hoped would translate into snowless miles. Fingers crossed.

After the long and late day, I decided to start the next day a bit later at 7:15 a.m. As I packed up my backpack, I happily bagged my micro-spikes in their handy little stuff sack and once again placed them deep in the bottom of my pack with a grateful smile.

As I started down the trail, I found myself in awe of the conifer forest I was hiking through. These were the tallest, straightest trees I had ever seen. None of them stood at ease, each tree was standing at full attention. It was overcast and I was getting wet, but I was unable to tell if it was actually raining or if the trees were just dumping what they had collected from the heavy rain the night before. A couple more miles of hiking and my next water source revealed itself. Hat Creek was not a creek at all. The melting snow from those tall surrounding mountains had turned the creek into a raging river with white-water rapids daring anyone to challenge it. I checked my guide just to confirm that I wasn't required to ford it and was happy to be able to put my mind at ease. After collecting and filtering some of the rushing water, I swallowed several large mouthfuls of the freshest, coldest mountain water I had ever tasted. A short time later I came to the side trail that led to the very small village of Old Station. Since it lay just two tenths of a mile off the trail, I thought I would grab an early lunch. The store was open, but the deli hadn't opened for the season yet—that would actually happen on the following day. Drat. One day too early! So, I treated myself to an ice cream bar and a Coke instead.

I hiked a few more miles and came to the difficult decision to stop for the day. It was only 1:30 in the afternoon, but I had finally succumbed to the groin muscle injury I sustained postholing two days earlier, which had become far too painful for me to continue hiking. I'm sure a doctor would have ordered rest, so that's what I did. I set up my tent so I could lie down. While in my tent, I tried to determine the number of snow-free miles I could look forward to. It looked like about 140 miles, and then it would be back to the higher elevations and the accompanying snow. This was now the third day I'd not seen another hiker on the trail.

I had started talking to myself.

A lot.

I ended up staying in my tent, resting, and sleeping for fifteen hours. It's a darn good thing I'm not claustrophobic, because my tent was not designed to hold a person for that long. But it worked.

I woke the next morning a bit tentative as to whether or not I'd be able to hike. There was a tightness and a sensation of a tug as I started off, but I was able to hike 25.2 miles. My first stop of the morning was at the beautiful and accessible Hat Creek Overlook. Lassen Peak, my injury-inducing arch-nemesis, was to the south. To the north was Mount Shasta. The iconic ancient volcano stood tall with a thick cover of snow fully enrobing it. It looked like a huge soft serve vanilla cone tempting anyone who would dare to climb it. Fortunately Mount Shasta isn't on the PCT, so it could go right on taunting me—I wasn't required to face that formidable beast so I really couldn't care less. To its credit though, it was really beautiful, especially on this clear morning with no clouds to hide behind. Mt. Shasta had chosen to fully present itself in all its glory. As I hiked on, I met a couple in a small motor home that was boondocked in the parking lot with that spectacular view as the backdrop to their campsite. Margie and Chris stopped me as I was about to step back on the trail.

"What are you doing?" they asked.

I explained that I was hiking the PCT, which they took great interest in hearing about. We chatted for a few minutes, and as I was getting ready to take my leave I thought to ask if they might have some extra water. I was quickly rewarded with my spare 750 milliliter bottle being filled, thus eliminating the need for me to trek down to Lost Creek, the only water source for the next thirteen miles. Lost Creek is off trail and requires a steep descent on a number of switchbacks, and my new friends had just helped me avoid it. Very helpful, especially after my recent injury which I did not wish to aggravate.

The views from the rim overlooking Hat Creek followed me for miles upon miles. I'd often have to stop dead in my tracks to take another peek. Breathtakingly beautiful! The mountain sunflowers were in full bloom on the rugged landscape. The transformation from the desert sands down south to the volcanic rock in the north was amazingly evident. The granite boulders of the desert landscape had been replaced by basalt boulders and lava rock with their distinct characteristics. Unfortunately, one of those characteristics is that it's difficult to walk on and very tough on one's hiking shoes, *my* brand-new hiking shoes.

And as I hiked on, I came across a number of signs posted that announced there was a prescribed fire ahead, and please do not report it. The burn area was an ugly mess, but I'm sure it could be an uglier mess if not managed. The good work that the Forest Service performs through controlled burns helps avoid potential disasters and wildfires that cannot be fought, such as the terribly scorched area I'd hiked through down south. Seeing such devastation, it's hard to remember that sometimes a fire is the best thing for a forest to survive and thrive. As long as it's managed, of course.

The next water source was a water cache. I was hoping Cache 22—haha—would not end up being a Catch 22. As is always the case, one should never count on a water cache because there is no guarantee any water will be there. But in this case, I had already met a southbound hiker who told me it was, indeed, full of clean, cold water—filtering recommended. As always, the unwritten rule was to carry your own and take from the cache only what you absolutely need. While at the cache I met Blue, a thru-hiker who had just skipped north as I had done. Blue was an interesting fellow from Switzerland, and as we chatted over lunch, we decided to hike out together.

While hiking, it became apparent to us that very few people had yet hiked this part of the trail this season. Under normal conditions, it would be another month or longer before this year's class of thru-hikers made it this far north. The trail was at times indistinguishable from the surrounding landscape. The trail bed had not been tramped down by the hundreds or thousands of hikers' feet, which would eventually clearly delineate where the trail was. Not to worry. Blue and I did our part today as we blazed the trail with heavy steps for the future hikers who were soon to come behind us.

That was the day I set a goal for myself—a goal that with some help I was eventually able to achieve. More on that in a bit.

Meanwhile, Blue and I hiked well with one another, and after battling it out with swarms of mosquitoes all day, we decided to make camp for the evening. We found a site which was in a mosquito-infested clearing situated under high tension power lines. It was flat land, but on solid volcanic rock which made driving tent stakes nearly impossible. The best I could do was to drive them in as far as they would go and then place rocks over the stakes to hold my tent erect. We jumped into our tents as quickly as we could, in hopes of avoiding the need for blood transfusions. Those mosquitoes tried their hardest to penetrate the screening on my tent. Thankfully their hopes of dinner were not to be realized.

While in my tent avoiding those pesky mosquitoes, I watched the evening sky that now warned of an oncoming storm. It was 1:15 in the morning when the sky finally opened up in all its fury. The thunder and lightning were like none I had ever witnessed. I thought for certain the wind would take down my tent, but I guess I'd driven those stakes far enough into the lava stone to stick.

When morning finally arrived, it was as though nothing had ever happened. I got myself packed and I could hear Blue doing the same. It looked like we would hike out together again. Fine by me, because I enjoyed his company.

Remember how I'd set a goal? This was it. The Burney Mountain Guest Ranch is a PCT favorite and it lay just six miles into our hike. Blue had told me he'd not been planning on going there, but I bribed him with the promise of a cup of coffee. I told him that after coffee and our second breakfast, we'd hitch the five miles to the town of Burney. When we arrived at the Burney Mountain Guest Ranch property, I saw it really was special. Duke, the owners' beautiful pure white Great Pyrenees greeted us first as we approached the porch. I rang the doorbell, and Linda opened the front door, offering a warm welcome. She took a moment and gave us the rundown as though we were planning on staying—where to shower and do laundry, where the resupply store was and how it's on the honor system.

"Just take a tally sheet and settle up when you leave," she said. Then she asked if we wanted breakfast. Ten bucks for eggs, sausage, potatoes, a fresh whole-grain waffle the size of a dinner plate, and fresh ground coffee sounded more than fair.

So, about my heart and my head on that day...

I'd been seriously struggling with a few things. Some I am not prepared to write or talk about for very personal reasons. But what I will share is that, although I am a risk taker of sorts, I'm not stupid. If I had known beforehand what I know now, I never would have attempted a thru-hike during this particular year. The snowfall and weather conditions had most, if not all hikers, seriously concerned about their personal safety. Few had hiked past Kennedy Meadows, California, which is considered the gateway to the Sierra Nevada Mountains. Meanwhile, the Sierras just received *another* five feet of fresh snow during two highly unusual May storms. The current trail snow from Kennedy Meadows to Echo Lake was well above normal at 210% of average. Some hikers had left the trail to wait for a melt, others had quit altogether, or jumped ahead as I had. I never had any illusions that jumping ahead meant no snow. The entire Sierra Nevada and Cascade mountain chains had received stupid amounts of snow. I had jumped ahead because the snow report had indicated there were 150 miles below 5000 feet that were mostly snow free. Hiking through a bit of snow would not remotely be like hiking through the High Sierras at ten thousand-plus feet, completely inundated with snow. It had been just four days earlier, at about 5,500 to 7,000 feet, that I'd hiked through a snowstorm and spent the entire day facing treacherous conditions...all by myself. I'm a strong hiker, but I just didn't want to place myself in that kind of situation again.

And now for that goal I mentioned. I had set a goal to go into the town of Burney and stay at the Life Assembly Church, which opens their gymnasium, kitchen, and showers to hikers. I was planning on asking if I could do a work-for-stay, which allows a hiker to perform work in exchange for room and board. My goal was to do this for a week or so while—hopefully—the snow levels dropped. I know myself, so I knew I couldn't and wouldn't just sit around doing nothing while waiting. Working for my stay would be a win-win.

Now, back to the Burney Mountain Guest Ranch. What I haven't mentioned is, there's a huge 40-foot cross on the property, erected where we had just made our initial approach hiking in. Seeing it, at that moment I knew I was exactly where I was supposed to be.

So, after breakfast I asked Linda if she and her husband, Mike, would allow me to work-for-stay. With a smile, Linda told me she had just that morning prayed for someone to come and help them. Perfect.

Blue and I said our goodbyes, and he hiked on toward his planned stop in the town of Burney while I settled in to what would be my home for the next eight days. I showered, did laundry, then went right to work. Honest, hard work. I had met my goal that day, but not without some Divine intervention.

Linda, Mike, and I had arrived at a fair and equitable agreement. They would provide me with a bunk in one of their cabins and feed me three meals each day in return for my work. My bunk was in one of the bunk houses, which held four bunk beds—so eight beds in total. There was a shared bathroom for the occupants, but I never had more than one roommate during my entire stay, and most of the time I had the room to myself. Most of the work they had in mind for me was a long list of tasks that needed to be completed prior to the busy hiking season. Other tasks were more wish-list things they hoped to achieve, but perhaps not necessities.

The next morning, I was up at my usual time, and by 6:30 a.m. I was dressed and sitting on the front porch, ready for the promised first cup of Linda's freshly ground brew. With no other hikers there and

Mike still asleep, Linda and I sat at one of the dining room tables and chatted for a couple of hours. Breakfast was fantastic, just as the beef tips, pasta, salad, and baked potato dinner had been the night before. I'd lost about fifteen pounds since starting my hike, and was now convinced that Linda was working on helping me gain back a good portion of that weight.

A full day of work ensued, which allowed the hours to fly by until it was time to call it quits. After cleaning up, I enjoyed another amazing dinner, then went to find rest in my bunk.

I was able to attend church that next morning, as well. I had asked Linda the day before if it would be possible, and she'd called a friend who kindly picked me up on his way to the service. The IM Free Church is a Baptist church with a congregation that made me feel very comfortable and welcome. This was very kind of the congregation, especially since the only clothes I had were my hiking clothes—not exactly Sunday best. Although recently laundered, they were tattered, pilling, torn in places, and had seen many better days. It's funny, but you never see a Tide commercial where they show how their product "can even clean a hiker's clothes." Ha. Never gonna happen. The pastor was a high energy preacher who gave a fantastic sermon, and the music was extremely uplifting. Truly what my heart and soul needed.

When I got back to the ranch, I changed into work clothes—my shorts and a loaner shirt—and got to work. I spent the better part of the day applying metal lath to the outdoor poolside fireplace. Concrete would be poured and applied a couple days later when the weather improved. Yes, it actually snowed up above 5000 feet that afternoon. I swore it was a conspiracy.

The days ticked by quickly with no shortage of work, which kept my mind off the fact that I wasn't getting any closer to Canada. Each day consisted of waking early and working late. I had completed the lath work, then mixed concrete for several days. I hung new blinds in the re-supply store, helped Mike prepare the swimming pool for the season by taking off the protective cover, and sweeping and vacuuming the pool, which was a huge undertaking. I also made repairs to failing and broken tiles, and helped Mike repair a leaking pump on a pool that I would never get to enjoy, but those future spoiled hikers who would soon arrive at the Burney Mountain Guest Ranch would. I installed a new bathroom counter and sinks. I cleaned and readied all of the swamp coolers for the upcoming summer season—a swamp cooler is similar to an air-conditioner.

It was a very productive week, and working with Mike and Linda was a pleasure. It was backbreaking work, but it was also fulfilling. I felt I was truly earning my keep, and I knew Mike and Linda appreciated my dedication. They fed me well and gave me clean accommodations with all the amenities I needed.

However, there was a constant reminder of what was still ahead for me on this journey. Visible from every window and every vantage point on this spectacular property was the snow-capped peak of Burney Mountain. While working each day, I couldn't help but steal a glimpse of the monster mountain that showed little to no change in the snow levels as the days ticked by.

During the week, a few other hikers who had also skipped the Sierras stopped for a respite at the ranch. Adam and his dog, Betula, showed up one afternoon, and unbeknownst to me at the time, they would soon become my unexpected hiking partners. Another hiker, Xena—though not the same Xena I had previously met—would also find her way to Burney Mountain Guest Ranch this week, where she too made a work-for-stay arrangement with Mike and Linda. Xena would also become a hiking partner in the days to come. Next, a young couple from Germany found their way to the ranch. Stephen and Mary were an especially kind couple that had planned their trip to the United States with hopes of hiking the PCT, but they were quickly reworking their plans because of the snow conditions.

I recall once overhearing Mary speaking with Linda about the beautiful towering cross on the ranch property. That morning was extremely foggy, and Mary pointed out how the fog-engulfed cross reminded her of how those who don't have Christ in their lives find themselves living in a fog. Mary's perspective was poignant and deeply meaningful to me. That beautiful cross will always be an image forever imprinted in my memory.

Don't live in a fog

After each full day of work, I would find my way back to my bunk for some down time. While relaxing before dinner, I would read, write in my journal, and sometimes just think. My thoughts brought me to realize it was getting to be time that I moved on. The temperatures had certainly warmed up, and it looked like there would be no additional snowfall. On Friday, I met with Mike and Linda over coffee to let them know that I would be leaving on Sunday morning. I had a few things to take care of, such as shopping for my next resupply, plus rain pants, and some Permethrin to ward off mosquitoes. Mike agreed to take me into town where I was able to get what I needed before my planned departure on Sunday morning. Fortunately, two young ladies who had arrived the day before had boxes mailed to them at the ranch, and ended up with too much food. This was fortuitous, and I was very happy to assist them with that problem. I was able to meet most of my resupply needs from the items they left in the hiker box.

The Burney Mountain Guest Ranch had been my home for eight days, but it was time to say my goodbyes to my hosts. Linda knew I wanted to get an early start, so she offered to make an early breakfast. I can't say enough about my hosts and work-for-stay employers, or how grateful I was that they were there in my time of need. Finding myself on their front porch was meant to be, and the time I spent there will forever be a meaningful part of my hiking experience.

I hoisted my pack at exactly 7:00 a.m. and hit the trail. Ten miles in brought me to the Burney Falls State Park. It was a bit early for lunch, but it was the perfect setting, so I took full advantage. The beautiful waterfall is fed by an underground reservoir which gets its seemingly endless water supply from seasonal snowmelts. The waterfall is only 114 feet high but very wide. One hundred million gallons of water flowing over it every day make it the most voluminous waterfall in the state of California.

Once I got myself moving again, I hiked with my usual purpose— to get more miles in. The hiking was great, with good conditions and gradual grades, which made for a nice first day back on the trail after eight days off. Afternoon thundershowers came at the seemingly regularly scheduled time of 2:30 p.m., with the sky opening up for about 30 minutes. Hardly worth the effort of putting on rain gear.

As I was hiking along, I ran into a hiker I had previously met by the name of Joyride. I had not seen Joyride since Scooby and I met him at the KOA campground nearly a month earlier. Joyride's trail name is quite an interesting story. As he tells it, he had hiked the Appalachian Trail in 2016, and at one point got a ride hitchhiking. The guy who picked him up was giving him the full tour of the town when the police pulled him over. It turned out that he had stolen the car! Joyride was arrested, as well, because the police assumed he was an accomplice. The charge against him was—yep—joyriding. He was able to convince the judge in the morning that he was just an AT Hiker at the wrong place at the wrong time, and all charges were dropped, but the trail name stuck. Joyride wasn't alone today. His lady friend's trail name is Bidet Day. I wasn't sure if there was a story to her trail name, and to be honest, not sure I wanted to know.

Close to four o'clock I found the perfect campsite, and decided that 18 miles was a good first day back, so I called it a day. With camp made, dinner enjoyed, and my food bag hung, it was time for lights out at 6:30 p.m.

Early to bed had me up at 4:00 a.m. and on the trail by 5:30. The hike started as a beautiful walk through the woods, but quickly turned into an afternoon of bushwhacking. The trail had not been used a whole lot this year, and it was pretty obvious there hadn't been a lot of trail maintenance either. In fact, a machete would have been pretty useful that day. At times I couldn't tell where the actual trail was, and had to use instinct...and of course my GPS. I eventually came to a clearing by some power lines, which offered some open sightlines. I was able to follow the trail again, which took me along a ridge. Suddenly, Mt. Shasta in all its glory came into view. The majestic volcano was probably more than a hundred miles away, but I felt as though I could reach out and touch it. I took a nice break with Shasta as the perfect backdrop. The warmer temperatures had the bugs buzzing about and the birds were happily chirping, making the whole scene welcoming, if a bit surreal. Distant mountains were further in the background, brushed in muted colors like in a paint-by-numbers painting that made them look like window dressing, with Mt. Shasta the star of the show.

As I reached elevations of 5,400 feet and higher, snowfields made their debut. This was where my challenging day actually started. I broke out the micro-spikes and it was game on. Progress was slow going and exhausting. There was plenty of snow melting, and portions of the trail were a deep creek that I would have to wade through. The unavoidable consequence was hiking in freezing cold, soaking wet socks and shoes. I wanted to get as much of this difficult section out of the way, so I kept moving. Eventually I was too tired to continue, so I found a fairly flat site at 6000 feet and pitched my tent on what looked to be about ten feet of snow. Not my first choice. but I was just too tired to go on. My plan was to take on the rest of this mountain in the morning after I'd had some rest and had a clearer head.

I've slept in snow before, but I guess I'd forgotten just how cold it can be. My air mattress insulated me from the ground, but I still needed my down jacket, toque, gloves, and socks on, all while hibernating deep under my quilt. That night at around 10:30 p.m. I heard a noise in the vestibule of my tent. There was just enough light from the stars and moon reflecting off the deep snow for me to be able to see a rabbit nosing around. Was this rabbit trying to get out of the cold? Was he just curious? Or, did he really even exist at all? I tapped on my tent and he took off, but quickly returned. I tapped again. He took off, but came back. We played this game of cat and rabbit for some time, until finally I got tired of it. Well, just tired in general. I finally let out a hare-raising primal yell—possibly more like the yell of a wild lunatic—and he finally left me alone.

In the morning I started hiking as soon as I had good light, which was at 6:30 a.m. It was a beautifully clear, warm day, which I was particularly appreciative of...especially considering how frustrating the day was destined to become. This section of the trail included Grizzly Peak, which was a true bear in that it was technically difficult. As evidence, it took me five hours to go 4.1 miles. It would have been impossible to get through without an ice ax, micro-spikes and GPS. Twice I failed to set my footing correctly, but thankfully was able to successfully perform a self-arrest. Planting my axe handle to find a good foothold was tedious work. I'll admit that it was exciting and provided an adrenaline rush, but it was also physically and mentally exhausting. Prior to my leaving Burney Mountain Guest Ranch, a group of four hikers had told me they skipped Grizzly Peak altogether and roadwalked instead—there is a dirt forest access road along that section. I should have done the same, especially since I was by myself. Stupid.

The questionable snow conditions had me second-guessing my purist approach to thru-hiking. While hiking the Appalachian trail I had decided that I wanted to see every white blaze, hike every mile, and do so with my full pack every step of the 2,189 miles. It had now become apparent that I would have to make some adjustments as to how I would complete the PCT. Once I got past that terrible five-mile stretch it was easy going, which was good because I really needed to get some miles in. I had originally planned on taking four days to hike this section, then resupplying in Dunsmuir. My problem now was, I had only packed out four and a half days of food. This section had me working hard, and my hunger had been relentlessly dissatisfied. I'd have to get creative and stretch what was left in what had become a very light food bag. Maybe I should have invited that rabbit into my tent, after all...

That night I slept to the calming and rushing waters of Butcherknife Creek—seriously, that's its name. When 5:00 a.m. arrived, I woke up and grabbed my disappointingly light food bag from my bear hang. There was so little food in it that a bear probably wouldn't have wasted its time trying to get to it. I wrapped my Pop-Tarts in a tortilla to add some much-needed breakfast calories, and washed it down with my morning coffee. I actually had just enough food to keep me going for the rest of the day, but it was slim pickings.

I had only two packs of Justin's peanut butter, two Starbucks Via coffee packs, and one tortilla left in the food bag when I arrived in Dunsmuir. I was hoping beyond hope that Dunsmuir had a McDonald's, because I believed I would probably order and eat my weight in Sausage Egg McMuffins.

That morning's hike took me along the McCloud River as it thundered by, swollen from the excessive snowmelt thousands of feet higher in elevation. Seasonal streams were now overflowing with cool, clear, fresh water providing thirst relief. There were streams where there weren't supposed to be streams, since all that snow had to go somewhere as the sun and warmer temps worked overtime. Unfortunately for us hikers, the snow was still not melting fast enough. When I reached a lower elevation, I had another rattlesnake encounter. I came upon this guy unexpectedly, taking him and myself by complete surprise. He politely warned me with a shake of his rattles, which had me stopping dead in my tracks. Still too close, I took two big steps backward and promptly tripped over my own feet. My eyes never left his, and his never left mine as he, too, backed up while still in his striking posture. He quickly lost interest when he realized that I wasn't a threat and casually slithered off the trail.

This was a big day for crossing paths with other hikers. I met Lowrick, Liza, Fat Ray, Mama's Spaghetti, and Bebo. All of them were southbound—aka SOBO—hikers, so I took the opportunity to pick their brains with extensive interviews. Where did they flip from and to? When did they flip? What were the snow conditions where they flipped to? Did they hike through the Trinity Alps or did they roadwalk? Every one of them said they skipped the Trinity Alps, roadwalking for their safety and self preservation.

Finally, at the end of my day and nearly 30 miles hiked, I met Austin. This young man of 25 was in his tent reading a book when I arrived at 7:15 p.m. He put his book down, got out of his tent, and made me feel like I was important. Austin was taking four days on the trail for a getaway before he started a new job. He offered and I happily accepted some wonderful dried sweetened mango slices, which at the time I believed were the most delicious thing I had ever tasted. It wasn't long before the mosquitoes found us, driving us both to escape to the comfort and safety of our tents. We talked for an hour or so through our tents about his new job with the Canadian Department of Fisheries and Oceans, and about where we have lived. We were surprised to learn that we had both lived in Athens, Georgia, which once again proved to me what a small world we live in.

My plan was to get to the town of Dunsmuir as early as I could, so I was up and well on my way while Austin remained sound asleep and loudly sawing logs. The 4.8 miles went by quickly as I daydreamed of a high calorie meal—alas, there was no McDonald's in Dunsmuir. As luck would have it, I caught a hitch in under two minutes. The trail follows Soda Creek Rd. which intersects with the I-5 freeway. It looked like my only option was to walk up the I-5 onramp, so that's what I did. I wasn't sure if I'd get a ride or if I'd be ticketed for jaywalking. Fortunately, Rob and Nathaniel pulled over in a van and picked me up. Nathaniel, an interesting guy with long dreadlocks, did a lot of business in the area and was very familiar with Dunsmuir just five miles farther up the highway. I would have buckled up, but there was a bed in the back in place of the car seat, which was really quite comfortable. The interior of the vehicle had the distinct odor of cannabis, which I've found to be a common theme in California. I imagined the California Highway Patrol pulling us over and finding out the vehicle was stolen, getting arrested with my two new friends, and having to change *my* trail name to Joyride. I honestly wasn't too surprised when I asked Nathaniel what line of business he was in when he nonchalantly responded it was cannabis. He would be the third person that I'd met while hiking that worked in this highly—haha—competitive business. Which I suppose made sense, since medical marijuana had long been legal in California, and the state had legalized adult use of cannabis in 2016.

When I asked if they would drop me off at a restaurant where I could get a good breakfast, Nathaniel suggested the Wheelhouse. When they dropped me off, they told me to tell the waitress that he had sent me. So, of course I did, and judging from her smile, the wait-ress seemed pleased that I was Nathaniel's friend. It's good to know people in high places. Today was June 6th, which happened to be my youngest son's thirtieth birthday. The perfect excuse for a celebratory breakfast beer with my breakfast burrito.

Dunsmuir is a relatively small town and easy to negotiate, but I was also fortunate to meet a mother-daughter duo leaving the restaurant at the same time I was, so I asked for a ride to the motel I had just booked. The Cedar Lodge Motel offered a fair rate of $70 per night, and the room was modern and very clean—well, until I arrived. Here is a busi-ness prospect for anyone in Dunsmuir: Open a coin-op laundry. With no Laundromat in town, the bathtub in my room had to fill the void. The afternoon had been taken up with shopping for my resupply, eating whatever I could lay my hands on, and studying maps of the upcoming trail section. I hoped to hike as much of the trail as I could that was safely below the snow line, then take Forest Service roads the rest of the way to California State Route 3, and finally roadwalk Hwy 3 into Etna.

That was the plan, anyway. For now.

Whistler, Adam and Xena

The following day was when Adam, Betula the dog, and Xena, whom I had not seen since the Burney Mountain Guest Ranch, re-entered my life. We caught a ride together out of Dunsmuir, took a selfie at the trailhead, and proceeded to beat that trail down. It was a pretty easy day, made easier by hiking it together. We paid a heavy price that night, though, with some high winds and frigid temperatures attacking us on the exposed ridge we'd called home. However, it was all well worth it the following morning when the sun came up from behind Mount Shasta. The winds had pounded my tent all night long, making the walls bow in and out as though it was a wild animal gasping for air, desperate to inflate its lungs. The tent flaps were whipping and snapping in the wind so loudly it should have kept me up, but I was too tired to allow anything to keep me from my slumber. I did wake up at 3:30 a.m. and thought about my food bag hanging in a tree about 50 yards from my tent. I just knew it had to be swinging in the wind like crazy, or possibly had already blown to the ground. I must not have been too concerned, since I didn't give it much thought but quickly turned over and went back to sleep. When I did get up, fortunately, it was hanging exactly where I had hung it the night before.

We hit the trail at seven, knowing we had a tough day ahead of us. The relatively easy day we'd experienced the day before was not to be repeated. While at the same elevation as the south face, the north face of the 7000-foot mountains made for some extremely difficult hiking. It was noon when we stopped for lunch, and we had only hiked 4.8 miles in five hours. There were some areas of steep angled snow that we cautiously traversed with micro-spikes and ice axes at a snail's pace. Xena seemed to have a natural knack for this kind of mountaineering, or maybe she was just fearless. Adam and I leaned more toward caution with an exceptionally strong will to live. There were several times we had to abandon the trail altogether and find a safer route, which included glissading down steep embankments and snowbanks for hundreds of feet or more down to the valley, then climbing back up to where it was safe to continue. This long, tedious process was exhausting, while at the same time extremely rewarding.

We continued to hike until we arrived at Parks Creek Trailhead. We took a break here and discussed the upcoming section known as the Trinity Alps. Every SOBO hiker we had met and spoken with—except for Happy Cowboy—had roadwalked this section because of the dangerous conditions and high level of difficulty with the snow cover. We'd met Happy Cowboy earlier that day and gained some great intel about what lay before us. He was able to give some good advice on how to approach some of the difficult sections we would encounter and—with his help—successfully traverse that day. While all his information was helpful, the upcoming Trinity Alps were still a major concern. In addition, the section just before the Trinity Alps was also reportedly sketchy, and required a decision to be made. Adam and I agreed we'd walk the Forest Service road that followed the path of the trail along the Trinity River but at a lower elevation, but Xena was undecided. She told us to go on ahead and that she might follow us after she made a few phone calls. As we left her behind, we could hear her talking with her dad, seeking his advice. Adam, Betula, and I hiked that long and winding Forest Service road, and as the hours passed Xena never showed up, so it was our guess that she'd decided to take the trail. I was not at all surprised, and neither was Adam. She was an ambitious, tough, and independent 27-year-old adventurer.

Meanwhile, Adam and I were of the opinion that there was a level of risk we were willing and prepared to take, and that the next section exceeded that threshold. Our best guess was that Xena would meet up with us in Etna.

Adam and I finally called it quits at seven that evening, and made camp at a beautiful spot beside the Trinity River. It was a clear, cool, and calm night, which provided a peaceful night's sleep. I hadn't gotten my coffee the day before because of the ridiculously high winds, but I did this morning, so now all was right with the world. Adam, Betula, and I hit the Forest Service road at 7:00 a.m. There would be no challenging mountain crossings, no traversing of snow-covered passes, no glissading, and no other high risks encounters, thank goodness. Just an awesome hike surrounded by beautiful mountains while following the thunderous sounds of the Trinity River. The miles ticked off quickly, bringing us closer to State Route 3, which would eventually take us into the small and popular trail town of Etna. Once we hit Hwy 3, we stopped at Scott Mountain Campground for a late lunch and a break. Betula was dog-tired and not the least bit interested in going any further. Adam thought it best to take it slow, and suggested I go ahead to the town of Callahan and wait there for them.

Callahan is a small town with a population of 250, just twelve miles from Etna. I walked those road miles like it was my job. It was a long, hot walk, and my thirst was difficult to quench, especially with the virtual non-existence of a water source. I finally came across a river that the highway crossed over, which easily met my hydration needs. I drank and hiked on. In the true spirit of humanity, car after car slowed to ask if I needed a ride. Guilt for skipping those miles of the Trinity Alps had overcome me, so I appreciatively but stubbornly refused any help. I arrived in Callahan at 4:45 in the afternoon and found a little pub called the Emporium, where I quickly found a cold beer to quench the thirst that developed after those long, hot asphalt miles I'd walked on Hwy 3.

Adam and Betula caught up an hour later and received a warm welcome from Chelsea, the pub's proprietor. Betula received a cool bowl of water, and Adam received a cool pint of freshly pulled brew. Chelsea took our dinner order, and our food was quickly delivered to the table along with another round. We discussed our plans for the next day, agreeing to get up at the typical time and roadwalk those last twelve miles into Etna. Why walk and not hitch you ask? Again, since we had skipped the Trinity Alps portion of the trail, our penance would be to walk those miles instead. An equal number of miles...just less dangerous. When asked about a place to camp, Chelsea suggested that we camp under the bridge—like trolls? —directly next to the Emporium. We actually found a really nice flat spot right next to the bridge that was secluded and quiet in the sleepy town of Callahan.

Our stealth tent sites next to the bridge were perfect for what they were. It was simply a place to be unobtrusive and unnoticeable by anyone who might happen by. Nothing special, no view, no fuss, no muss, just a place to sleep. Morning came, and it was time to start the daily routine. I took a few minutes to call Annie, while Adam and Betula started the twelve-mile roadwalk into Etna before I had even broke camp. Adam had been having some serious issues with blisters, his feet overall, really—roadwalking is really tough on your feet—so it was understood that I would catch up. I eventually did catch up at about mile three, and we made the best of the roadwalk along Hwy 3.

Once we reached the Etna city limit sign—population 727, elevation 2,950 feet—we were immediately accosted by the locals. Do you guys need a ride? Do you know where you can stay in town? Do you need to know where the brewery is? Do you need to do your laundry?

We stopped at the local gas station and a guy pumping gas gave us the rundown on the entire town. I thought the town council must have called a meeting with all 727 residents in attendance and made certain they were all going by the same playbook. Not sure what it says about a town that small, but Etna has two breweries and a distillery. Everyone sure seemed happy.

So, where did I stay? I stayed at the town park, where they allow hikers to pitch their tent for a five-dollar fee. There are clean bathrooms at this park. For an additional five dollars—plus a ten-dollar deposit—you get a clean fluffy towel, shampoo, conditioner, and soap for the hot shower they provide. For an additional three-dollar fee you can rent a locker for your backpack, which includes a charging station in the locker for your electronic devices—no need to carry your pack all over town—just brilliant. These amenities are arranged at Ray's, the local grocery store. This town gets it. They understand that hikers are good people and openly accept them, knowing the hikers will in turn spend money in their town. Win-win.

But, like most towns in the world today, there can be a dark side. After performing my in town tasks, I returned to the park, where I found a young lady passed out in her own vomit by the park restrooms. I asked her if she was okay, but it was obvious to me that she was in a drug-induced condition. This was so disheartening to witness, and I knew I had to do something quickly. I could see an active ballpark close by, so I ran over and asked if someone could call for help. Being a small town, the first guy I spoke with had a friend who was a police officer on speed dial, and help was on the scene in minutes. The girl couldn't have been more than fifteen and was totally out of it, while other girls her same age were no more than 50 yards away playing softball. How did she slip through the cracks? How does this even happen?

Meanwhile, Adam and Xena met up at the R&R Bunkhouse, where they were able to stay for free with a work-for-stay agreement. Adam and Betula would stay for three nights to heal their feet, while Xena was planning on leaving in the morning. Xena didn't roadwalk as Adam and I had, she took a hitch. Her plan was to hike the Trinity Alps southbound then hitch Hwy 3 back into Etna, and eventually hike out with Adam when his feet recovered. The three of us met for dinner at the Paystreak Brewing Company where we talked about our adventures together. While there, two other hikers I had not seen since the Burney Mountain Guest Ranch showed up. Alex—no trail name yet—and Tang joined our table and shared some of their own adventures. Having gotten my laundry done, my resupply taken care of, and a few postcards mailed, I decided that I'd be hiking out first thing in the morning. Alone again.

I was waiting at Ray's front door at 6:30 a.m. to return the locker key and towel, and to get my deposit back. Unfortunately, the store didn't open till 7:00 a.m. But wait, the woman who had helped me the day before saw me from inside, smiled, unlocked the door, accepted the key and towel, and gave me back my deposit. Now all I needed was to get coffee, but they didn't open till seven, either. But wait, the coffee shop owner saw me, smiled, and let me in early. It was almost as if they appreciated my business. What a concept.

I was able to secure Xena and me a ride up to the trailhead from a guy I met while camping at the park. Dennis drove the two of us up the ten-mile access road called Sawyers Bar Road, which in itself was a 3000-foot climb. Xena was hoping to hike the 39 miles south to Hwy 3. Those were the same miles that Adam, Betula, and I had roadwalked the day before. As far as we knew, Happy Cowboy was the only hiker we'd met to complete that section.

I was planning on continuing hiking north from there. Dennis pulled over, we all got out, took photos, and said our goodbyes. My progress north started off well. I took a break at noon for lunch, and checked to see if I had phone service. I had just received a text from Xena that she was back at the hostel. She had only been able to hike 2.5 miles on the trail before having to turn back around. As we'd all heard, it was just too dangerous. One thing I knew for certain—if Xena, as fearless as she was, had turned around, I'd definitely made the right decision to skip the Trinity Alps. Xena also sent me photos of mountain lion footprints she'd found in the snow as she hiked back to the trailhead where Dennis had dropped us off at just hours earlier. Those footprints had not been there when she started out. In other words, that lion had been following her. Yikes. Xena had made exactly the right decision to turn back.

Meanwhile, I finally hit the snow I was anticipating at about 6,600 feet. Nothing too serious at that point, but enough to really slow me down. With micro-spikes on and ice ax in hand, I was back to a slow crawl. The snow was soft and slushy, making it slippery too. The sun was blazingly hot, so the snow was melting fast and water was pouring off the mountain like someone had left the tap running. I had set a goal for where I wanted to camp, but when eight o'clock came, I was still nearly four miles from that site, and I had to stop shy of my goal. I was too tired and hungry to go any farther. I found a small clearing that was half on the trail, pitched my tent, and had dinner to the setting sun's spectacular light display on the surrounding mountains. I felt bad about placing my tent on the trail, but I hadn't seen another person all day and figured I wouldn't be in anyone's way. The beautiful setting sun let me know I had made a good decision. I had hiked until so late that I didn't even attempt to journal. Instead, I woke up at 4:30 the next morning to write about my previous day. Once that was taken care of, it was coffee time. I enjoyed that cup as I watched that sunrise from my tent where I had watched it set the night before.

The hike ahead of me was like entering the unknown. What would the snow conditions be like? Lately, that always seemed to be the big question of the day. Would the trail take me on the north face of a 7000-foot peak, or the south face, which would mean less or even no snow. I was hiking today through the Marble Mountains, which just weeks earlier had been reported impassable. I got lucky and met six southbound hikers. We were all eager to share intel for what was coming up, respectively. My leading question was, of course, about the snow conditions. We had all come to hike the trail, not to go mountaineering. My next question was about water sources. The last bit of information the group provided me was about the trail conditions leading into Seiad Valley. More about that in a bit.

The other advantage to my meeting up with the six SOBO hikers was that they had recently blazed the trail. Which meant...*footprints*! Their footprints lay before me and would save me some time in navigating over the vast snowfields. Now I could concentrate more on not falling. I kept my micro-spikes clipped to my backpack waist belt for quick and easy access. It was a constant game of on again, off again, most of the day. The good news was that I didn't need the ice ax as there were no dangerous traverses. The dangers today were simply from hiking through the melting snow, since it was melting so quickly, which causes postholing conditions and snow bridges that cave in. Snow bridges form over hidden, fast-moving water, like creeks under the snow. The quickly melting snow adds huge volumes of water to the creeks that you can't see but often can hear under the snow. If enough of the bridge melts, it will cave in under your weight.

I also found myself hiking through large areas of burned out forest during the last two days of my hike. The wildfires of yesteryear have left huge scars on these mountains. The recovery is slow, and the remains of the fire's devastation reminds us of those tragic events—the huge loss of natural resources, loss of homes...the loss of life.

When I finally found myself free of the snow, I don't believe I could have been happier. Based on the current elevations and snow reports, it looked like my hiking should be close to snow free for the next hundred or so miles. Excellent!

So, back to that bit of information from the six SOBO hikers regarding the trail conditions leading into Seiad Valley. They gave me the heads up to expect that around 20 miles from the town of Seiad Valley I would encounter the worst trail conditions imaginable. It ended up that this was not an exaggeration. There were hundreds of fallen trees on the trail that required me to go over, under, or around. The trail was so overgrown that it was indistinguishable from the forest that surrounded it. It was obvious there had been zero trail maintenance on this section for years. I guessed that it would take the PCTA, an army of volunteers, and hundreds, if not thousands, of hours to bring that section of the trail back.

My overnight camping accommodations that night was simple and functional at best. Nothing special about the place other than it was flat and close to water. I was now just fourteen miles from Seiad Valley, where second breakfast and a Coke were waiting for me. It was kind of remarkable that the day before I was hiking at just under 7,000 feet, and when I arrived at Seiad Valley I was at just 1,374 feet.

That morning's hike down to the valley was still a bushwhacking experience, but not nearly as bad as the day before. The trail followed Grinder Creek pretty much the entire way giving that lull-you-to-sleep, rushing water noise. The trail crosses the creek several times, employing beautifully constructed pedestrian bridges. Day hiking that trail would make for a great outing if not for the poor trail conditions, so I doubt many of the locals ever hiked that trail.

The last 6.5 miles of the trail takes you along a dirt road and then a paved road right into the town of Seiad Valley. I passed a number of home-steads along the way, with expanded properties providing the owners with wilderness living. Once I arrived in the *very* small town of Seiad Valley, I made a beeline for the cafe. Four southbound hikers had just received their breakfast as I sat down. We struck up a conversation about the obvious. Yep, we each wanted to know what the trail was like up ahead, and it didn't take long for the conversation to turn to questions about snow.

I was about to order my breakfast when the waitress let me know they were now serving lunch. Well, okay then, lunch it was. As a side note, this cafe is known for their Pancake Challenge. If you order the five pounds of pancakes menu item, and you eat it all, you'll get it for free. And to think I just missed ordering breakfast! Since they were now serving lunch, I ordered the mushroom and Swiss-smothered burger with a bottomless glass of Pepsi—sorry, no Coke.

Home of the Pancake Challenge

Back to the SOBO hikers. As best I could tell, no one had skipped ahead farther and started southbound north of Ashland. I guessed I'd just have to go see for myself what the trail conditions north of Ashland would be like. While everyone else I'd met at the Café was planning on staying in town, my plan was to keep going. I did a quick resupply at the little convenience store and hiked on. I really thought I was motivated, but I hit the wall at 2:30 p.m. after I'd started what seemed a near vertical climb out of Seiad Valley and discovered that I just wasn't feeling it. I got one and a half miles up that climb and came to a water source. I pointed out to myself that I had just passed a lovely tent site that was a mere one-tenth of a mile back. I don't know if it was that mushroom and Swiss-smothered burger weighing me down, the gallon of Pepsi I drank, or if I was just plain tired. I debated going further, and after a 30-minute debate with myself, I hiked back to that tent site and pitched my tent. Tired won over. I was just 34.2 miles from the California-Oregon border, but as I said, tired won over.

I started fresh at six the next morning, finished the 4000-foot climb I'd started unsuccessfully the afternoon before, and headed for Oregon.

Once I got to the ridge, it was hiking as hiking should be. Cool breezes, a nice tread, and bright, clear skies. I walked through a beautiful forest that had obviously been severely damaged from a fire, who knows when, but was now in a recovery stage. There were huge conifers with charred bark but full canopies, thick and green. Proud survivors of a fire which had taken many of their kin.

I met a good number of SOBO hikers that day, and picked up some bad news regarding the trail. Crater Lake was still snowed in with six to ten feet of snow. One group had to skip a 50-mile section. I was truly at an impasse as to what I should do. I just wanted to be able to hike, and it seemed like obstacles kept getting in my way. For now, I would hike the remaining miles to Oregon, get to Ashland, and make my plans from there while off the trail and away from any distractions.

What distractions? Well, I was lying in my tent trying to think, and the birds were singing and chirping, and the cool, calm winds were keeping me from being able to seriously consider my dilemma. And— as if I needed another reminder of how time was marching by—I found myself looking up at my *third* full moon while on this trail. Still, what beautiful distractions.

I woke up the next morning excited by the idea that I was just fourteen miles from the Oregon border. That excitement was quickly diminished after I called my wife. Annie let me know that a dear friend and neighbor had passed. She was a kind and gracious woman that we would all miss dearly. I hiked on with sad thoughts throughout the morning, particularly concerned for her husband, a friend who also happens to be a hiking partner of mine. My heart ached for him, their two daughters, their granddaughter, and of course, all the many people who knew and loved her. This day reminded me that life and tragic death continued on in my absence.

At last I got to the Oregon border sign...and found the entire experience a bit anticlimactic. The loss of our friend was still weighing heavily on my mind, but there were other things, as well. The fact that I wasn't really finished with California, for one. There were over 600 miles I had skipped because of that darn snow in the Sierra Nevadas. Also, there was no one around to share the state border crossing with. No celebrations, no fanfare, no photos, other than the lonely selfie I took. Hey, by the way Oregon, you need a new sign; the one at your border is falling apart.

Crossing into Oregon

I did have one moment today that took my breath away. I was exactly one mile from Oregon, and found myself hiking through a beautiful meadow. I was accustomed to looking down—to make sure I didn't fall on my face—but I would look up from time to time to check out my surroundings. You don't see too many high mountain meadows on the trail, and this one took me by surprise. It looked like something out of *Little House on The Prairie*, stunningly beautiful. Once in Oregon, I learned that state wasn't exempt from receiving snow. A welcome to Oregon snow-covered ridge was waiting smugly for my arrival. But I was not in the mood, so I kicked that snow's butt. Unfortunately, there was plenty more of the white stuff a bit further up the trail, starting with Crater Lake.

The mysterious workings of the trail had me run into a couple I hadn't seen since the desert. Milla and 173 had flipped up north, and were now southbound. It was really special getting to see this wonderful couple and catch up on trail news. They had flipped up to Cascade Locks and tried to hike south from there, but guess what? They hit too much snow. So, they went a bit farther south to Ashland, and were now southbound from there.

I'd been leapfrogging a hiker that goes by Tai-Chi these past three days. We'd end up at the same camp each evening, so tonight we had our sights on a small campsite, big enough for just two tents. I arrived before he did, and found a couple of section hikers. A friendly couple called Bluejay and Sparkles, were already there with a huge three-person tent set up. The early bird had gotten the worm...and our tent site. Fortunately, there was an old Forest Service road just above the campsite that was fairly flat. Tai-Chi and I enjoyed our dinner together and made plans to meet at Callahan's Lodge for second breakfast. This was where I also hoped to catch a ride to the Ashland post office where yet another pair of new shoes and a box full of goodies from my daughter-in-law, Lauren, and my granddaughters, Blakely and Katy Ellis, were waiting for me.

Fourteen miles never went so fast. It certainly helped that about twelve of them were heading down the mountain. When I arrived at the trail junction for Callahan's, it was a bit convoluted, so I thought it best to wait for Tai-Chi. I knew he didn't use a GPS. When he caught up with me, we found that getting to Callahan's Lodge was ridiculously confusing, but we finally found our way there.

The lodge was much bigger than I had expected, and really way too nice for stinky hikers. Yet, they treated us like regular people. In fact, they treat hikers better than regular people, evidenced by their offer of a free beer to all thru-hikers. Their hiker lunch special is a bottomless serving of spaghetti, a choice of three sauces, salad, and bread, all for sixteen dollars. Tai-chi and I both had three very healthy servings.

After lunch, I knew I had to get to the post office, and also to do a major resupply in Ashland. Tai-Chi did not need to resupply, so we agreed that he would hike on and we'd try to meet up at Fish Lake in a couple of days. I asked Jeff, the manager of the lodge, if he could suggest a way that I could get into Ashland, 20 miles further. Without hesitation, he said that he would drive me there. Trail magic at its best. He dropped me off at the post office where I picked up the new trail runners that my wife had ordered for me, as well a box of goodies from my daughter-in-law and handmade cards from my two beautiful granddaughters. I have to say, that box was one of the highlights of my journey.

With my shopping done, it was just past 5:00 p.m. and the town post office had closed. I needed to get to the Rite Aid Pharmacy where there was a satellite post office that was still open, so I could mail my next three resupply boxes. I walked to the first car I saw backing out of the Safeway supermarket parking lot and asked the driver if he would drive me there. The driver, Alex, was a seventeen-year-old young man who told me to hop on in. But first, I told him I also needed a canister of stove fuel. He drove me to two separate locations to find the fuel I needed, and then to the Rite-Aid before that post office closed at six o'clock. He also helped me carry my boxes in because he wanted to make sure the post office was still open. People, don't give up on our young people—they are amazing. All I can say is, this young man's parents have done a terrific job raising him.

Now, how to get back to Callahan's?

I tried to hitch, but it was a very busy town and I found it diffi-cult to catch a ride, especially with my destination being 20 miles away. So, Uber it was. My driver, Stephanie, got me safely back to Callahan's Lodge in about 20 minutes for $23 plus tip, which was money well spent.

Finally, while pitching my tent I met a hiker from Germany. We hit it off pretty well. We talked for over an hour and agreed that we would hike out together the next morning after breakfast. He had a unique trail name. This guy got his trail name from when he applied for his PCT permit. That random permit process selected him as the first person, number one in the lottery to get a permit, hence, the trail name First One.

It ended up being a long and interesting night. There were four tents set up on the beautifully manicured lawn at Callahan's. The lodge was playing host to a large group consisting of 20 or so teachers on a retreat. It was probably more like a celebration, now that school was out for summer. If a lodge measured its success by how much alcohol it poured in a single evening, Callahan's had a hugely successful night. The party moved from the lodge patio after the restaurant closed for the evening, up to the balconies of the group's apparently adjoining rooms. The balconies were directly above the tenting area of the lawn we hikers were now camped on. Oh, and they had music—1980's music—and of course they knew all the words to every song. I've found that the more alcohol consumed, the better people think they can sing, and naturally, they have a need to sing louder. It was 11:30 p.m. when I finally put on my shoes and my headlamp, walked over, and politely asked if they might be done anytime soon.

"Oh, sure we are just about done."

At 12:30 a.m., I called Joel at the front desk. At 12:32 it fell silent as the party came to an abrupt end. Thank you, Joel.

First One and I had agreed to meet for breakfast, so I skipped my morning Pop-Tarts and had the hiker special of three eggs, three slices of bacon, coffee, and unlimited pancakes. They had me at unlimited. I still had a couple of postcards to fill out, so we didn't get on the trail until 9:30. That was okay, though, because we still got in some great miles. We also had the opportunity to talk while we hiked, which honestly helped the day and miles fly by. When it came time for lunch, we stopped at a great coldwater spring where cold water was literally shooting out of the ground. First One insisted on sharing his French baguette loaf loaded with ham, cheese, and fresh tomato. Who am I to refuse a gentleman's kind offer?

When it came time to call it a day, we stopped at our predetermined camp. Hyatt Lake Campground is a state run, pay-to-stay campground. When we arrived, it was clear that something was wrong. The campground looked abandoned. What had apparently once been a nice campground now looked like a ghost town. We were about to head back and continue on the trail when a car pulled onto the campground road. I gave a wave to ask for help, and the driver rolled down his car window. I asked if he knew anything about the campground and he told us that it had been like that since the year before. There had been a discovery of contaminated water from insecticides used in area farmlands. The state campground had shut off all water sources, but had kept one area open to primitive camping. The development has had a huge environmental and economic impact on the local area, while also explaining why the campground was almost completely abandoned. Luckily, the section C loop was still open, and the driver said we were welcome to camp on his reserved site. We happily camped with our new friend Dennis on site 43, which was situated on Hyatt Lake and had spectacular views. I pitched my tent lakeside with the flaps wide open, which provided me with a beautiful view of the open sky and setting sun. Saved by another trail angel.

A little more about our gracious host. The reason Dennis was at the Hyatt Lake Campground was because he was meeting a large group that would be performing a butterfly census. He and 20 or so of his colleagues were going to be checking on butterfly populations. I'm not really sure how they go about this whole process, but I guessed it was work that needed to be done. Dennis did more than give us a place to pitch our tents that night. As there was no water at the campground—the lake water was also considered to be contaminated—he shared the drinking water he'd brought with him. That gave us what we needed to cook our dinner and also what would be needed in the morning to hold us over until we got to the next reliable water source.

When we finally found good water—I sure hoped it was good water—we filled our bottles and drank the cool water with great enthusiasm. The trail was very kind to us that day, which was good because First One was not feeling his best. Our discussions, and honestly our entire focus these last two days, had been about what to expect regarding snow before and including Crater Lake, and beyond. Snow reports are good for an overview, but firsthand knowledge is always best. There had been so few SOBO hikers so far, and almost all of them had started out south of Crater Lake. The few we had crossed paths with painted an ugly picture. Still, the recent temperatures had been pretty hot, so we were hoping that some of all that snow would melt before we got there.

It was now June 19th, and that evening we camped at the South Brown Mountain Shelter. This log cabin structure is used by folks in the winter on snowmobiles or cross-country skiing, and during hiking season by PCT hikers. There is just a small handful of shelters on this trail compared to the Appalachian Trail where they averaged about ten miles apart. Those who know me would know I'd avoid this shelter and sleep in my tent where I always slept best.

The day before and most of the hike today had taken us through beautiful forests, with limited changes in elevation. There were periods this morning that had us trekking over several miles of trail with a lava tread. While walking on the lava I felt as though I was walking across a giant barbecue, because it looked exactly like the lava that comes with a home propane grill. After those long lava miles, it also became apparent that this was where shoes go to die an early death.

We made the first ten miles quickly, which took us to Oregon Route 140. Just two miles down the highway is Fish Lake Resort where we were to meet Tai Chi and hopefully enjoy an ice-cold Coca Cola. We would attempt to hitch the two miles, but if we were unsuccessful, we would walk back into the woods and hike on. The trouble with the highway was, there was too much traffic so it wasn't conducive to hitchhiking. However, the pull of a cold Coca Cola was too strong for either of us to handle, so we roadwalked the two miles. Unfortunately, we were unable to find Tai Chi. First One ordered a double cheeseburger with his Coke. My food bag was still pretty heavy, so I ate out of it and washed my lunch down with that precious cold Coca Cola. When it came time to head back to the trail, we got lucky; the third vehicle to come by pulled over and drove us back to the trailhead. Satisfied with our full bellies and Cola fix, we quickly added to our daily total miles. We climbed over a number of small snowfields and suspected they were a pretty good indicator of what was to come the following day as we ate up the distance to Crater Lake.

That was a great day to be a mosquito. The Whistler smorgasbord was open for business and those pesky creatures had their way with me. In the meantime, it was a good thing I still had my winter gear—weather reports were calling for freezing temperatures that night.

The next day we came across a young couple we had been leap-frogging for a few days. Anders and Tuva from Norway were hiking Oregon and Washington, and had just started their trek four days earlier. They had been with us on the side of the highway trying to hitch-hike to Fish Lake. We had also camped in the same place the night before. In the morning we all said our goodbyes, and I truthfully didn't expect to see them again anytime soon.

The morning got off to a strange start. First One and I started out at what had become our usual start time of 7:00 a.m. Similar to when Scooby and I hiked together, it had become the norm for me to take lead. It didn't take long before I noticed and brought to First One's attention that it was unusually quiet. No birds were singing their morning songs, no wind blowing through the trees, just a still and noiseless morning. I have to admit the stillness fit my mood. I had been feeling a bit anxious all morning, knowing what we were hiking toward. The high snow levels in the coming miles had been the topic of conversation between all of us hikers. The latest PCTA snow report showed there would be lots of the white stuff waiting to greet us.

First One

It probably wouldn't have seemed so intimidating, but we had places coming up with names like Lucifer Mountain and Devils Peak. Are these names really necessary?

We conquered Lucifer by climbing above the steep snow traverses and working our way across the ridge, then carefully down a scree field back to the trail. Devils Peak required that we take it slow along the long-angled traverse. When we thought we were finished with it, we walked around one last switchback...and blurted out a few choice and expressive words. Just minutes earlier First One had uttered, "I feel sorry for the Norwegians because they don't have micro-spikes."

At that very moment, Tuva came walking around the corner all aglow with Anders directly behind her. We chatted about the challenges of the day so far, and then we all stared up at the deep and steep snow that lay before us. We were at 7,400 feet, and the trail hidden somewhere under all that snow would bring us down to 6,000 feet. If we could find it. Even so, First One and Tuva carefully started to hike their way down the mountain.

With no trail in sight, I decided that instead I would make the descent by way of glissading. I put my rain pants on, stowed my trekking poles, sat down, and held my ice ax beside me like a rudder to slow my descent on the semi-steep and icy snow.

I was just about to push off, when out of the corner of my eye I saw Anders literally skiing down the mountain on nothing but his shoes. It was the most fantastic thing I had ever seen. Not surprisingly, afterward we were told that Anders had learned to ski in Norway before he could walk.

I pushed off in a sitting position at a pretty fast pace, but not anything as impressive as Anders. I controlled my descent speed with how deep I pushed the axe blade into the icy snow. It was a crazy fun way to make a quick descent, and I went from an anxiety-filled morning to one of my greatest memories of the trail.

We were now just sixteen miles from Crater Lake National Park, which would prove to be one of my fondest memories of my thru-hike.

The general store at Crater Lake served Starbucks coffee…but didn't open till 7:00 a.m. Needless to say, we got a late start. First One and I had agreed the night before that we would hike the seven-mile alternate trail to the Crater Lake Rim Trail as opposed to hiking the PCT. Taking the alternate trail was doubtless what most would do because it was considered a once in a lifetime experience. Once we arrived, we took time to have a second cup of coffee and a snack. We observed multitudes of visitors driving up to the crater in their cars.

It reminded me of when I hiked up Mount Washington while on the Appalachian Trail. I hiked up while most others drove up. There was even a bumper sticker for sale at the gift shop that read, "My Car Made It to The Top of Mount Washington." What this all actually reminded me of was how blessed I was to have my health and the legs needed to carry me up those mountains.

Crater Lake exceeded my greatest expectations. It was one of those rare times in my life that I found myself dumbfounded by the beauty before me. How a once explosive volcano some 7000 years ago became this peaceful, tranquil lake—the deepest lake in the United States—couldn't possibly be a mistake. It had to be part of God's plan. First One and I were like giddy school boys. We couldn't stop laughing and taking photos. Hiking the rim with the lake on our right made it very difficult to watch where I was walking. The lake would change with every single step we took along the trail.

Crater Lake will forever be imprinted in my memory, and would certainly be one of the highlights of my entire journey.

Crater Lake

We hiked as far as Watchman Overlook, where we were told by the rangers there was a risk for avalanches beyond that point. We took the road and walked until it intersected with the PCT again, seemingly walking on air in total disbelief of the amazing day we'd had. There were still miles to hike, though, so we got right to it. Water was an issue. It would be a nine-mile hike to the next water source, which was a cache that was apparently very reliable. This section would take us through a forest that was surely home to the world's largest population of mosquitoes. Our best defense was to basically run the nine miles. With First One taking the lead and his legs practically on fire, we literally went over four miles per hour to the water cache. It was abundant with several hundred gallons of water, and the frustrated mosquitoes never got the first drop of my blood.

The water cache was the perfect place to make camp since ten ounces of that precious liquid would be used at breakfast for my early cup of coffee. The trail does provide.

I awoke the following morning with a thought: If every day was a Crater Lake day, would I still truly appreciate it? Had I appreciated that day more because I'd hiked up to the rim instead of driving?

I think the answers to those questions would be a resounding yes. After seeing Crater Lake, we had a long hike through a very nondescript forest. In fact, I've hiked hundreds of miles that were bland and boring, and I doubt I could give the briefest of details of those miles. It's the total of all the miles hiked that adds huge value to those few very special sights, and make each and every one of the boring miles worth the effort. So, in support of those thoughts, that day we hiked 29.9 miles...and it was clearly one of those nondescript days.

It was still a good day, though, for First One and me to simply talk as we walked. It had been one week since we started hiking together, and as I've mentioned before, it's difficult to find someone you can hike with comfortably. First One and I agreed we have similar hiking philosophies and practices. We were able to hike at the same speeds and the same distances, although, being eighteen years my junior, he could definitely outpace me. What I'd found after hiking about 2000 miles with my friend Scooby, and now a week with First One, was that the sum of two hikers is greater than the two individuals.

I'll try to explain. We each have to carry our own weight, and we still have to hike each of the steps taken by ourselves, but there is a greater drive to take those steps when you are teamed up. If I am in front leading, I know my hiking partner is behind me and is counting on me to keep moving, thus keeping him moving. But there is more to it than that. There must also be mutual goals. There has to be the willingness to be flexible and agreeable. What I knew about Scooby, and now about First One, was that we respected one another, were kind to one another, could joke with one another and enjoy each other's company, all while moving toward those mutually agreed-upon goals. First One and I both agreed that we were similar, yet different, and that we have also enjoyed hiking by ourselves in the past, and who knew, we might again in the future.

Interestingly, as we were talking, he shared a German saying that goes something like this: Luck and happiness are doubled if shared.

As with my many miles with Scooby, and those most recent miles with First One, we had enjoyed double the luck and, I daresay, double the happiness in our experiences.

My thoughts the following morning took me back to when I had first started this journey. You may recall that I'd had the pleasure of staying with trail angels Scout and Frodo in San Diego. During the two evenings I was there, they would serve dinner in their backyard for up to 40 hikers. During and after dinner, they would offer up stories and advice. Scout suggested on that first evening, if you hike into the Sierra Nevada with one or more other people, you should all make a pact. He recommended that if even just one person was uncomfortable with the trail conditions and their personal safety, everyone in the group should support that person and turn around, get off the trail, and head to safety. On the next evening, he told a story of when he was leaving for the Continental Divide Trail. He told us that Frodo's last words to him were not, "I love you." Her last words were, "Make good decisions."

First One and I made a really good decision today. We decided to avoid a fifteen mile stretch of snow at and above 7000 feet. The Oregon Skyline Trail runs parallel to the PCT, but lies 1000 feet or more below it, and is considered the alternate trail. We enjoyed lunch that afternoon at a horse camp that had picnic tables, where we warmed ourselves under the sunny, clear sky. You may recall that I mailed myself three drop boxes while in Ashland. I inadvertently shipped the first box to Willamette Pass, where I had thought I'd take my next zero, but I had now changed my plans since I was hiking with First One. We decided to split up after lunch with First One heading for Shelter Cove—our newly planned destination—while I hiked the additional seven miles off trail to Willamette Pass to pick up my resupply box. I'd hiked about three miles when Kevin, Amanda, and their dog Bailey stopped, offered me a ride, and drove me the rest of the way. This wonderful couple had just finished a camping trip and were headed home, and as luck would have it, these great trail angels were there to assist me in my time of need.

The Willamette Pass Inn accepts PCT hiker boxes, and according to the owners Judy and Brad, they had done so for eighteen years. They took it exceedingly personally when we discovered my box wasn't at their Inn, and they jumped into action to help locate it. The post office tracking reported it as having been delivered, so Judy called Patty at the local post office. Patty told Judy that Jim the postman was actually off the day it had reportedly been delivered. So, Jim's wife had delivered the mail that day. Gotta love small towns. I was told that Jim would arrive at the local post office boxes by 1:30 p.m., so I waited patiently. When Jim got there as scheduled, he looked up and pointed at me while practically yelling, "Monk, your box is at Shelter Cove." Yep, the exact location First One was hiking to. I politely asked him why it was there as opposed to the address I had placed on the package, and his reply without hesitation was that he "Must have mis-delivered it." Period. End of story.

Alrighty then. So I started my long walk along Oregon Route 58 toward Shelter Cove. I tried getting a hitch back to the trail, but this is a very busy highway with cars unable to stop even if they wanted to. Using my GPS, I found an alternate route that would take me along Odell Lake by way of the railroad tracks. It seemed a bit odd, but the topo map clearly showed this as a direct and certain way to get there. I must admit, this was not how I had envisioned my day, but I knew that I had to get to Shelter Cove so I just kept hiking.

When I finally reached the tracks, I had walked along the rails for several miles when up ahead I could see someone sitting on the tracks. I kept moving forward, and saw the person stand up. It was First One. As it turned out, he had gotten misdirected and lost on the trail, so when he'd come across the railroad tracks, he'd sat down to take a break. Finding First One in the middle of nowhere, in the very last place I had ever expected, truly helped lift my spirits. We hiked the remaining five miles together along the tracks, only having to leave them twice because a couple of trains actually used them for their intended purpose.

Once we arrived at Shelter Cove, we found our friends Anders and Tuva already there. Sadly, Tuva was dealing with shin splints. But we enjoyed our time together as we caught up and shared our experiences since last seeing them.

Shelter Cove is one of those old-time resorts that serves skiers and snowmobilers in the winter, and campers plus PCT hikers in the summer. There had to be a hundred or more campers there—everything from pup tents to 40-foot motor homes. The general store was stocked floor to ceiling with anything and everything you might want or need. The restaurant was serving the masses with freshly made meals. I chose to eat out of my food bag again because I was still carrying more than I needed. That additional food was heavy, but it allowed me to enjoy two breakfasts, two lunches, and two dinners every day, which helped slow my excessive weight loss.

First One and I agreed to a later than usual 9:00 a.m. departure. We had been burning up the trail at close to 30 miles each day, and decided to step it back a bit. After breakfast, we said our goodbyes to Anders and Tuva since they were taking a few days off the trail to allow Tuva's shin splits to heal. I hoped that I would meet up with them again, but again it seemed unlikely.

Once we left Shelter Cove, our hike took us through a beautiful, healthy, and lush forest. We hiked along the shores of Odell Lake, and Lower, Middle, and Upper Rosary Lakes. This reminded me of the numerous ponds and lakes I had passed, and once enjoyed a swim in, while hiking through Maine on the Appalachian Trail. Hiking along the daisy chain of Rosary Lakes, I imagined the hikers coming up later that summer would undoubtedly be swimming in these crystal-clear waters. As the day wore on, and because I was feeling quite energized, I hiked on ahead of First One. At lunchtime, I came to the Maiden Peak Shelter, which is maintained for the use of winter skiers. It's left unlocked so hikers can use it, as well, for shelter against a storm or to just drop in for a place to sit and enjoy your lunch...as I now did. I took my time and hoped First One would catch up. When he never showed up, I figured I would hike on ahead and meet him at our agreed-upon campsite.

But as the day wore on, the sky darkened and the air temperatures changed. It wasn't long before I was being pelted by hail, snow, and sleet. Thunder claps were so loud they shook the whole mountain. Reality struck, and I knew I had to pitch my tent somewhere to escape the threatening weather. I found a perfect spot near Charlton Lake, but it was secluded and I feared I would miss First One if he came by later that night. Luckily, he eventually found me, quickly pitched his tent, and was in it before the winter mix started to fly—hail, snow, sleet, and rain, too, as though the clouds couldn't make up their minds what to drop on us unsuspecting hikers. The storm lasted all night and into the early morning, but with barely any accumulation since the ground temperatures were just above freezing. I was well prepared with my rain gear at the ready, but the sun came out just before we started hiking, a timely appearance that provided a perfect accompaniment to the lake fog that slowly skimmed and drifted across the lake.

Charlton Lake was a gorgeous spot, and we both agreed it was one of the most beautiful campsites on the trail.

Our hiking took us through more of the lush green forest, but then the landscape quickly changed. It wasn't long before we found ourselves hiking across a disastrously scarred ridge which was a huge contrast to the verdant forest. Thousands of fallen trees littered the mountainside as though they'd been picked up and haphazardly tossed about by some giant. I don't know what could have caused this type of carnage, but it looked like a strong winter storm must have had its way with the mountain. Trees had been snapped in half as though they were twigs. We hiked through this eyesore of a forest for about three miles. The scenery improved greatly later that day, and we found ourselves hiking around more beautiful secluded lakes and ponds. Clear water, abundant from the snowmelt higher on the mountains, had those lakes cresting at their maximum holding capacity. I did my part by taking all that I could drink as I hiked lake to lake.

This day marked the second day that we had not seen another hiker on the trail. How was it possible to not see another living soul on the PCT for two whole days? It was a mystery to me. It had also occurred to me that it wouldn't be long before I started passing the SOBO hikers who had started their southbound pilgrimage at the northern terminus just weeks earlier.

The following day would take us to above 6000 feet to Sisters, a small resort town, and Three Fingered Jack, a formation at the summit of a Cascades volcano. We knew we'd be hitting some major snow in this 20-mile stretch, but that would be the end of the deep snow for the rest of Oregon, and possibly Washington, if the snow continued its fast summer melt before we arrived.

As was now our habit, I hiked on ahead of First One, with the usual plan to meet at our agreed-upon campsite. Once I arrived, I made my camp at a spot close to a small pond, collected water, and waited on First One. When he never arrived, I fixed my dinner and got ready for bed. Had he fallen too far behind? Or had he somehow gotten ahead of me? I kept expecting to hear him walk up and make camp near me, but he never did. I decided that I would head out at 5:30 the next morning to see if he was just past my campsite, but I never found him.

Was I worried about him? Not really. We had already discussed that he was going to hike into the town of Sisters to purchase new shoes. I felt pretty sure that we would see each other again. Hiking with First One reminded me of how I'd seen others hiking together, starting together in the morning, but tending to separate as the day went on, only to meet toward the end of the day, and then start all over again the next day.

As it turned out, First One and I would eventually cross paths again, but it wouldn't be for a very long time.

In the meantime, my early start allowed me to take advantage of the frozen snow before the sun turned it into a slushy mess. It was a good strategy, but as the day went on, I found myself wishing I had started even earlier—say, like at midnight. The sky was clear and it looked like the rain and winter mix I'd been caught in these past two days were behind me now. It was actually a perfect day for a tough hike.

South, Middle and North Sister mountains lay just ahead, and I'd soon find out if they were evil sisters.

The early morning climb took me from 5,300 feet to 6,500 feet in just three miles. A short time later I was walking through an expansive meadow surrounded by snow-capped mountains, while the meadow was virtually snow free. Lunchtime came and went with me not wanting to stop. I was starving, but I couldn't make myself stop because of how perfect this place was. It was just too beautiful, too perfect, to sit down. I was also anxious to see what would soon lie around the next turn. I finally stopped for lunch when I remembered I needed to dry the gear I'd had to pack wet from condensation that morning. So, I sat next to a winding seasonal stream as its cold waters meandered past, trying their best to lull me to sleep while my gear dried in the warm sun and cool breezes. A lunch of tuna on a tortilla never tasted so good. Before I left that spot, I pulled and filtered a liter of cool water to enjoy later, and as a reminder of that perfect tranquil place.

As I walked away, I turned around for one more look, and simply shook my head in wondrous disbelief.

But I guess it's true when they say every rose has its thorns. Not five minutes after leaving my special lunch spot, I crossed into a burned-out area that confirmed I had stopped at exactly the right place and time.

The rest of my day proved to be exhausting and extremely difficult. The snow was deep, steep in places, and it went on for miles upon miles. The snow was so soft from the afternoon sun that I sank in up to my knees too many times to count. My biggest fear was that I would posthole down to large rocks or tree stumps hiding under the soft, slushy snow. There were a few traverses, but none that required I pull out my ice ax. It was slow going. I had to stop and pull out my GPS to confirm my direction every few minutes. Following footprints from hikers before me had not always worked out too well, and couldn't always be trusted. Why follow someone who had no better idea where they were going than I did?

As difficult as it was, I was determined to get through most of the snow that day. My intended camp was at mile 1,974.8, and I had no idea if I'd be pitching my tent on dry land or mushy snow. My last chance for water was Glacier Creek at mile 1,973, which I found to be buried deep under the snow and totally inaccessible. I still had three-quarters of a liter and could make due, but it had become my habit to drink one to two liters while at camp to rehydrate. When I arrived at the camp-site it was high and dry, and as luck would have it, I heard the steady sound of an ice-cold snowmelt stream running close by. I had hiked till six o'clock, making for a long, tiring but very productive day with 27 miles hiked. I knew I would have just about seven more miles to challenge me in the morning, and that would be pretty much it for the snow. I would be a liar if I said anything other than I would not miss that snow one bit.

I woke up that next morning, stretched my legs, and pulled them out from under my quilt. I glanced down at my feet which, just the night before, had been shriveled up prunes from being in the wet snow all day long. They now looked like brand-new feet. Looking down at them, I said out loud, "Thank you, feet." Yep, I was talking to my feet—a hiker's best friends.

I started out at six-thirty that morning, and attacked what little snow was still before me. I felt really good, especially after a long and grueling hike the day before. I came upon a pretty steep traverse, but I figured I needn't bother with my micro-spikes because it was only about a hundred feet across. I got about ten feet out on the icy snow, looked down to my left and saw jagged lava stone sticking up. I start-ed thinking that when they found my mangled body, the search and rescue people would say something like, "What an idiot. He had mi-cro-spikes and didn't bother to put them on." I turned back around, sat down, and put them on. "Use 'em if you got 'em," was what I then said out loud. Little did I know that this comment would soon come back to haunt me. I eventually came to the Dee Wright Observatory in the Willamette National Forest, where I stopped for lunch amongst all the observatory visitors. As I enjoyed my meal, I was pleasantly surprised when Anders and Tuva came driving up. A wonderful trail angel who had been taking care of Tuva as she continued to take time off for her shin splints to heal was taking them sightseeing. We sat together, got all caught up, and finally said our goodbyes.

Whistler, Anders and Tuva

Hiking on later that day, the mountain air changed and got much colder as lightning and thunder cracked the sky wide open. At the time I was hiking through what ended up being about five miles of lava fields. I was on an exposed ridge as the lightning lit up the sky accompanied by loud claps of thunder, immediately followed by hail that was bouncing off of me and the ground like popcorn. The whole time I was thinking I was in a pretty precarious position, especially because I was hiking holding two conductive aluminum trekking poles. My solution was to hike faster. Faster than lightning. The last thing I needed was to get struck by lightning. That would have been extra bad because it happened to be the day before my sixtieth birthday. I definitely wanted to reach that milestone.

My plan was to get to Big Lake Youth Camp to pick up my next resupply box, shower, and do laundry. As I hiked the approach trail to the camp, I met a woman who asked if my name was Whistler. I was somewhat surprised by this, especially when she went on to explain that my wife had called the camp to ask that they help make my birthday special. Annie managed to get one of the staff members to agree to drive me to a pub in the town of Sisters for a birthday dinner. Was I surprised!

When I arrived at the Big Lake Youth Camp I checked in as required. The PCT receptionist greeted me by name, wished me a happy birthday, and made me feel extremely welcome. This camp is without a doubt the most hiker-friendly place you could ever imagine. They have a building specifically set up for hikers that has a full kitchen, two bathrooms with showers, laundry facilities, hiker lounge, and so much more. I was invited to have dinner and breakfast the next morning, and lunch, too, if I wished. They do this for all hikers, even when they also have a hundred-plus kids there for the summer camp. All of these PCT hiker services are by donation—no set price. Oh, and they also accept mailed resupply boxes for hikers, which was good because my next five days' worth of food was waiting for me upon my arrival.

In addition to my resupply box, my wife had also mailed me a birthday surprise package. I accepted the kind folks at Big Lake's offer and joined them for dinner. As much as I knew I would have enjoyed the dinner Annie had planned for me in Sisters, I decided to camp at Big Lake, have dinner with the camp staff, and hike out in the morning. I didn't want to take a zero for my birthday as my wife had suggested, I wanted to hike on my birthday. As it turned out, that was another decision that would haunt me.

The following morning, my birthday, started off well with a delicious breakfast at the Big Lake Youth Camp and a perfectly clear day—a great day to hike. It was made even better when my son Brian called to wish me a happy birthday. We talked while I hiked, and I really wished he was there hiking with me. The miles rolled off quickly, but I also took the time to speak with local day hikers I met on the trail who were enjoying their Sunday hikes. I felt like a million bucks because it was my birthday and I was where I loved to be—on the trail.

I met a fine young man named Ryan who had just started a section hike of Oregon. We'd leapfrogged a couple times, and would have another chance meeting later that day. I stopped at a beautiful lake called Rockpile Lake which was just before Mount Jefferson. My Guthook app indicated that this would be the last place to collect water before my planned campsite. I was excited because the campsite I had selected reportedly had spectacular views of Mt. Jefferson. Ryan happened along just then. We chatted a bit, and I let him know that he might want to collect water here as well. I shouldered my pack, said goodbye, and hiked on.

I'd hiked a few more miles when I came across a portion of trail covered with snow. By this point on my thru-hike I'd crossed literally hundreds of miles of snow, and I thought this small traverse would be a cinch. The thought of pulling my micro-spikes out of my pack never even occurred to me. It would have been a short traverse and not a "use 'em if you got 'em" moment. I could see where someone before me had kicked into the snow for footing and I did the same with my right foot. As soon as I lifted my left foot, I quickly slipped down the side of the trail and over the embankment, then tumbled downward hard and fast. I was now falling head over heels down the steep embankment over rock and brush. With each tumble and roll I could hear my own grunts, groans, and cries of pain. I can still close my eyes to this very day and see my fall as though it were occurring again. The worst was the knowledge that I could do nothing to stop myself. When a tree finally stopped my precipitous descent, I knew that I was seriously hurt. I lay there on my back for what I knew was just a few moments but which felt like an eternity. Finally, I was able to unstrap my pack.

I slowly stood up while taking a cursory inventory of the damage I'd done to my body. I estimated that I'd fallen approximately 50 to 60 feet. I had abrasions, cuts, and I was pretty certain some broken ribs since I was unable to lift my pack.

I had no choice but to work my way back up to the trail, so I inched my way up by pulling on tree branches and roots, slowly and methodically, while dragging my pack behind me. I'd stop along the way to retrieve items that had fallen out of my pack during my violent fall. I'd also lost my eyeglasses which, ironically at the time, seemed to me to be my biggest problem. Finally, my grunts and cries of pain caught the attention of that great young man, Ryan, who at that same moment happened to be making his way across the snow traverse. Unable to see me, he called out, "Is there someone down there?" I let him know it was me, that I'd fallen badly, and that I needed help. Once he reached me, he assessed my situation, then asked if he could pray with me. Ryan's timely arrival and thoughtful prayer gave me the strength I needed to make that climb back up to the trail.

Vince, another hiker who'd been heading southbound, saw what was going on and assisted me as well. How many times had I hiked all day, or even days, never seeing another person? How fortunate was I that these two guys happened to come by at the exact time I was in desperate need of help?

Once back on the trail, the three of us determined and agreed that there was no way I could hike on. My breathing was shallow and painful, making hiking the distance to a trail exit physically impossible. I had my Garmin InReach and would have been able to SOS for help, but I also had phone service, so I called 911. My call was quickly forwarded to the local authorities responsible for search and rescue in that geographic area. The Jefferson County Sheriff's Department assembled a team of volunteers led by a deputy. It would take twelve hours for this dedicated volunteer rescue team of four to arrive.

In the meantime, Ryan and Vince stayed with me all night, doing their best to keep me comfortable. I was laid out on the trail on a sleep mat, and kept warm with two sleeping bags. My missing eyeglasses were still stupidly important to me, so Ryan made several attempts at finding them, but with no success. They built a fire and kept it burning all night. They never slept. I was able to doze off but only for brief periods of time. That night while lying on my back, I witnessed the most beautiful sunset, and later, a star-filled cloudless sky. I thought to myself how I'd not taken the opportunity to cowboy camp on my hike—meaning sleeping on the bare ground under the stars—and how sorry I was to have missed out on those past opportunities. I realized then that today I might well have taken a hike-ending fall.

When day broke, we could hear the rescue team as they made their way up the same trail I'd been happily hiking just the day before. It didn't take long for them to assess the situation and determine that they would need to call for the Air National Guard out of Salem. While we waited, I jokingly mentioned my lost glasses, and three of the volunteers unhesitatingly made their way down the steep embankment in search of those elusive specs. Five minutes might have passed when one of them came over to me with my fully intact glasses in hand. Unlike me, there wasn't a scratch on them.

A few hours later we heard the approaching rhythmic sounds of a Black Hawk helicopter in the distance. The rescue team had already put out a bright signal cloth to provide the pilot with a visual target, and were now communicating via radio. It was a surreal scene for me to be looking skyward at the hovering beast above while still lying on my back. There was no place to land, so a medic repelled down to our location and started to run my vitals. The crew in the helicopter lowered the Stokes basket, and with a great deal of assistance, I was strapped in, lifted up, and finally pulled into the belly of that amazing machine. The medic was lifted up next, along with all my gear. As

I was lying on the stretcher the medic continued working on me. I tried to thank him, but I was just too choked up, and it was too loud for him to have heard me anyway. Just then, he looked down at my face and he caught me attempting to speak. He simply put his hand on my shoulder and mouthed, "I know." Nothing else needed to be said. He and his crew were doing the work they were trained to do, and I was the beneficiary.

Air lifted

The trip to the National Guard Airbase in Salem was made quickly, and an ambulance was waiting on the tarmac to transport me to the Salem Health Hospital. Once there, I received the best care I could ever have asked for. Their efficiency and professionalism were soothing and comforting, and there was no doubt I was in good hands. I received full body scans, X-rays, blood work, and a literal head-to-toe inspection. I was told that someone would be coming in a moment to take my blood, and a person would miraculously appear to take my blood. Next, I was told it was protocol after a major fall to be placed in a neck brace. Seconds later a person walked into my room with a neck brace. My ER physician, Dr. Barr, constantly kept me informed of all their findings.

During all this, I received a phone call from Annie. I had not yet let her know about my fall because I hadn't wanted her to worry. Of course, I had not sent my customary evening text the night before, nor my early morning text, either. She was already worried, and must have known something was wrong. We spoke for a few minutes, then she asked if we could FaceTime. I didn't want to do that because I was looking pretty rough. There I was, lying in a hospital bed with cuts, abrasions, blood all over, and now in a neck brace. Not a good picture. She handled it pretty well, though. So well, in fact, that when I told her I guessed my hike was over, she gave me what was really not an unexpected response.

Annie simply said, "Bill, your hike isn't over. Just come home, heal, then go back and finish it." Yep, I'm married to that girl!

When all the blood was cleaned up and all the scans and test results came back, I had miraculously only sustained two broken ribs, along with lots of cuts, lacerations, and bruises, which made me look like a human punching bag. By mid afternoon, I was told that the head of the trauma unit was going to review my file to determine if I would need to stay overnight. When she came in, she reviewed my file, ran some cognitive tests, was satisfied with the results, and agreed with Dr. Barr that I could be released.

One of the nurses who had been taking care of me brought me a menu and invited me to select whatever I wanted to eat. I told her that I'd just been given the go-ahead to be released. She looked me up and down and said in no uncertain terms that I wasn't going anywhere until I got a good meal in me.

I've posted in the past of how I'm the luckiest man alive. There you go—proof that I really am the luckiest man alive. That fall could have cracked my head wide open and easily broken every one of my limbs, but here I was, about to walk out of the hospital less than 24 hours after that fateful misstep. It was a true miracle.

Well, now what?

My luck continued. As it happened, I had dear friends who were coincidently vacationing at their summer home in Wenatchee, Washington. With just one phone call, Ian and Maureen readily agreed to do whatever was needed to help me. Wenatchee was a six-and-a-half-hour drive from the Salem Health Hospital, so I took a seat in the waiting room to await their arrival. As I was sitting there, a gentleman sat down next to me and asked, "William, how long before your friends pick you up?" I did a double-take, as I couldn't quite place who this person was at first. I quickly realized that it was Dr. Barr, the ER doctor who had cared for me, but he was now dressed in civilian clothes. I gave him the approximate time I was expecting my friends, at which point he invited me to his home for dinner with his family. I was once again overwhelmed by the kindness and generosity of the people I'd met along my journey. I had a special home-cooked meal with a humble, caring physician, his sweet wife, and their young son. Dr. Barr shared that I was the very first patient he had ever taken home. I asked why I'd gotten so lucky, to which he replied that he found me "intriguing." Ha. There you have it. I'm intriguing. After dinner, Dr. Barr drove me back to the hospital where my friends, Ian and Maureen, picked me up a short time later. Ian loaded up me and my gear, turned the car around, and drove the six and a half hours back to Wenatchee—a thirteen-hour roundtrip just to help this piece of hiker-trash (hiker-trash…a term of endearment in the hiking community).

Another reminder of how blessed I am.

My plan was to spend a couple of days with my friends for some rest and recovery, and then fly home. My hope was that I could fly back to Oregon when I was healed, and finish up what I had started on April 11th. I wanted—well, in truth I needed—to finish my thru-hike of the Pacific Crest Trail.

My stay with Ian and Maureen gave me time to plan my travel back home to Nova Scotia, which included a shuttle to the Seattle airport and my flight home. There was no way I would have been able to travel with my backpack because of its weight and my inability to lift it. Ian agreed to hold on to it for me and to await further instructions. My flight home was bittersweet—bitter in that I was no longer on the trail, but sweet that I was going home to see Annie for the first time in two and a half months. When my flight arrived in Nova Scotia and I first saw her at the airport, I thought she was truly the most beautiful thing I had ever seen.

It was genuinely nice to be home, to see friends and neighbors, but I knew I didn't want to be home. I wanted to finish what I had started.

Annie continued with her daily routines while I helped as best I could by staying out of her way. As time passed, we agreed that we would no longer call my accident a fall; instead, it would now be referred to as The Incident. I was still in pain, with getting in and out of bed the most difficult. At about week three, I had a chance meeting with a friend, Donna, whose husband was a doctor at our local healthcare center. I told Donna about my hopes to return to the PCT and complete my hike, at which time I detected a look of deep concern. Later that day, her husband phoned to tell me that he was coming over for a house call. When Dr. Conyers arrived, he brought along his resident, so I guessed he was going to use this as a teaching opportunity. Dr. Conyers reviewed my medical records from the Salem Health Hospital, which were available online. He and his resident had me take off my shirt, and they proceeded to poke and prod me. They ran several tests including taking an oximetry reading. They promptly started laughing when they saw the oxygen level in my blood. Dr. Conyers told me it was evidence of my good lung health, and that my blood oxygen levels couldn't be higher— one good residual effect of hiking 1,300 miles prior to The Incident. Then he shared with me that before actually examining me, he'd been prepared to tell me I had no business of returning to complete my hike. Instead, he gave me a list of tasks he wanted me to work on before going back, which included taking day hikes carrying a pack on my back, and lastly instructions to come to his office in a couple weeks for a final check-up. That was good enough for me. There was now no doubt in my mind that I was going to return to finish my hike. And I was now on a mission—a mission to regain my strength and the ability to hike the remaining half of the PCT. I started hiking every day, with a light pack at first, and eventually working my way up to my full pack weight of 35 pounds.

At close to five weeks since The Incident, it was time for me to make definitive plans. I was feeling good, strong, and ready to pick up where I'd left off. Getting back to Oregon and to the trail itself should have been a logistical nightmare, but this was where old and new friends provided selfless acts of kindness and generosity which continued to amaze me.

My friends Ian and Maureen still had my gear in Wenatchee, and they agreed to mail it wherever I needed it to be sent after I had made definitive return travel plans. With my plans in motion, they packed and shipped my backpack to some unexpected new friends. You may recall that Annie and I own a bed and breakfast in Nova Scotia. Several months earlier, Annie had taken a reservation from a couple, Janet and Steve, who happened to mention they lived in Bend Oregon. Annie told them I was hiking the PCT and apparently piqued their interest. These future guests told her to have me call them when I got close to Bend. They told Annie that they would pick me up, take me to their home, feed me, and give me a bed for the night. Well, after The Incident, Janet and Steve contacted me—because of my journal postings—and offered their help if and when I returned to the trail. So, Ian and Maureen mailed my backpack to Janet and Steve's home in Bend, and they in turn agreed to pick me up from the airport when I arrived. As planned, I was picked up and taken to their home for that meal and bed they'd offered months earlier. And just to be clear, I'd never actually met these people, but nevertheless they were willing to help me, this crazy hiker and perfect stranger, in his time of need.

Trail angels Steve and Janet

Section four

Santiam Pass, Oregon to Cascade Locks, Oregon
miles 2,000.9 to 2,147.1

BACK IN THE SADDLE

Undoubtedly, the pressing question of the day was whether or not five weeks had been enough time for my broken ribs to heal. The problem was that I was running out of hiking season. I still had half the trail to finish, and I knew winter would do all it could to keep me from completing my hike. It was a delicate balancing act. I would have liked to take a bit more time to heal, but I found myself racing the calendar. My current plan was to finish hiking Oregon, travel back to Ridgecrest, California, and hike those 679 miles through the Sierra Nevada, and finally, travel back to hike Washington...and hopefully beating the snow.

After picking me up from the Redmond airport on August 5th, Janet and Steve drove me to the REI store in Bend, where I had an order waiting for me. My order of new socks, water filter, stove fuel, and a bottle of Deet was waiting for me at the customer service counter. Steve also took me to a local grocery store where I was able to get the food I needed for my resupply. After a delicious homemade dinner and ice cream dessert, we chatted for a bit, but I finally hit the wall. My early flight, nearly fourteen hours of travel time, and the four hour time difference, totally wiped me out. My hosts offered up an early breakfast, and had me to the trailhead by 7:30 a.m. the next morning.

The closest crossing of the trail and a highway was U.S. Route 20 at Santiam Pass, which meant I had to re-hike fifteen miles of the trail in order to get to where The Incident had occurred 37 days earlier. Hiking those same miles was a déjà-vu experience. I recognized so many of the landmarks and geographical features, the only difference being the absence of snow. I found the exact location of my fall with ease, and stared down into the abyss. Seeing it again served as a harsh reminder of how lucky I was to have ended up with only two broken ribs.

It was pretty obvious, as expected, that I had lost my hiking legs. It was actually not as bad as I'd thought, but my lung capacity was definitely not what it had been five weeks earlier. Another observation was that I didn't return with my hiker hunger. I was sure it wouldn't take long for hiker hunger to return, but on that first day back to the trail, I ate like a mere mortal. I was surprised by, and actually lost count of the huge number of southbound hikers I passed. A number of them told me they had started their hikes on June 30th...which was my 60th birthday and the day of The Incident.

I stopped that first day back on the trail at five o'clock after hiking 22.7 miles. I ate dinner and climbed into my tent by six o'clock for some much-needed rest. I was pleased with myself for those miles hiked, and was hoping for a good night's rest and an early start in the morning. That first afternoon had been really hot, and I was looking forward to a cool early morning and some big miles.

I was a bit tentative on my first creek crossing the following morning. The rushing waters from the snowmelt of Mount Jefferson were deep and rapid. My concern was tenfold what it would have been five weeks earlier. Apparently, I had a newfound healthy fear of falling and re-injuring those ribs. When I arrived at the second creek crossing it was even bigger and faster than the first. I took perhaps an excessive amount of time with my foot placement, after first apprehensively walking up and down the creek searching for the best place to cross. If I crossed using the log that reached across the span would it be too slick from the splashing waters, thus assuring a fall into the creek? If I rock-hopped instead, would the result be any different? In the end, my caution paid off. Both crossings were uneventful, while also helping to boost my confidence.

Hiking through Jefferson Park took me across some of the most beautiful meadows I've ever seen, with nearby Mount Jefferson watching my every step from high above. A steep climb to 6,888 feet took me to the Mount Hood Wilderness Area and the promise of spectacular views of Mount Hood. However, wildfires to the east spread a thick smoke screen between me and the monstrous mountain, obscuring those promised views. Coming down the north side delivered me to two snowfield crossings that again had me using exaggerated caution. I had hiked hundreds of miles through snow, but these two hundred-yard fields were the most nerve racking. I knew my ribs were not completely healed, and that a simple fall would mean the true end of my hike. Fortunately, there was little to no snow left after being off the trail for five weeks, so my fears were actually greater than the reality of the situation.

A special treat later that day was arriving at Olallie Lake where there is a camp store stocked with snacks and plenty of cold soda. It was just one tenth of a mile off the trail, and the lure of a cold Coca-Cola was exactly what I needed on that extremely hot day. With just four miles left to my planned camp, I made quick work of it. My goal was to make camp at Jude Lake and go for a cool swim. When I arrived at Jude Lake, I was the only person there, so I took the swim in just my birthday suit. The water was cool, refreshing, and the perfect way to end my day. I also used the opportunity to wash my clothes as best

I could. It wasn't five minutes after I had gotten out of the water and put on some clothes when a whole parade of hikers started showing up. Whew! Good timing, Whistler.

I was in my tent by seven, but the steady stream of hikers arriving at camp all decided they needed to have a party. While staring at the ceiling of my tent in the golden hue of a full moon—another one!—I learned one hiker was lactose intolerant, heard what everyone's favorite trail food was, how the hiker with the trail name Gasman got his name—if you use your imagination, you'll probably be correct—and I got to listen to the philosophical teachings of the hiker who went by the trail name Plato. The idea of sleep finally occurred to this group at around 10:30 p.m. When I got up at my usual time of 4:30 a.m., I didn't feel too bad about the noise I made breaking camp. I did hear a few huffs and puffs from deep within their tents, though.

I was hiking by six, and the trail conditions allowed me to have fifteen miles behind me by 11:30 a.m. The perfect trail conditions included long miles through beautiful, lush forest, walking over trail tread of deep forest duff. I was able to average three miles per hour pretty much all day. The morning was exceptionally nice with a deep and heavy fog that kept temperatures in the high sixties and later in the seventies.

Later on, I hiked along one of the biggest lakes I've ever seen. Timothy Lake is a multi-use lake with people boating, swimming, and camping along the shoreline. The PCT follows the shore of Timothy Lake for miles, and the cool breezes made it a hiker's paradise. Shortly after having passed the lake, I came to the spur trail that leads to Little Crater Lake. It was just past 5:00 p.m. by this point, and I still had to hike four miles to my planned camp, but I took the time to see this geological feature. Unlike its big sister, Crater Lake, it is a very small lake. It was formed by a volcano and the shifting of a fault which forced an underground spring to create it. It's just 45 feet deep, with the water temperature at a consistent 34 degrees. No one swims in that water! Like big Crater Lake, the water was the clearest and bluest you could ever imagine. It was well worth the little side trip to see this attraction.

And finally, what better way to end a hiker's day than with trail magic? Trail Angel Mad Baker had a set-up on Forest Service Road 58 for hikers that included cold drinks and plenty of great snacks. Yep, it was a great day!

But what kind of a hiker would I be if I didn't set goals? My goal for the next day was to get up early—what a surprise, right? —and hike to Timberline Lodge. This is the iconic landmark used in the filming of the movie *The Shining*. It was just over fourteen miles away, but I wanted to get there early because I had a whole laundry list of things to do while there.

While hiking along, I had some difficulty because of a bit of foot pain. I had a blister that had formed on the bottom of my right foot, I was close to losing the nail on my right big toe from stubbing it countless times, and I had a deep cut on my left ankle. Of course, I was still hiking because they happened to be the only two feet I had, but admittedly, I was feeling a bit sorry for myself. About then I saw a man and woman with full packs hiking toward me. When they got closer, I noticed the man was hiking with a prosthetic leg. He was wearing a United States Marine Corps hat, so I could only guess how he lost his leg. Perspective is an ironic thing. There would not be a whimper from me about my stupid feet from that moment on.

When the lodge came into view, I was mesmerized by its architectural beauty and mammoth size. It had been built at the base of Mount Hood, providing lodge guests with a million-dollar view. It served as a winter ski lodge, and apparently also as a very popular summer vacation destination, based on the large number of guests I witnessed.

Here's Johnny

My day got really interesting as I was walking through the parking lot toward the lodge entrance. I heard someone yell out, "Whistler!" so I turned to face him. I knew this person, but was unable to place him immediately. He reminded me that his name was Scott, with the trail name Rokk. I'd met Scott on the Appalachian Trail in 2017. We'd kept in touch by way of emails over the past two years, but he was not someone I would ever have expected to see here because he lives in Pennsylvania. He had been on vacation while also following my journal, and unbeknownst to me decided to surprise me. He had been waiting and looking for me for two days! Let me attempt to explain how monumentally impossible it should have been for Rokk to find me. There were hundreds of people visiting the lodge, with numerous restaurants, bars, and public areas. How at this exact moment we end up almost walking into one another, I'll never fathom. The encounter was just short of a miracle, and was truly one of the kindest acts I could have ever imagined. Rokk, his wife Peggy, and their friend Randy gifted me with some serious trail magic. I was treated to an incredible lunch and the largest ice-cold beer a thirsty hiker could only dream of.

Once we parted, I got to that laundry list, which started with me finding a bathroom to wash my socks and underwear in an actual sink. I know, classy right? I'll admit I got a few stares, especially when I used the hand drier to dry my clean clothes. Other items on the list included postcards for the grandchildren, cleaning my water filter, finding Band-Aids for my feet that I'll never complain about again, charging my electronics, responding to my inboxes of greatly appreciated emails, text messages, and messages sent via trailjournals.com from friends and followers, and most important, calling Annie to catch up and ask her to order me new hiking shoes.

With my chores all done, it was time to get back to why I was there in the first place—on the trail. It was now close to four o'clock, and I had already decided I would only hike five more miles, then make it an early day and rest my bones. As I lay in my tent writing in my journal, there was a huge thunderstorm rocking the entire Cascade mountain range. I was at a tent site just big enough for one tent, situated next to the raging waters of Lost Creek which was being fed from the snowmelt off Mount Hood. Once again, I believed I was the luckiest person on the planet to be in such an amazing place.

The thunder, lightning, and rain did their best to keep me from my much-needed rest, but nothing could have prevented me from a deep sleep. I didn't get up until five the next morning, and when I did, I enjoyed my coffee and Pop-Tarts to the same creek sounds that had contributed to my deep slumber.

The rain clouds had rained themselves dry, but a fog hung thick and heavy in the air. Sandy River lay in wait for me as I descended from 5,486 feet down to 2,804. The roaring sounds of the river could be heard long before it came into sight. There ended up being a group of six of us preparing to ford Sandy River at the same time, with each of us offering encouragement as the next person crossed, and then the next, until finally I was the last one to cross. The current was swift with the melting snow off Mount Hood combined with the heavy rains of the night before. We high-fived one another once we were all across, no longer strangers.

Prior to The Incident, I would not have hesitated to cross, but I still had a concern about falling and possibly breaking ribs number eleven and twelve again. I knew I could possibly fall, but I already felt far more confident, and I was in a place that I knew I'd pick myself up, dust—or dry—myself off, and hike on. Getting back in the saddle was the best way to conquer that fear, and I was feeling pretty good in the saddle.

Soon came Muddy Fork, and it was an even deeper and faster river, but the crossing was made easily with the aid of two huge trees that lay across the river along with the heavy rope a kind hiker of yesteryear had placed there for future hikers to hang onto.

As I hiked that day, I found myself marching across miles of trail with a gravel tread. It crunched with each step, which gave a strong audible sound to my presence. A short time later I was hiking on deep forest duff, which silenced my steps as though I wasn't even there.

Late in the day I came across wild blueberries and golden raspberries. I ate handfuls, and finally had to stop myself. I still had a lot of miles ahead of me. I camped that night at Wahtum Lake which was just over sixteen miles from the Cascade Locks and the Bridge of the Gods on the Washington state boarder. It rained a soft, gentle, but constant rain all night.

By morning there was just what I call "tree rain." Heavy rain-laden tree branches deposited drops that thumped my tent with a now-familiar tune. I pulled out my rain jacket and rain pants, and geared up for those saturated plants and branches that would be hanging heavily over the trail. My 6:00 a.m. departure from camp was under cover of darkness. It was too light to use my headlamp, but just dark enough to stumble on unseen rocks and tree roots. The only evidence I would see of other hikers at this hour were the few tents nestled along the trail, with their inhabitants still sleeping soundly. There was a beautiful mist hanging heavy through the forest that provided me with several photo opportunities I couldn't pass up.

Section Five

Cascade Locks, Oregon to Manning Park, BC, Canada
miles 2,147.1 to 2,653.1

Washington State

This was a big day for me. It was the day I would exit Oregon and enter the state of Washington. I had a bit of pep in my step knowing I would soon be walking over the Columbia River by way of the iconic Bridge of the Gods. The descent from where I started at 4,300 feet to the bridge at just 77 feet above sea level—the lowest point on the PCT—was sixteen miles, and it took five hours. When I arrived, I had lunch at The Alehouse—highly recommended—then shopped for my resupply and completed a couple of other essential chores.

With my to-do list taken care of, it was time to head for that spectacular iron girder bridge. When I arrived at the bridge entrance, I asked the woman at the toll plaza what I was supposed to do. There isn't a pedestrian walkway, so I wasn't too certain how to get across. The woman kindly told me to use the crosswalk and carefully walk across the bridge while facing the oncoming traffic. I received a few friendly honks and thumbs up, which told me the people there were used to sharing the bridge with us thru-hikers. It was another surreal moment for me. I'm not a big selfie kind of guy, but I took a few that day. It was a day I would not soon forget.

Crossing The Bridge of the Gods

Once I crossed, it was time to put my head down and get in some more miles. It was almost four o'clock and I still needed to hike nine miles to my planned campsite, and as was usually the case, it was a typically big climb out of town. Once at camp, I was still pretty satisfied from the big lunch I'd had in town, and extremely tired from a long day, so I decided to have a small snack and skip dinner.

Remember, when hiking under such adverse conditions, a hiker has got to be flexible. In this case I was flexing my plans. I wrote earlier that I was planning on completing Oregon, flipping back to California to complete the section I'd skipped, which included the Sierra Nevadas, and then come back to hike Washington. Well, I changed my mind. I decided to hike Washington now, before the heavy rain season started in September. This would also save me a couple of travel days, as well. So, when I crossed the Bridge of the Gods yesterday, I just kept going.

So, what was it like in Washington? It really was different than Oregon in some surprising and interesting ways. Of course, I had only been hiking Washington state for a day and a half, but these were my initial observations. For one, it almost had a tropical rain forest feel to it. Huge ferns and broad-leafed plants covered the forest floor. Wild blackberries, raspberries, thimble berries, blueberries, and huckleberries lined the trail, providing too much of a temptation. Even the birds sounded like they belonged in the jungle.

I had recently been told that I hiked too fast to enjoy the experience. I'd had a few comebacks, but I restrained myself and just let it go. I do hike fast, it's my nature, but I also didn't feel as if I'd missed anything that was important to me. I look at the trail as a superhighway, and my legs as the vehicle I use to get me to where I want to be. Superhighways have lots of exits, but we don't get off at every one of them. When I hike through miles upon miles of deep, lush forest, I don't need to stop or even walk slowly. I've seen hundreds of miles of deep, lush forest already. That doesn't mean I don't have an appreciation for the forest, it's just that I have limited time and so many other things to see. Using an analogy, there is a Starbucks coffee shop at just about every exit. I don't need to stop at every Starbucks...though my wife might disagree. Some miles are dull and boring—at least to me— but I hike those miles to get to the special places. If every mile were special, would any of those miles actually be special?

Here's another random thought. My wife and I have borrowed a line from a funny video we saw together some time ago. A young boy had just come from the dentist and was still under the influence of laughing gas while his parents drove him home. His perspective of everything he was seeing was now different. Sitting in the backseat he called up to his parents and asked, "Is this real life?" I've lost count how many times I've seen beautiful views and had to ask myself, sometimes even out loud, "Is this real life?" So, to those who might believe I hike too fast, I say to you, I sincerely hope you are enjoying your hike as much as I am enjoying mine.

And now...a poem.

THAT IS YOU, THIS IS ME

I've listened to what you've had to say,
But let me be clear to you today.
I may go fast, while you go slow.
Who is right? We neither know.
I wake each day with my goal,
while your days are a random roll.
To judge each other, we are free,
but please remember, that is you, this is me.

Last night after hanging my food bag, I was ready to hit the hay. My campsite was secluded, and I could hear the sounds of the soothing waters of Panther Creek. It was still early with daylight out, which added to my inability to find sleep. Rest finally came shortly after nine o'clock, which was frustrating because I was hopelessly tired. At 3:37 a.m. that morning I heard some animals running around my tent. I could tell they were not large animals, and I suspected they might just be a couple of squirrels. I did my best to ignore them, but then a thought came to me that I couldn't ignore. What if those vermin were climbing the tree where I had just hours before hung my food bag? This was the food I absolutely needed for the next five days until my next resupply at White Pass. I've seen squirrels figure out technically difficult situations. I've had squirrel-proof bird feeders that they eventually learn to get into. My wife has often said that we have sped up the evolution of the squirrel by giving them difficult problems to figure out, such as how to get into a squirrel-proof bird feeder. I'm pretty sure I've seen squirrels in a tree in our yard with a slide rule and a calculator, working out their desired solution to the problem before them. Back to my dilemma. Naturally, I put my shoes on and crawled out of my tent with my headlamp on to check on my provisions. With everything safe and sound, I returned to my tent and attempted to re-enter the world of slumber. I gave up at 4:15 a.m., made coffee, ate a Pop-Tart, got dressed, broke camp, and with headlamp on, started hiking at 5:30.

My first nine miles were tough, nine miles of climbs that just plain wore me out. I had planned a 30-mile day, but between my early wakeup call and several big climbs, I accepted 26 miles and called it a day. What aided my decision to call it quits was when I stopped at Bear Lake to pull and filter water. Was that not a perfect tent site overlooking the pristine lake? I closed my eyes and could picture myself camped right there. Decision made!

Not too far from where I'd found that perfect and private tent site, I could see a family camped and swimming in Bear Lake. They had camp chairs and a couple of huge family-style tents set up on the beach. I could see and hear the kids having a great time, and I imagined that this may be their last summer fling. What I didn't understand was how they'd gotten there. There was no road...that I was aware of, anyway. Perhaps there was a spur trail that only they knew of. Their own little family secret. Their own personal lake that only their family knew of, its secret location handed down from one generation to the next.

Early the following day, trail conditions were such that I was able to hike some pretty fast miles, my enthusiasm driven by the knowledge that I would soon catch my first glimpse of Mount Adams. A gradual grade and soft tread made for a good morning and afternoon. It wasn't until late afternoon that I realized I had set my goals a bit too aggressively. As I started getting closer to Mount Adams, the trail got sloppy, rocky, and consequently a lot slower to negotiate. My situation now was that I had already identified where I wanted to camp. I only had one liter of water and thus had to continue on to the campsite I'd selected because it was close to a water source—Riley Creek. I'd been hiking since six fifteen, and by five o'clock I was spent, but I still had another hour before I reached what would be home for the night. The last hour was made a bit more palatable because I was hiking around the western side of Mount Adams. This magnificent, still snow-capped majestic mountain took my mind off those painful lower extremities I have vowed not to mention again. I ended up camped just north of Riley Creek in a beautiful meadow. No real impressive views, just tall spruce trees surrounding and watching over me at full attention as I slept. Views? I had plenty of those while hiking that day, and like the views before them, they would stay with me forever.

Mount Adams

Another notable difference between Oregon and Washington was that I had left mountains made up of lava and basalt behind me and was now hiking over beautiful granite. Grey, deep purple, and beautiful pink granite made up the geological formations of the mountains I was now climbing.

When I awoke the following morning, I sat up with my sleeping quilt wrapped around me to stay warm while I prepared my coffee in the vestibule of my tent. The jet-engine sound of my stove temporarily drowned out the sounds of Riley Creek's waters. Once the water had come to a rolling boil, I turned off the stove. With my mug held tightly in my hands, I turned off my headlamp, sat in the stillness of the morning darkness, and listened...just listened.

The PCT Trail Days were to be held on the coming weekend back at Cascade Locks. The three-day festival would start on Friday, which meant the trail would be abandoned by most hikers...with the one exception being Whistler. I ran into a number of hikers who were on their way to Cascade Locks to enjoy a break from the trail and to take in the festivities. I wasn't about to turn around to head south, though. No, I was focused on Manning Park, Canada.

How was it possible that each state could possibly be prettier than those before? After I had hiked the Appalachian Trail, people would often ask me what my favorite state was. To this day I would respond that Maine was my fave, and that the Appalachian Trail Conservancy had saved the best for last. Oregon was beautiful, but it was definitely second to Washington. I still had to be fair and refrain from judging California, though, because I had not completed that state yet. I would have to wait and see what the High Sierras had to offer.

This morning's hike took me all along the western face and then the awe-inspiring north face of Mount Adams. It was one of those situations where you'd find yourself constantly stealing sideway glances and looking up while hiking, and realizing that it just kept getting more and more beautiful. I couldn't help but stop to take photo after photo, convinced that each was better than the one before.

Eventually I made my way toward Adams Creek. Mount Adams gives up its winter snow into this steep and fast-moving namesake creek. Prior to arriving at the creek, I met Toasty Hands who was southbound. She had just crossed the creek, and she shared that she waited to cross for an hour, ever hopeful that another hiker would come along. When I asked why, she responded so they could help her cross, or at least tell authorities where to find her body. Toasty Hands let me know there were two logs crossing Adams Creek upstream and east of the trail. When I got there and was able to assess the situation, I threw my trekking poles across to the other side—my way of committing. I found a large, heavy branch that I was certain had been used many times by previous crossers of this creek. I stepped onto the logs, which were no bigger than eight inches in diameter, and planted the tree branch firmly into the creek rocks below. I started across using that branch to steady me, with the deafening sounds of Mount Adams's snowmelt rushing beneath me. I was across to the other side, safe, and dry in no time, where I left the tree branch for the next SOBO hiker. I picked up my trekking poles and hiked on, the best part being that I had crossed that raging creak with no hesitation, and had felt no anxiety. There really is something to be said about getting back in the saddle.

Speaking of saddles and horses… When my tramping through the mountains of Washington was nearly finished that day, I met Tammy and Gordon on horseback. This part of the trail was a shared equestrian footpath. Tammy and Gordon were a wonderful couple and fit the image you would have of a cowboy and cowgirl. We chatted a bit, then I continued on for a short distance to my camp along Walupt Creek, which made this a 29.7-mile day. A short time later they arrived at the creek, where they watered their horses. Tammy asked if I liked red wine.

I almost responded, "Is the pope Catholic?" But instead, I said, "Yes, I do."

Tammy yelled over her shoulder, "Gordon, grab a can of red wine out of your saddle bag for Whistler." Gordon produced a can of wine along with a Kit Kat candy bar, and handed them down to me while still high in his saddle. Two firsts here. This was the first time I had received trail magic from trail angels on horseback, and who ever knew wine came in a twelve ounce can?

Trail angels on horseback

I had been anticipating the following day for a week now. In fact, I had strategically hiked extra miles the day before in order to place myself at the perfect starting point. Why? This was the day I would hike Cispus Pass and Goat Rocks. But a problem unexpectedly presented itself that morning. When I woke up, I said to myself, "It sure is dark out." I poked my head out of the tent and found that the beam from my headlamp hit a wall—a wall of fog. It was so densely fogged in that I doubted I would be able to see a goat, rocks, or even my feet on the trail, for that matter.

First came Cispus, exactly three miles from the campsite at Walupt Creek. Well, at 6,469 feet there was nothing to see there. Thank you very much *fog*. I was reminded of when I thru-hiked the AT in 2017 and had highly anticipated seeing McAfee Knob, the most photographed location on the trail. Wouldn't you know, there was dense fog that day, as well. So, with nothing to see at Cispus, it was time to hike on, Whistler, hike on to Goat Rocks. While en route to Goat Rocks, I first heard and then saw the first of many pikas. A pika is a small mountain-dwelling mammal found in Asia and North America. With short limbs, a very round body, an even coat of fur, and no tail, they resemble their close cousin the rabbit, but instead with short rounded ears. The sound they make is like a squeaky toy you might give your pet. I heard plenty of marmots, as well, with the loud whistling sentinel warnings they make, but they remained elusive.

So, guess what paid a visit as I approached the climb to Goat Rocks? Yep, the sun finally made a grand entrance. I got those views after all. I took an alternate route that reportedly offered better views, and to be honest, it would be difficult to imagine a better view. Old Snowy Mountain required taking a slightly higher route, then trekking across the Knife's Edge with its deep drop-offs to the left and to the right. The hike up called for some minor snow crossings when I was there, but I imagine it would have been treacherous if blanketed by snow in the early hiking season. The Knife's Edge was simply amazing, and offered some of the best views I have ever seen. When I finally completed the descent, I had the desire to turn around and do it all over again. I didn't see a single other thru-hiker. I'm guessing they were all at Trail Days. But there were plenty of local day hikers taking in the sunny, clear day and perfect views. As I bid farewell to Goat Rocks and hiked on, I came across countless streams flowing down steep embankments. I couldn't help but think of the plentiful sources of water. Like the blood pumping through our veins, this water provides the lifeblood for every living plant and creature along its path.

At The Knife's Edge

Hardly another hiker crossed my path the next day, but I did come across two hunters, all dressed in their camouflage gear, making it pretty obvious they were not out for a hike. Well, the rifles helped give it away too. I asked what they were hunting, to which they replied, "Bear." In fact, they had just spotted one and were tracking it down.

"Are there a lot of bear around here I asked?"

"Oh, definitely. Too many, in fact," was their response.

Hmm, I thought to myself, I had best hang my food bag a little higher tonight.

I dry camped that evening just five miles from White Pass, carrying water in because there was no water source at my campsite. That night around 9:15 p.m. a couple came into where I was camped speaking quite loudly and shining their headlamps directly into my tent, so as to assure themselves they had successfully awakened me from my deep sleep. Uncertain as to what was going on, I spoke up and said, "Hello?" while still in a sleepy haze.

Raindrop was very excited about her day and wanted to introduce herself.

"Hello Raindrop, nice to meet you, but a hiker is sound asleep here."

Raindrop received the message and I immediately felt terrible. She was guileless and just trying to be friendly, and my reaction was so unlike me. Before getting back to sleep, I thought perhaps I could meet her at the Kracker Barrel store at White Pass where I would formally introduce myself and apologize for being short with her.

The Kracker Barrel would also be holding the box Annie had mailed, bringing the new shoes she'd ordered for me. This popular hiker pitstop also offered showers, laundry, a restaurant, and food resupply. My plan was to get there early the following day, take care of business, and still hike a few more miles.

I was up early and very careful not to wake Raindrop...although the dark side of me wanted to stand outside her tent to introduce myself. "Good morning Raindrop, I'm Whistler"

I was on the trail by six. With only 5.2 miles to White Pass, I arrived at the trailhead at U.S. Route 12 by 7:30 a.m. A section hiker called Hicker was standing by his car and asked if I wanted a beer. "Sure," I replied. Yep, beer, the new breakfast beverage. The Kracker Barrel gas station and convenience store caters to hikers and does a great job stocking most of what a thru-hiker needs. My first need was a breakfast sandwich and a Dr. Pepper. With that need met, I happened to mention to the cashier that there was no ice in the fountain dispenser.

A few minutes later she came over to where a group of us were sitting. She told us that she had a hurt shoulder and asked if someone could fill the ice machine for her. Of course, I jumped up and was more than happy to help. Once I finished, she invited me to select anything out of the hot food case. A second breakfast sandwich definitely hit the spot. Need met again.

It had been eleven days since I'd last washed my clothes properly, though I'd rinsed them in lakes and creeks a couple of times. So, I did my laundry, and met that need, as well. It had also been eleven days since my last real shower, not counting my lake swims, so I was able to take a shower at the Kracker Barrel. Huge need met. As I said, they cater to hikers here. Before shopping for my resupply, I checked to see what was in the hiker box. It was pretty common for a hiker to have a resupply box mailed to themselves here, and quite often they are mailed too much. I was able to get nearly a four-day supply of food from the hiker box. Check off that need met as well. Recharging my electronics and battery banks takes a long time, so I ended up staying at the Kracker Barrel through lunch, and only got back to the trail by 1:30 p.m. I really needed to get in some more miles, so I hiked another 13.7, for a total of 18.9 miles that day, which wasn't too bad considering I took a five-and-a-half-hour break. Another need definitely met.

That night I found camping along the Bumping River to be peaceful, with sleep coming quickly and deeply. Up at 4:00 a.m., I went about my morning chores. Before going to sleep, I had picked a campsite 25.5 miles ahead for the next day's conservative goal, but I would go farther if my legs agreed. The morning's climb took me from the depths of the dark forest to the heights of open and clear skies. A light fog hung over the treetops like a blanket, soon to be chased away by the warmth of a new rising sun.

I soon found myself at 5,700 feet, which came with the added bonus of indescribable views of Mount Rainier that just couldn't be beat. Every time I turned a corner I'd have to stop and take another photo. I was reminded of when I had visited the Grand Canyon and a friend had asked me to describe it. Similar to the Grand Canyon, it would be impossible to describe the views of Mt. Rainier. If I hadn't seen it with my own eyes, I would never have believed a mountain could be so beautiful.

Mount Rainier

I eventually got serious about moving on and doing what I was there to do---hike. My trek brought me to Chinook Pass where it passes Washington State Route 410. Being a Sunday and a beautiful clear day, there were literally hundreds of day hikers hiking this popular destination. Although I had just showered the day before, the crowds parted quickly to allow me to pass. They all smelled of soap and shampoo while I'm pretty sure I had taken on the pungent odor of day-old road kill. I decided to stop at the parking lot where I could sit and enjoy my lunch while watching the multitudes. A nice woman I had met just a short time earlier while still on the trail pulled up, stopped her car, called me over, and gave me a cold can of lime sparkling water. That was an unexpected and appreciated treat, which added to my ever-growing love for the good people of this earth.

The latter part of the day required hiking mostly up and along a poorly-maintained trail that sloped away from the mountain with a great many washouts and very loose scree. Cautious and careful foot placement along this deteriorating section of the trail demanded my full attention. The trail was in dire straits and could have used a strong dose of some volunteer loving. But as always, a sincere thank you to the sometimes-underappreciated trail builders and maintenance crews for even making my hike possible. I hit my targeted campsite and still had some fuel in the tank, so I hiked an additional 2.9 miles for a total of 28.4 miles that day.

The following morning, I climbed with vigor and purpose. I knew the same cell tower that had provided service the night before was in a clear line of sight and would allow me the opportunity to FaceTime Annie. As we were catching up it occurred to me that I was seeing a mountain goat ahead and in the distance, high on a ridge. I couldn't believe my eyes. It was standing statue still, so I started second-guessing myself. Maybe it was just a white rock that looked like a goat. Just then it turned around and walked into the woods. It wasn't a rock. I'd seen my first mountain goat!

The next morning's hike took me through another burned out area of forest. It was the site of the Falls Creek Fire of 1988. It had been accidently started by loggers, and was eventually brought under control by the Forest Service and crews from the Washington Department of Corrections, but not until over 3,000 acres had been destroyed. The damage was still evident today. While walking through these burned out areas you try to avert your eyes and just walk. But, inevitably like a tragic accident on a highway, you slow down and look. It takes witnessing the carnage firsthand to truly understand that fire is a harsh reality in the Pacific Northwest.

Hiking a 2650-mile trail can sometimes put you into a trance, or take you to a place of mindless, one-foot-in-front-of-the-other boredom.

While in one of my hiking trances, I thought back to a conversation I'd overheard at the Kracker Barrel. Someone had asked another hiker why they were thru-hiking the PCT. The response given was, "To see the beauty of these mountains, and to see what I am made of."

I hadn't thought much about that response until today. I realized that if asked, I might have given exactly the same response. I was witnessing some of the most spectacular scenery this country has to offer, some of which can only be seen by physically walking there. The seeing-what-I'm-made-of part was also a bit curious to me, and required some more thought. What I and other thru-hikers do is difficult. It requires tenacity, drive, motivation, a bit of arrogance, and some honest humility. I was hiking ten to twelve hours and 20 to 30 miles each day. I'm going to use the analogy that my legs are my vehicle again. There were times I had a steep ascent that included a gain of several thousand feet. My legs required that I oxygenate the blood my muscles needed by taking deep, full breaths. During those times I thought my lungs would explode and that I couldn't continue, but I did. I would push down on my trekking poles while lifting my legs, push down, lift, push down, lift, repeat, repeat, repeat. I wouldn't look up ahead because that would have been just too discouraging and would have messed with where I needed my focus to be. Instead, I watched where I was about to place my feet and the trail directly in front of me. Push down, lift, and repeat. When I eventually reached the peak and my heart felt like it was about to burst out of my chest, I would take a backward and fleeting glance to where I had just come from and say to myself, "That's what I'm made of."

It was 6:00 a.m. the next morning, and I hadn't been on the trail five minutes when I saw an approaching SOBO hiker heading my way. I told him I thought I was the only one crazy enough to be hiking that early. He laughed and said he'd just been thinking the same thing. My goal was to hike another 30-plus mile day, and you have to start early to achieve that number of miles.

When I'd left White Pass 15 days ago, I had intended to hike to Snoqualmie Pass and take my first zero since returning to the trail August 6th. My progress over the past few days had been very productive. I'd felt strong and motivated to hike long days and miles. Hiking past Snoqualmie and on to the next town of Leavenworth was dependent on one thing—my food bag. I usually try to have an extra day of food in my bag for an emergency, and as it happens, I actually had a bit more than that, and could even stretch it if I hiked some long days.

The miles hiked today were just that—plain miles. No scenic views to speak of, just lots of pointless ups and downs—a.k.a. PUDS. The trail conditions reminded me of the Appalachian Trail in that there were a lot of rock scrambles and a bunch of tree roots doing their very best to trip this unsuspecting hiker. I must admit, though, that I did make multiple stops to pick and consume what had recently become my daily requirement of huckleberries, blueberries, and raspberries. I was starting to believe I would need an intervention to help me with this problem. If I saw ripe berries, I felt it was my duty to pick and eat them.

As it turned out, the trail took me under the ski lifts in Snoqualmie, and then ran directly to Interstate 90. I recalled reading on Guthook that the Aardvark Restaurant boasts great curry, and that thru-hikers get their first beer free. It was getting late at 6:00 p.m., and I still had over four miles to my targeted campsite. I decided that buying dinner would help stretch the food I had left for the next two days. I went in and had the best curry I've ever eaten. I stopped at the one free beer, then made my run up the mountain and finally ended my long day. Starting at six o'clock in the morning and ending at close to eight o'clock at night pretty much guaranteed a deep sleep.

There had been some talk while I was in Snoqualmie of rain overnight and all day long. Rain was inevitable; this was Washington I was hiking through, after all. The overnight rain never developed, but when I checked the radar in the morning, it was obviously going to be a long, wet day. The rain started at about eight o'clock that morning and looked like it would last all day. It was a light but constant rain that made sure every bit of me got a good soaking. To top it all off, the first eight miles of the day were a rock scramble. Fields upon fields, mile after mile of little rocks on top of big rocks, sharp rocks, slippery when wet rocks, and most of all, hard rocks. Slow methodical steps through the rain made for very slow miles.

And who lives among rocks? The elusive marmot does. I saw and heard plenty of them today. The sound they make is that of a sharp whistle. It's actually pretty irritating to listen to their loud whistling all day long. I fantasized about throwing rocks at them—Lord knows there were plenty of rocks laying around—but of course I didn't, so I took lots of photos instead.

At almost exactly noon the rain actually stopped, which was perfect timing because I was starving. My hiker hunger was back with a vengeance. I sat up on a high ridge overlooking one of many lakes I'd pass that day far below me. It was breathtakingly beautiful. My simple lunch of tuna with cheese on a tortilla tasted like a gourmet meal. Why does food always taste better when you are outdoors?

Once again, I saw very few hikers. Probably most had enough sense to stay in town and wait out the rain, but not me. I just kept pounding the trail like I was on a mission...probably because I was.

The rain from the previous day made another appearance and continued all night, which made sleep come easily. When morning arrived, the rain finally gave way to the rising sun. The air felt different, brisk, cool, and fresh, in what was certain to be a glorious day. Was this a new season? Had fall come? As I hiked on this morning, I passed several hikers just starting to stir about their camps. I passed one young lady attempting to dry her gear in the swift breeze and early sun, a task I planned to take on at lunchtime.

There was a big climb this morning with countless switchbacks serpentining their way up the mountain. At one point I heard the *click clack* of another hiker's trekking poles somewhere behind and farther down the mountain, working their way up to me. I was moving quite quickly, not just to get early miles, but also to build up some body heat to ward off the cold air. As if from nowhere, a voice behind me asks, "Is that you, Whistler?" I turned around and saw it was Tarzan.

I'd met Tarzan at the Kracker Barrel in White Pass. I had ordered two slices of pizza as a snack before heading back to the trail, and after 40 minutes I learned that the clerk had never put in my order. I was a bit disappointed and had just asked her to cancel the order when this guy, Tarzan, stands up and asks if anyone wanted the rest of his pizza. My hand went up first. We chatted as we hiked together for a bit, but I have to be honest, even being a pretty fast hiker, I still had a difficult time keeping up with him. I'd see him a couple more times as we leap-frogged throughout the day, but I suspected I probably wouldn't see him again after that, and I was correct.

That was a good day, and the trail was kind to me. It was well-groomed, flat, and smooth in places, allowing for some fast and easy miles. I usually only took 30 minutes for lunch, but I was making good time and needed to dry my gear, so I opted for a full hour. The more I hiked through Washington, the more it reminded of the similarities to Maine. The countless lakes and ponds, each doing their best to lure me to stop and abide awhile. Not today though; I had miles ahead that I knew I must put behind me or I'd never make it to Canada. I hiked till 6:30 p.m. to a campsite that was just over 14 miles from Stevens Pass, where I planned to get a hitch into Leavenworth. There was a package from a good friend waiting for me at the post office, and I was hoping to take a day off the trail. I needed to give my weary body a day off. But I'd soon find that wasn't going to happen.

The next morning, I was desperate to get to Leavenworth. Once I made it to Stevens Pass, I was able to get a hitch in about ten minutes. It was a 35-mile drive to Leavenworth, but this kind couple was going to be driving past there anyway, and went out of their way to make me feel welcome and comfortable. I wish I could have said the same about the KOA campground in Leavenworth. But more about that situation in a bit.

The couple driving me to Leavenworth dropped me off at the post office, where Joe, my lifelong friend and best man at my wedding 40 years earlier, had mailed me a package of hiker goodness. With my package in hand, I grabbed lunch and then made my way to the local KOA.

That KOA was literally the worst experience I had ever had regarding customer service and human compassion. I guess it might have been my ragged outward hiker appearance, but it was made abundantly clear that they just didn't want me there. When I arrived at the campground office, there were two ladies being helped by a Sarah, the service clerk, about wanting to leave two days early because their site was too small for their camper. They were told that they would have to forfeit a refund because of the KOA 48-hour cancellation policy. Fair enough, I get that.

These kind ladies overheard that I would not have a place to stay because the campground was fully booked, so they told the clerk that they changed their minds and would stay. Then they offered for me to stay at their site. They had arranged a cabin rental in the next town over and were leaving the campground without a refund, but knowing they were helping a hiker in need. What would be the harm…right? These kind people gave me food, beer, snacks, and firewood, then they loaded up and left.

As soon as they were gone, a golf cart came driving up, and I could hear the conversation over the driver's walkie talkie. "The people who booked the site just left, and the hiker who's there now needs to leave."

Mr. golf cart man offered to drive me to the office, where he proceeded to browbeat me after giving me a lecture on rules all the way there. When I was delivered to the office, Sarah got her manager, who harshly proceeded to tell me that if I didn't leave, she would call the sheriff and have me escorted off the campground. Just to be clear, I was nothing less than kind and polite. In other words, the only thing ugly about me was my outward appearance. Admittedly, I really needed a shower. She then told me that I could pay her for the site, at which time I politely reminded her that it was already paid for. I told her that my new friends paid for the site and offered to let me stay there since they were leaving without a refund, so the site was officially still theirs. She then told me that I couldn't do that because I had not arrived in their vehicle with them. Throughout this ridiculous exchange I remained calm, and without another word, I made an about face and left. It was obvious there was no reasoning with this verbally abusive, aggressive, and threatening person.

So, it was now about six o'clock and I had nowhere to shower, do laundry, or worst of all, get some much-needed rest. With Annie working the World Wide Web and Whistler wandering aimlessly around the streets of Leavenworth, I was finally able to find a room at the very beautiful and expensively priced—in hiker terms, anyway—Bavarian Lodge. Although it was a bit pricey, the associates were warm and welcoming despite my outward appearance. The sleep I received that night was the kind of sleep that rejuvenates a person. Peaceful and quiet uninterrupted sleep was exactly what this weary wayfarer needed.

I didn't actually go to bed until just past ten o'clock because I was determined to get most of my chores done. As nice as the hotel was, it didn't have laundry facilities. But it did have a large and deep vanity sink. I washed my clothes in three separate sink loads. Once washed, rinsed, and rung out, I hung them in the bathroom with the heater on. Because my hiking socks were wool, they required a bit more work. I carry three pair with me, so I had quite the assembly line going. Once cleaned, I placed a sock over the blow drier and turned it to low. It took about ten minutes per sock, but they were clean and dry. I had a beautiful, clean room, a great night's rest, and a breakfast buffet included in the room rate that definitely contributed to my daily calorie requirement. I was up by 6:30 a.m. and enjoyed my first breakfast from the buffet—eggs, potatoes, sliced Black Forest ham, biscuits, orange juice, and really good coffee. After breakfast, I walked just over a mile to the local Safeway grocery store where I shopped for my next five days' worth of food. The customer in front of me at the checkout lane and I started to chat. One thing I've learned while on this hike was not to be afraid to ask for help, so I asked if he would consider giving me a ride back to the Bavarian Lodge, and he readily agreed. Once back at the lodge, I went straight to the dining room and had my second breakfast, then back up to my room to sort and pack my provisions. With that taken care of, it was almost 10:30. That was when they stopped serving breakfast. As quickly as I could, I ran down the stairs—because the elevator would've been too slow—with just ten minutes left for me to enjoy my third breakfast. Afterward, it was back to my room to load my backpack. Checkout was at 11:00 a.m., but the night before I had asked the desk clerk, Kim for a late checkout, which she had graciously granted. I now had time to write out a couple postcards, call Joe to thank him again for his perfect hiker box of goodies, and to call Annie for her help with planning my future transportation back to California. Annie also ordered my next pair of shoes, and a bear canister that would soon be required to hike in the Sierra Nevada Mountains.

For the record, the staff at Leavenworth KOA were the only people I met on this entire journey who demonstrated what I call the ugly underbelly of society. I've had the absolute pleasure to meet the kindest and most gracious people throughout my hike, for which I was and still am so appreciative. I believe that, in the end, greed and the lack of autonomy led the staff at KOA of Leavenworth from doing what most would consider right, decent, and kind.

So, I never got the zero I had planned and hoped for, but I was already itching to get back on the trail anyway. I waited in the Bavarian

Lodge lobby and asked a few of the guests who were checking out if they might be heading towards Stevens Pass, and if so, would they consider giving me a ride to the trailhead? I got a few odd looks, and I'm guessing a few were wondering why I was at that really nice hotel instead of the KOA. But no ride. It was time to thumb it on U.S. Route 2 and try my luck at hitching the 35 miles back to the trailhead. In about two minutes a guy called Paul pulled over and took me halfway, since he was turning off and driving to Fish Lake which was heading away from Stevens Pass. I now found myself at a busy intersection for three and a half minutes, after which a man named John picked me up and took me the rest of the way. I was pretty sure if John had been unable to take me the rest of the way to Stevens Pass, that George or Ringo would have shown up so I could get by with a little help from my friends and complete my hitchhiking pilgrimage.

By 1:40 p.m., I was back on the trail, where life was far less complicated and felt right. I hiked just under ten miles and found the perfect campsite on Lake Janus. My spirits were soaring, and the following day couldn't come soon enough. When I arrived at Janus Lake that night, I hiked down a side trail that lead to some campsites. There were already three tents set up, but with plenty of room for another five or six. A woman saw my approach, jumped to her feet, and asked if I was looking for a campsite. I looked around and saw plenty right in front of me, but she pointed up another side trail and suggested I try there.

Well, I can take a hint. Once again, I believed I wasn't welcome. I should have asked if she worked for KOA...

The next morning brought a heavy fog and mist, keeping all the views at bay. As I hiked up to higher elevations I would hope for a view, but there would be nothing to see, so I kept moving. I had been looking forward to Grizzly Peak, which is known for its views, but there was nothing to see there, either, so I kept moving. Finally, around noon the sky finally cleared, and it was now time for a view-fest. I couldn't believe how beautiful northern Washington was with its endless, wide-open views requiring frequent stops and providing spectacular photo opportunities.

I was now above 6000 feet and headed toward 6,500 where clouds were covering the higher peaks. I felt as though I could literally touch the clouds. The sun was putting on a light show by casting different shades of light and shadows on the mountain face. Meanwhile, I could hear the marmots' loud and haunting whistles from deep in the valley as they echoed up to the highest peaks. It was cold and my plan had been to hike just 25 miles, but the sun had come from behind a cloud and warmed my face so I continued on. I felt the conditions were too perfect and that it was too beautiful to stop hiking. I couldn't wait to see what would come next. As I walked in absolute wonder, I asked myself what I was feeling at that exact moment. You do things like that when you are by yourself. What I was feeling was a huge sense of humility and privilege to be where I was at that very moment.

It was seven o'clock when I finally gave in and made camp. A new day would soon come and the mountains would still be there.

My tent ended up pitched pretty close to another hiker, so I did my best to pack up quietly. I was on the trail by 6:30 a.m. and went immediately from my high mountain perch to a deep descent into a beautiful verdant forest filled with water features like the White Chuck River and a beautiful waterfall. The trail crossed creeks and rivers several times. Sometimes there were foot bridges, other times logs were the required method for crossing. I'd gotten so accustomed to these crossings again that I practically ran across them. I was once again fearless, as if The Incident had never occurred. Today there were several huge blown-down trees crossing and blocking the trail, slowing my progress to a snail's pace at times, having to climb over, crawl under, or detour around them. The circumferences of some of the trees were so large that it would have taken three or four men to wrap their arms around them.

I had skipped my morning coffee because of how loud my cook stove was, and I hadn't wanted to wake my camp-mates. When a perfect spot showed up at nine o'clock, I decided to make that cup of joe, and now all was right with the world. There was a photo to be taken at every turn, but the problem was, the camera was incapable of truly capturing what my eyes saw in person. But that didn't stop me from attempting to document my hike by taking photo after photo.

As the day went on, I eventually made it to Mica Lake. This pristine lake reflected the tall mountains of the background in its deep, clear, sapphire-blue water. Again, I took photos, but they also failed to stand up to what my eyes saw. I camped that evening at Dolly View, which opened up to a wide display of mountains that spoiled me as I enjoyed my dinner. Dolly View was high on a ridge with full exposure, and the last place you would want to be if the weather turned bad. But it was a beautiful, clear night, making it the first place I wanted to be. The view didn't end after dinner because my vestibule faced the east and the next morning I was treated to a beautiful, clear sky and an epic sunrise that included a crescent moon. It was the kind of sunrise you could only hope and pray for. When it was time to break camp and I was packing my gear, I caught myself taking upward glances to get as much of the sunrise as I could before starting my day's hike. When I hiked on, I watched as the sun quickly jettisoned the mountains behind as it headed for higher sky.

When I had planned my hike for that day, I'd realized I was only 121 miles from Canada! The trail was good to me that day and allowed me to hike 16 miles by noon. I took a well-deserved hour lunch break, where I took my shoes off to rest my paws. There was still plenty of snow in the high mountains, which translated to plenty of water in seasonal streams. It also meant there were some soggy trails.

The following day's hike would be just over twelve miles, taking me to the small town of Stehekin where I would do my last resupply in

Washington. Those provisions should take me as far as Manning Park, British Columbia, Canada. Only 93.1 miles from Canada, Stehekin was another of those iconic small towns close to the trail, and one I looked forward to visiting—especially the famous Stehekin Pastry Company. I could almost smell those croissants when I woke up at four o'clock that morning, but I would have to hike those twelve miles first if I wanted to enjoy eating them.

It was an easy hike to Stehekin, going mostly downhill. Stehekin is a popular vacation destination for those in the Pacific Northwest, located on Lake Chelan, the third deepest lake in America. It is accessible only by foot—my chosen form of transportation—float plane, ferry, or boat. A handy shuttle bus picks up hikers four times a day. Sixteen dollars round trip gets you a ride into one of the greatest towns you could ever imagine. As luck would have it, the bus first makes a stop at the famous Stehekin Pastry Company bakery, about one and a half miles from the town proper. That stop alone was worth my sixteen dollars. We were back on the bus after seriously overdoing it at the bakery, then dropped off in the center of town.

Thank you Stehekin Pastry Company

My first stop was the public showers where a coin-operated shower timed my two, much too short two-and-a-half minute showers. Next was laundry, and then on to the visitor information center where I got the permit needed for the next sixteen miles of my hike. The permit is free, but it is required if you planned to camp along this sixteen-mile stretch of the PCT. My final stop was the general store, where I did my final resupply in the state of Washington. My purchases were a bit on the pricey side, but that was understandable since they must ship everything in by ferry. They did have a great selection of bottled beer for two dollars each. I couldn't pass up the bargain, so I had two IPAs on the deck overlooking the beautiful lake. The general store also offered Wi-Fi. For a five-dollar fee, you got a pass code that gave you 24 hours of Wi-Fi service or one-half gigabyte, whichever came first. I needed to upload four days' worth of journals and catch up on my email, so I paid my five dollars, and although the connection was very slow, I was able to get caught up.

With all my tasks completed, and being highly motivated to reach Canada, I caught the 5:30 p.m. shuttle back to High Bridge. I ended up being the lone hiker on this full-sized bus. I guess the attraction of two-dollar beers was just too much for the rest of the hikers I'd left behind. I hiked another five miles and made camp at Bridge Creek Campground, a designated camp as required by my permit, around eight o'clock. I was in a great position to get an early start to chip away at those final miles to the Canadian border, which was now just 75.8 miles away.

When I received my permit from the ranger's station, I had been informed by the ranger that there had been a bit of bear activity in the area where I was planning to camp. He warned that I should be certain to use the bear boxes provided at the campsites to stow my food, cook pot, and anything else with a scent. I followed his instructions exactly. Okay, maybe not exactly. I knew I'd be up for another hour or so while I worked on my journal. What harm could there possibly be if I brought that bag of M&Ms into the tent with me? Well, the ranger had let me know about the bears, but he'd failed to mention the mice. It was just past midnight when I felt a mouse running across my sleeping quilt. I quickly armed myself with a shoe and my trusty headlamp. That little booger had chewed two holes in the netting of my tent. Then the vermin dived through one of those holes, never to receive the shoe leather—actually rubber—he so richly deserved. He was guilty of breaking and entering into my humble abode and chewing the M&M package into little pieces, no doubt in frustration because there were no M&Ms left since I'd made a pig of myself and eaten the whole pack. The holes he'd made were no bigger than the size of a dime, so I put some Gorilla Tape over the holes and fell right back to sleep.

When I'd done my resupply in Stehekin, I had purchased foods that wouldn't require cooking. My fuel canister looked to have just enough fuel for morning coffee and not much more. After a 29.8-mile day, I was now just 46 miles from the border. I knew I wouldn't have been able to fly back to California with a full can of fuel in my pack, so I made due with what remained in my nearly empty canister.

When I reached Rainy Pass, I followed the sounds of loud car and truck traffic for about an hour where Washington State Route 20 and the trail parallel one another. As I continued up that very long climb, I felt as though I'd been transported back in time, or experiencing another déjà-vu moment. This section looked and felt just like the Southern California desert with its high, treeless ridges and expansive trails that let you see for miles. Even this far north it was desert hot, and I was fully exposed to the sun for hours. The only obvious difference from California was that northern Washington didn't have Joshua trees or rattlesnakes.

During my last few miles of the day, my foot caught on a tree root that brought me down. It was one of those falls that makes absolutely no sense. I got back up and looked around to make sure nobody saw me fall because it was embarrassingly stupid. I had hit the ground pretty hard and bruised an upper rib where my water bottle had caught me just right. Yep, another stupid rib. I was still able to hike, but taking a deep breath was a little painful. I just hoped it wouldn't slow me down since I had some big climbs coming up the following day.

When I got up at 4:00 a.m. the next morning, I awoke to the sounds of a light rain falling on my tent. I was still on the trail by six o'clock, but it was under a dark and dreary sky. I called up a weather report on my Garmin, and was pleased to see it was calling for a sunny day with cool temperatures. It was ten o'clock when the sun finally made its grand entrance and the sky cleared to a bright blue with light, wispy clouds. It was going to be a beautiful day after all.

The trail was once again kind as it gifted me with gradual climbs and descents, which was greatly appreciated, especially with my new rib injury. Shouldering my pack wasn't a problem early in the day, but it became increasingly difficult the more miles I hiked. I hiked some good miles, but as the day was coming to a close, all I could think of was setting up my tent and crawling in.

The hike itself had been beautiful. That day reminded me of when you go to a fireworks display and at the end there is always a grand finale, or at a baseball game when the score is tied at the bottom of the ninth and both teams step up their game. It was as though the state of Washington was putting on its grand finale with unprecedented panoramic views. This state had really stepped up its game. Climbing from 4,300 feet to 7,000 feet sets a hiker up for a great show, and I had the best seat in the house. Well, except I wasn't sitting, I was hiking like a crazy man.

I was now just 19.6 miles from the monument at the Canadian border, and then an additional eight miles to Manning Park. At this point, I was not nearly as excited as I thought I would be. When I'd hiked the AT, I was thrilled with the idea of that Mt. Katahdin summit. There was a huge difference here because I knew I would still have 679 miles to hike through the Sierra Nevada. So even though I would soon be in Canada, my hike was far from over.

I woke up the next morning after getting the most sleep I'd had in weeks. The night before I was in my tent and asleep by 6:30 p.m. and would have remained sleeping if not for a couple of hikers who arrived at 9:30 and stayed up to all hours in the night, not remotely concerned about my need for sleep. While in my tent and now wide awake, I learned about all of the ingredients in my camp neighbor's dinner, that she actually didn't lose her socks, oh, and she found the crackers she couldn't find at lunchtime. They were in her mug, and now she could have them tomorrow with her lunch, whew. It went on and on and on, until just past midnight. I don't believe I'd ever wished that a bear would jump out of the woods and eat another hiker until that very evening. When I did get up at 4:00 a.m., I fired up my jet engine cook stove and made myself a really loud cup of coffee. For some reason it tasted especially delicious.

Upon waking, I evaluated my injury, which felt much better than the night before. My unprofessional opinion was that I didn't crack or break a rib on that fall, but had simply bruised it. That was my story and I was sticking to it, because I was going to finish this hike.

The final gorgeous views of Washington while hiking that day and on the day before had been as if I'd gone to a double header. The state of Washington seemed to be saying, "So, you think what you've seen so far was awesome? Well, check this out!"

I've mentioned that I wasn't too excited about getting to the northern terminus monument. I knew I'd be much more excited if it were actually the end of my hike, but I wasn't done...not yet. As the day wore on and the final miles dwindled to no more than a few, I grew a bit more excited, especially when I came to a clearing two miles from the border and realized that for the first time in nearly 2000 miles, I was looking at Canadian mountains.

When I approached the monument, I realized there was no one else there, so I took my time and enjoyed the moment. I signed the PCTA journal with my name, trail name, and start and arrival dates. I put the journal back in its dry box and sat for a bit while I made myself lunch. It was a very private and contemplative time being alone there. But a short time later, two young ladies I had been leapfrogging for several days, Lone Wolf and Emily, showed up with champagne in hand and I watched as they celebrated. Lone Wolf was a thru-hiker, while her friend Emily had come to hike this last section of Washington with her. When I asked, they were very happy to take some photos of me at the monument. I returned the favor, and then it was time for me to step over the border and into Canada. To be honest, I felt pretty special. Canada is my adoptive country—Nova Scotia is where I now call home. My thru-hike hasn't exactly gone as I had hoped or planned, but that's okay, because life doesn't always go as we hope or plan. I have still walked to Canada from Mexico. Mostly. I just needed to go back and hike those 679 more miles required to make my journey a true thru-hike.

Whistler at the Northern Terminus Monument

Those last 19.6 miles got me to the Canadian border, and an additional 8.1 miles took me to Manning Park...but those last 8.1 miles didn't count toward the PCT. I tried explaining that to my feet, but they didn't buy it. At the Manning Park resort, I went to the lodge to see about a room. No luck, they were fully booked. But they were kind enough to tell me where I could camp. Ugh. The campground is called The Corral. There are actual corrals nice and close to the campsites, which offer campers a lovely horse manure scent to sleep by. That is, if you can get to sleep at all because of the traffic noise and the late-night party that a group of car campers carried on with past midnight. The fee for this zero-amenities campsite was $25. With no office or paid associate on site, an attendant drove through to collect the fee. The attendant apparently came by while I was showering and doing laundry at the nearby Manning Park resort, thus missing me all together. The following morning, after a nearly sleepless night I made a command decision to pack up and leave the site at 7:00 a.m., before the attendant's possible return. Did I feel guilty about this decision? Absolutely not. The place was a dump. I walked back over to the resort and had a huge hiker breakfast that I happily paid for. My objective was to hitch to Vancouver, or as close to it as possible. I wanted to book my flight to Southern California, but obviously couldn't until I knew how and when I could get to the Vancouver airport. In the meantime, my belly was full and my rib injury was feeling a bit better.

While enjoying a bottomless cup of coffee after my hiker breakfast, I made a decision. I decided I wasn't going to thumb a ride. I decided I was going to walk table to a table, introduce myself, and come right out and ask if I could hitch a ride. The first table was a strikeout because the couple I spoke to were going in the opposite direction from Vancouver. My next stop was at the table of a father and his fourteen-year-old son. I introduced myself and asked if they might consider giving me a ride. The father, Keith, politely let me know their car was overloaded. I thanked them both and wished them a good morning. As I walked outside, Keith's son, Owen, came after me and told me they would try to make room for me. Keith offered to take me to the town of Hope where I could easily use the bus system to get myself to Vancouver. Sometimes you just have to ask.

Owen, Whistler and Keith

After getting to Hope, the three of us enjoyed a cup of coffee and dessert together, and spent an hour or so talking about a variety of topics. It was now time for me to take my leave and to start making the rest of my travel plans, so I said my goodbyes to my trail angels and new friends, Keith and Owen. I found a fairly reasonably-priced motel that was just around the corner from the bus stop, checked in, and finally booked a flight to Reno, Nevada, and a rental car for the drive from Reno to Ridgecrest, California. I was deliberate in how I scheduled the trip, while still being cognizant of my need for additional time to heal. I felt positive about my overall schedule because I had, in my opinion, banked some days with my vigorous hiking since returning to the trail. Since The Incident and subsequent return to the trail, I had hiked 25 days straight without taking a day off. During those 25 days I hiked 657.5 miles, for an average of 26.3 miles per day. I had also sustained an injury to the big toe on my right foot. It had started with me stubbing it on rocks countless times each day, regardless of how careful I was. I found that the more careful I was trying not to stub it, I'd sure as heck smack it against a rock instead. Each night, my sock would be stuck to my big toe because of all the blood. I could tell I was close to losing the toenail, so I would do my best each evening to clean it, treat it with an antibacterial cream, and wrap it to keep it from getting infected. It was painful enough to walk on, but stubbing it would almost bring me to tears and want to scream. In order to continue, I'd have to make sure I was healthy and would need to back-off my current pace which I knew was unsustainable, especially at the higher altitudes and anticipated challenges of the High Sierra.

The budget motel in Hope was clean, quiet, and very comfortable. That evening, I took advantage of the tub in my room and soaked my feet in some Epsom salts. After about 30 minutes, I reached down and pulled the toenail off my right foot. I slept extremely well and woke up late, knowing I wouldn't be hiking a single mile that day. My mode of transportation wouldn't be my feet, instead I would be taking the E-Bus to Vancouver. Once the E-Bus dropped me off, I purchased a three-dollar pass for the Skytrain to the Waterfront stop, and then the Canada Line to the airport. I arrived at 2:00 p.m., but my flight wasn't until 7:00 a.m. the following morning. I went ahead and checked in, got my seat assignments, and boarding passes. Now all I needed to do was wait patiently at the airport for my departure...which wouldn't be for another seventeen hours. It was going to be a long night.

A very long night.

At one point I heard, "Hello? Hello, sir. I'm with airport security. Can I see your flight itinerary please?"

Well, that got my attention and took me from a deep sleep to being very wide awake. I'd been scoping out a tucked away area at the airport where they stored the porters' carts since having first arrived on the previous day. It seemed so perfect, being tucked away from all the noise, hidden and quite private. I stealthily found my way there at about ten o'clock that night after the large numbers of travellers had thinned dramatically, and made myself comfortable. I blew up my sleep pad, pulled out my sleeping quilt, and stuffed my down jacket into its sack for a pillow. The only part of my sleep system I didn't use was my tent—that might have drawn unnecessary attention, and perhaps have been a bit overboard. It was just after midnight when the security guard politely woke me, but I could tell right away he was a kind person and was just going through the motions of what he was mandated to do. Seemingly satisfied, he politely returned my boarding pass and ID, at which time I asked if I needed to pack up. He got a funny little smirk on his face and chuckled a bit, looked around, then back at me, and said I was just fine where I was and to have a good evening. My first thought was how appreciative I was, my second thought was that this guy needed to teach a customer service lesson to the jerks at the KOA campground in Leavenworth.

My Vancover airport campsite

I eventually had to get up around five o'clock the next morning because a whole lot of people were arriving and starting to make noise. It was so noisy, in fact, it was as though they all had flights to catch or something. I broke camp and walked over to the counter where I checked my backpack, then made my way to the gate for my first leg, the flight to Salt Lake City, Utah. A connecting flight then took me to Reno, Nevada, where I picked up the rental car for the long drive to Ridgecrest, California. Miraculously, it was a flawless day of travel with every detail going according to plan.

The six-hour drive from Reno to Ridgecrest was mostly on U.S. Route 395 at the eastern foot of the Sierra Nevada Mountains. This was the same route Scooby and I had traveled in May when he drove me to Chester, just going the opposite direction. Surrounded by high mountains for the entire 600-plus miles, I was feeling incredibly intimidated by them. In May the mountain range had been fully cloaked in deep, treacherous snow. Now there was a limited amount of snow, but the mountains appeared no less intimidating. These were the 10,000-plus-foot peaks I would soon find myself hiking, and they seemed to be looking down at me, just waiting for me to leave my footprints on them. As it got dark, they turned into black silhouettes backlit by a pale and muted sky, making them look even more sinister.

I checked into my very inexpensive motel at eight o'clock, showered, and crawled into a real bed for some much-needed sleep.

Section Six

Walker Pass to Chester, California
Mile 652-1,331

The Sierra Nevada Mountains

Today was a great day because, with Annie's diligence through numerous emails and phone calls, I was now the proud recipient of a valid, updated PCTA hiker permit, which Annie had faxed to my motel. The thought that my PCTA-issued hiking permit would expire prior to finishing the trail had never occurred to me. It had also never occurred to me that skipping the Sierras with a plan of returning to hike this section later, would be considered altering the hiking itinerary noted on my permit. My objective, and that of most hikers this year, had been to flip past the Sierras for safety reasons due to excessive snowfall. Permit-related issues therefore became a real concern to this year's class of thru-hikers. I had recently received a text message from Scooby warning that he'd spoken with several thru-hikers who'd had park rangers checking their permits, especially in Yosemite and on the John Muir Trail. Some nightmare stories included hikers being fined, or even told to leave the trail because of expired permits. I had assumed, along with many others, that there would be some forgiveness and understanding due to the severe snow conditions that year. But at the end of the day, it also made sense that there was accountability and restrictions with regard to the management of the permits. Otherwise, why even have a permit process in the first place? Some hikers took their chances, while others had elected to seek individual park permits to complete their hikes. The other way around this issue was to request a change to a permit itinerary along with a date extension. Which was what I had done, with Annie's help.

With my hiking permit issues put to rest, I used the rest of my day off for rest and healing, planning, resupply, and returning my rental car. The Kern County transit bus that I would need to take to Walker Pass only ran on Monday, Wednesday, and Friday, so it looked like I would be taking an additional day—Thursday—off, as well. A double zero would have me energized and ready for the final leg of my hike.

On Friday it was time to get back at it. After my days off for travel and for rest, I was definitely ready to get back to my purpose. The Kern County Transit bus that was scheduled to pick me up at 7:05 a.m. from the front of the Ridgecrest Wal-Mart arrived on time with no other passengers on the bus. The driver got off, locked the doors, looked over his shoulder at me and said he'd be back soon, then disappeared into the store. Thirty minutes later, he returned to the bus with a full shopping cart. He explained that his wife had given him a shopping list that morning. So much for keeping to a schedule. I paid my three bucks, took a seat, and we were finally on the road at 7:30, which was five minutes past the scheduled drop off time at Walker Pass. Again, so much for keeping to a schedule. We made all the stops that were on the itinerary, but there wasn't a soul waiting at any of them. Perhaps they'd gotten tired of waiting for the late bus. Right. So much for keeping to a schedule.

Whistler waiting for the driver to finish his shopping

It was a 25-mile trip from Ridgecrest to Walker Pass, so my fare of three dollars divided by 25 miles comes to twelve cents per mile. My best guess was that the bus driver got paid, and the bus burned fossil fuel, and there were maintenance costs associated with the bus, and that there was a support staff behind the scenes. I sure appreciated the generosity of the Kern County tax payers for the use of their unsustainable public transportation system.

As you may recall, Walker Pass was where Scooby and I had gotten off the trail on May 20th, then caught a hitch into Ridgecrest and rented a car. Scooby then drove me to Chester, which was where I'd skipped the Sierra to start hiking north from, while he drove south to the L.A. airport for his flight home.

Returning to Walker Pass felt right, like I had now returned to finish what I had started. Those 679 miles from Walker Pass to Chester were all I had left. This was truly the final leg of my journey.

The 102-degree temperature and some steep climbs made for a difficult and slow first day back on the trail. Fortunately, there was plenty of water through this section of the trail, and I definitely drank my fair share. My senses were on high alert and my eyes wide open, and I did my best to take it all in. The differences between the forested mountains of Washington state and the high desert of California were dramatic. Everything smelled different now, too. While the air in the forest of Washington was damp and humid, the air of the desert was dry, and the scents of sage and the dry flowers was strong and pungent. I found myself sniffing the air, trying to identify what I was smelling. The sounds were also distinctly different than what I'd heard in Washington. Each different bird had its own distinct song. The leap from one geographical area to another was sharp and immediate, not gradual like a slow and casual hike would ordinarily be. One moment I was in the beautiful forest of Washington, and the very next moment in the beautiful high desert of California. The geological, faunal, and floral differences were shocking to the senses.

There were also long periods of peacefulness. In fact, I had only seen one other person on that first day back. A southbound hiker passed my northbound trek, and I could tell he was too hot to stop and talk. I certainly understood because I was feeling the same way. As he passed me, he told me I was the first person he had seen all day. I seconded his comment and told him to have a great hike. It was then I realized just how we had passed each other so rapidly. If we were both walking two and a half miles per hour, we'd passed each other at five miles per hour! He was gone in an instant, and we both kept on moving, so fast yet so slow. The thought also occurred to me that we may have passed one another with the same exact number of miles to the completion of our thru-hikes. If he had started at the northern terminus, he would have had right around 660 miles to the southern terminus, while I had just about the same number of miles left until I would reach Chester. Kind of weird…

I was up at 3:30 the next morning and went right to my phone to finish my journal entry from the previous day. I had a big mileage day planned, and as usual, was motivated to get an early start. Kennedy

Meadows was just over 29 miles away, and the earlier I started the earlier I'd get there. When I exited my tent at 5:30 a.m. it was still dark, and it was the stars that were lighting up the early morning sky. It looked like it was going to be another clear and very hot day. With my headlamp on, I was on the trail at 5:45 a.m. and hiking directly toward a beautiful sunrise. The morning was cool, and those early miles came easily. The cool morning hours were always my favorite, but they were short-lived in the desert. It wasn't long before I was once again hiking through triple digit temperatures.

The timing of my flip back to California apparently had me ahead of the SOBO hikers who had started at the northern terminus. Again, I only crossed paths with one hiker on that day. It felt as though I had the whole trail to myself...peacefully to myself.

Welcome to Kennedy Meadows

I was excited to get to the General Store at Kennedy Meadows for a of couple reasons. First, it's considered the gateway to the Sierra Nevada. Second, it's another one of those highly-anticipated iconic landmarks along the trail that I'd read about and seen enough videos of to know what to expect. What I didn't expect was to arrive on the same day as their annual Chili Cook-Off. Twelve teams had set up to compete for a top prize and trophy, all based on the votes of the attendees. Who could resist? I love chili. As an attendee, I walked from team tent to team tent making my judgement as to who had made the best chili. I voted #7 by far. Dinner was taken care of. I picked up my shoes and bear canister, set up camp—camping was free for PCT hikers— and transferred my supplies from my food bag into my new anti-bear contraption. I eventually hit the hay with the loud live band continuing to play a short distance away for the chili-consuming fans, but nothing could have kept me awake.

The idea of a big hiker breakfast was tempting, but the trail was calling me. So, instead of waiting around for the general store to open up, I found myself packed up and taking the one-mile roadwalk from the General Store back to the trailhead at 6:30 a.m.

The elevation at Kennedy Meadows is 6,149 feet, and my climb that day took me to over 10,500 feet. It was a pretty big climb, but modest in Sierra Nevada terms. Still, it wore me out and set me up for another night of deep sleep and recuperation. The hiking was incredible, and included a meadow that went on for several miles. I could see a homestead off in the distance, along with a huge herd of cattle. My guess was that the PCTA worked out an arrangement with this private land owner to allow the trail to cut directly through his land. One thing was obvious, the cattle grazed along the trail, evidenced by the fact that I hopped, skipped, and jumped over hundreds of cow patties. I tried to imagine what the trail had looked like in May covered in a deep blanket of snow. But the snow was now completely gone and I was enjoying the Sierra in all its glory. Trail conditions were nearly perfect and water was plentiful. Seasonal streams continued to flow with beautiful cool, clear water. I took my lunch break at the Kern River Monache Meadow. I sat on the foot bridge with the river flowing below me and enjoyed my break with a cool breeze under a cloudless sky. I hiked till 6:30 p.m. when I had finally arrived at my destination, Death Canyon Creek. I was tired and ridiculously hungry. After dinner, I wrote in my journal, and was asleep by 8:30. Death Canyon Creek was at 8,959 feet, and I would have a big climb to over 11,000 feet first thing the following morning.

It was 36 degrees waking up the next morning, and getting out from under my sleeping quilt was a difficult chore. It was so cold that I started my hike in full winter gear—down jacket, gloves, and toque. But it wasn't too long before I'd worked up enough body heat and started stripping down. It was another clear and cloudless day, another perfect day for a hike. I'd been conflicted all day as to whether or not to take the side trail to the summit of Mount Whitney. Mount Whitney stands at 14,505 feet and is the highest mountain and highest point in the contiguous United States. The opportunity to climb this mountain would most likely never present itself to me again. So why the conflict? Food, that's why. I had previously made the decision not to get off the trail in Independence for a resupply. Getting off there required a nine-mile side trail—18 miles round trip—to Kearsarge Pass and to the Onion Valley trailhead. From the trailhead you still need to hitch into Independence or Bishop, which is at least another 25 miles. Making this resupply run would take at least a full day. So, I thought I would skip Mount Whitney and stretch my food a bit and hike to the Muir Trail Ranch and resupply there instead. Muir Trail Ranch—affectionately known as MTR—is a popular family-owned guest accommodation used mostly by John Muir Trail hikers. The JMT and PCT share this portion of the trail. At 98 miles up the trail, I would have had just enough food to get there. Unfortunately, this decision would also mean that I could not summit Mount Whitney, which is a side trip off the PCT and would require another full day and another full day's worth of food.

Conflicted? Yes. Enough so that I decided to sleep on it and to make my final decision in the morning.

Because this section of the trail is shared by the JMT, there were a lot of section hikers, mainly because of its popularity and accessibility by way of three nearby passes. The views were beautiful, but I knew the next few days coming up were going to be truly spectacular. If I chose to skip Whitney, I would instead reach Forester Pass. At 13,200 feet, Forester Pass is the highest pass and the highest point on the PCT—because Whitney isn't actually on the trail.

The trail continued to work its magic. I happened to run into a couple of thru-hikers whom Scooby and I had first met while hiking the Southern California desert. I had not seen Pierre and Diesel for close to 2000 miles, and yet here we were, crossing paths again. I couldn't believe that after all those months and all those miles on the trail, I would run into them in the Sierra. The trail indeed works in mysterious ways.

Diesel and Pierre

Finding sleep that night was a struggle. I just couldn't stop thinking about Mount Whitney. Do I hike on and skip it, or do I summit the king of mountains and figure out the food issue later? It was right at two thirty in the morning when I made a decision: I just had to summit that quintessential mountain. With that decided, I realized there were only eight miles to reach the base camp of Whitney, called Crabtree Meadows. For me, that would almost be like having a day off. So I decided to sleep in. I finally woke up at 6:30 a.m.—which was sleeping in for me—and immediately felt great about my decision. I made coffee and had not one, but two tortillas with peanut butter and Nutella—I couldn't believe it had taken thousands of miles hiked for me to discover Nutella, the greatest invention of all time. I had a couple camp-mates close to my site, and they were just starting to stir. I said hello to one lady, Ann, a solo hiker like myself, as she exited her tent. After introductions, I told her about my indecisiveness and my struggle with Whitney because of my concern over not having enough food. Ann looked at me and said, "Whistler, I'm finished with my section hike and I have way too much food left over." Well, there you go, the trail does provide.

As I hiked my minuscule number of miles, I saw a SOBO hiker coming my way. I knew immediately who it was, and he recognized me at that same moment. It was First One! I had not seen him since late June when we had inadvertently been separated near Sisters. We took our packs off, and sat and talked for half an hour. Knowing I only had eight miles to hike was so liberating. It made sitting down to talk with First One feel like what a normal person would do, not what a crazy hiker would do. First One had made it to Canada, then he flipped down to Chester where he'd started hiking southbound through the Sierras. Now he only had about 60 miles to Kennedy Meadows left to complete his thru-hike. Having gotten caught up, it was time for us to both hike on, but not until we hugged one other and took a couple of photos.

Whistler and First One

Once I arrived at Crabtree Meadows, I set up my tent and rinsed clean my dirty shirt and socks in Whitney Creek. My plan was to get up at 11:30 p.m. and start hiking at midnight in order to reach the summit of Mount Whitney in time to watch the sunrise. I would leave my tent and most everything else at Crabtree so as to lighten my pack. In my pack would be some food, water, warm clothes, and my cook stove, because I would be having my morning coffee at 14,505 feet.

I was in my tent and under my sleeping quilt by six o'clock, but unfortunately, two other hikers made camp right next to me and they were not starting their hike at midnight like this crazy hiker was. They stayed up late while having a deep, long, and loud conversation, which kept me up and only allowed for two and a half hours of sleep. No blame, it was just my unfortunate luck.

There was no doubt I was also very excited, so I woke myself up at 11:25 just before my cell phone alarm was to go off at 11:30 p.m. The night before, I had put everything together that I was taking with me except for my sleeping quilt. Once packed, I was soon on the trail with my headlamp leading the way. There was a nearly full moon, but it was not bright enough to light the seven and a half miles of steep trail up Mount Whitney. It was slow going because of the dark, the steepness, and the effect that the high altitude had on my ability to get enough oxygen. I started noticing some minor difficulty in getting enough air after I reached about 10,000 feet. I never felt lightheaded or nauseous, just a slight shortness of breath. I found myself taking short pauses that I wouldn't ordinarily need. The trail was more difficult to follow the further up I got in elevation because of some snow and ice patches. As I looked far below, I could see a whole train of other hikers making their way up the trail with their headlamps lighting their way.

I reached the summit of 14,505 feet right at 4:30 a.m. Way too early for sunrise. When I arrived, the temperature was just 18 degrees, and it was extremely windy and still very dark. The sky was perfectly clear and filled with billions of stars and the moon. I took a moment when I realized I was standing at the highest point in the contiguous U.S., and I would never be closer to the stars and the moon than I was at that very moment. I sat with a few other hikers on the east side of the stone-made emergency shelter to break the high winds, wrapped in our sleeping bags and quilts, waiting and watching for the sun's arrival. It looked like it was going to be a long wait, so I made coffee for myself and my new sunrise friends.

When the sky started to turn a bright orange on the horizon, someone mentioned that they actually had cell service. I checked my phone and saw that I also had data and cell service, so I thought I would FaceTime Annie so she could see the sunrise too, while nice and warm at home. Once the sun had made its grand entrance, it was time for photos, and then to head back down the way we'd come. The hike down was beautiful, and I stopped often to take photos along the way. I'd been by all those beautiful sites on the way up, but never saw them because of the inky darkness. All I saw on the way up was the trail—and that was questionable at times—and my feet.

Whistler at the summit of Mount Whitney

After I'd made it back to Crabtree Meadows, I packed up, ate lunch, and was now determined to hike some actual PCT miles. Just as I was getting up to start hiking, Ranger Bob came by and asked to see my permit. It felt so good to know that my permit was updated. As I hiked on, I couldn't help but feel proud of myself. Not proud that I had climbed to the top of Mount Whitney, but proud to have taken what was likely to be the only opportunity I would ever have to hike up that majestic mountain. Hiking a long trail takes planning and coordination, and I had almost let my fear of running out of food keep me from a once-in-a-lifetime opportunity. I was proud that I had allowed myself to take a risk that ordinarily I would not have considered, but which paid off with one of the greatest experiences I have ever had.

Because I was exhausted from both the lack of sleep and the strenuous hike up Mount Whitney, I only hiked 8.4 miles that day, which did set me up for a couple of big climbs the next day.

MY SUNRISE

Up at midnight with open eyes,
today's the day for my sunrise.
It's that time, this I know,
to climb Mount Whitney, I must go.
The tallest mountain in the forty-eight,
to see my sunrise, I must not be late.
At fourteen thousand, five hundred and five,
I'll climb that mountain stride by stride.
The air is thin from the altitude,
with no effect on my attitude.
At the summit with the moon and stars,
a brand-new day, not too far.
In the distance on that horizon,
a new day here, the sun is rising.

I was in my tent and tucked under my sleeping quilt by seven o'clock that night, and slept for nine much-needed hours. When I got up at four o'clock, I went to retrieve my bear canister and was shocked to find I was now surrounded by tents that had not been there when I'd gone to sleep the night before. I'm normally a light sleeper, but I never heard any of those hikers coming in and making camp.

It was going to be a big day, with Forester Pass to start and Glen Pass to finish off the day. The hike up to Forester started off as a gradual ascent. At one point I could see the pass, but couldn't see the trail leading up to it from where I stood below. It appeared to me like a puzzle with lots of missing pieces, but they became apparent as I followed that long and winding trail up to the pass.

As I was mindlessly hiking, I couldn't help but wonder about the thousands of man hours that must have gone into building that trail. The blasting of this one mountain alone to place a clear trail over it must have been a monumental task. At 13,200 feet, Forester Pass is the highest pass on the PCT. It took me two and a quarter hours to climb the 4.8 miles. It wasn't a difficult or very steep climb, but it was a slow, methodical ascent for me after reaching 10,000 feet because of the high altitude. It felt like I couldn't catch my breath, which required that I go a bit slower than I was accustomed to. At the pass there is a cornice of jagged rock that was reminiscent of the Knife's Edge at Goat Rocks. There was sheer nothingness below me to my immediate left or right. I tried to imagine what it would have been like to cross this pass if it were deep in snow with high winds. It would have been treacherous. The views were okay, but I was looking forward to Glen Pass, where the views were reportedly out of this world.

The hike down the north side of Forester took me from 13,200 feet down to 9,500 feet. Then the climb up to Glen Pass took me back up to 11,950 feet. This time, it wasn't the altitude that slowed me on the way up, it was the incredible views. I found myself stopping to look so often that I thought I might never get there. The views from the south side were amazing, and definitely lived up to their reputation. Then I reached the pass and saw what was on the north side. It was at that point that I realized it was going to be a very long day. This was not a section of trail to rush through. No, I would need time to take it all in. The lakes from above were absolutely magnificent, then the trail takes you directly to and around them. Hiking around the Upper and Middle Rae Lakes was surreal and peaceful. I stopped often, to capture and commit it all to memory, while also taking a crazy number of photos. At one point I told myself that I simply had to stop looking up. If I didn't get back to looking down at the trail, I knew I would never finish hiking it. The place was that astonishingly beautiful.

As said, it was a long day. I didn't get to my campsite till 7:30 that night, two hours later than I had planned. Believe me, it was worth it.

A common question family, friends, and neighbors ask is, what was it like to hike alone? It's funny, I've hiked hundreds if not thousands of miles by myself, but I never actually felt alone. For example, before leaving camp on that particular morning, a fellow hiker had asked me if I had any duct tape. I did, of course, but I first asked why he needed it. He explained that his water bottle had sprung a leak. I had a better solution, and that was to give him one of my extra bottles. Another hiker was experiencing tooth pain along with some swelling, so I offered and she accepted some Ibuprofen and Tylenol. A couple of days earlier, Ann gave me some of her extra food. These are just a few of the many examples of hikers helping hikers, and testimony that we are never really alone.

After my big day going over Forester and Glen Passes, I ended up camped at the Woods Creek Suspension Bridge. Who doesn't love a suspension bridge? This bridge is truly an impressive feat of engineering. Even with a limit of one person at a time, the bridge swings to and fro when walking across, and may not be all that comfortable for some people—especially if you easily get seasick. I'm not certain of its length, but I would have to estimate it to be at least 150 feet long.

Woods Creek Suspension Bridge

Shortly after crossing Woods Creek by way of the resplendent bridge, I came to the Woods Creek Water Slide. This long granite stone "slide" could be a seductive water feature, but would be a sure way to seriously injure oneself. Neat to look at, though.

On the following day, I would be taking on both Pinchot Pass—pronounced Pin-cho—and Mather Pass, both over 12,000 feet. The approach trail to Pinchot Pass was seven and a half miles with a gain of 3,700 feet. The pass itself is at 12,100 feet, making it a pretty difficult climb. It wouldn't have been so bad if there were some decent views after all that work, but unfortunately there really were none. This may have been unfair because I knew I was probably going to compare the rest of the Sierra to my new gold standard, Glen Pass. In any case, I guess the climb was good exercise...like I really needed more exercise.

After Pinchot, it was time to make my way to Mather Pass. This pass starts with a six-mile approach trail that is a gradual ascent, which was greatly appreciated after one already big climb for the day. The gain in altitude is about 2000 feet, putting Mather Pass right at 12,100 feet above sea level. The still waters of those sapphire blue lakes alongside the approach trail to Mather reflected the sparse snow that remained on the mountains. The snow was still melting and keeping the creeks swollen with the resource most appreciated by all late season hikers. Clear, ice cold water was still plentiful in what would ordinarily be considered late in the hiking season. When my Guthook guide listed a creek as seasonal and likely dry, I usually found it with a heavy flow. The many creek crossings were easily negotiated during these weeks by rock-hopping, but the snowmelt must have made for dangerous crossings for hikers in the spring and early summer. Each day here told me that I was hiking the Sierra at the perfect time.

That night, the mountains completely surrounded and wrapped around my campsite. As I sat outside enjoying my dinner, I took a 360-degree scan, and all I saw around me were those huge, beautiful mountains. The late-day glow of the setting sun exaggerated the peaks and valleys as shadows crept across the face of the grandiose mountain range. The view evolved as the sun continued its descent, with the shapes of the mountains shifting and morphing minute by minute. I had camped countless times in places where I was all alone and I'd never really felt unsafe, but for some reason I felt exceptionally safe surrounded by these incredible mountains. It didn't hurt having the sounds of the thundering Palisade River nearby helping me find another night of deep sleep.

The next morning, a full moon and rising sun simultaneously led the way along the trail. I couldn't actually see the sun because of the high surrounding mountains, but the sky started taking on just enough ambient light to allow me to see where I was going. The seasons were changing, and it was getting light later in the morning and dark earlier each night. It was now September 14th. Fall was coming, and this year's hiking season would soon be coming to an end.

The famous and iconic Muir Shelter

My hike that day took me over Muir Pass, creating yet another of those iconic memories. I'd been looking forward to hiking Muir Pass for as long as I had been planning this thru-hike. I'd seen photos and videos of the pass, along with the famous Muir Shelter, and anticipated seeing it for myself. The beehive-shaped shelter had been built by the Sierra Club in 1930 to commemorate leading conservationist and trail namesake John Muir as its first president. This shelter has provided safe refuge for countless people during stormy weather, and most certainly saved many lives. I woke up that morning knowing it would be a sixteen-mile hike up to Muir Pass and Muir Shelter, and decided that was where I would be having my lunch that day. I arrived at 1:30 p.m. extremely hungry, enjoyed my lunch, took countless photos, and lingered a bit before finally heading over the north side for my descent. When I arrived at another creek and a beautiful campsite, I decided to call it a day. It was only 5:15 p.m., which was pretty early for me, but I had to sew up a hole in my shorts, rinse clean some clothes in the creek, eat dinner, and finally, to journal about my day.

The past few days had taken me to some extraordinary heights. I'd seen some of the most beautiful landscapes you could ever imagine, and still had so many more ahead of me. But at this moment, all I could think about was getting a good night's sleep.

The next day, I set a goal to reach the Muir Trail Ranch by lunchtime. I was in desperate need of a resupply, which was actually a big gamble. More on that later.

I had only hiked a few miles that morning when I came to Evolution Creek. In high snow years, this creek is one of the most dangerous crossings in the Sierras, especially in the spring and early summer. I looked back at comments posted in July of this year on Guthook, where hikers had reported that the creek waters were chest high. There is a patch of huge cascading rapids a bit further downstream that can be fatal if the current sweeps you away. One need only to Google "deaths on the PCT" to see how many hikers had lost their lives crossing dangerous creeks like Evolution Creek. Fortunately for me and my fellow late-season hikers, the creek was now just ankle high. No drama for Whistler that day. Thank goodness. I'd already had enough drama on this trip, thank you.

So, back to Muir Trail Ranch. MTR is a popular accommodation and resupply location for many John Muir Trail hikers. MTR accepts your mailed resupply package, and will have it waiting for you at the Ranch when you arrive. Because the location is so isolated, they charge $85 for that service. The operators of MTR go to great lengths to pick up these hiker packages, a.k.a. buckets, from the post office. And when I say bucket, I really mean bucket. They require that when you mail your resupply package you must mail it in a five-gallon bucket with a secured lid, like those sold at home improvement stores.

Let me explain what I meant earlier when I said I was taking a big gamble with my resupply. PCT hikers all know that JMT hikers must ship their resupply as I just described, and we also know that those hikers tend to put way too much in those packages. All that extra food and supplies, first aid, personal care products, and so on, are then put into hiker boxes—or in this case hiker buckets—and made available to PCT thru-hikers for free. My big gamble was taking the chance that I'd be able to meet all my resupply needs from these extra hiker buckets. Luckily, my gamble paid off bigtime. I was easily able to gather the needed seven-day resupply of food, and also to get the AAA batteries I needed for my headlamp. Most important, I scored the roll of two-ply, high-quality toilet paper that I desperately needed—and all for *free*.

While I was there at the ranch, I figured I should eat lunch, so I pulled a jar of peanut butter and a large package of saltines out of a bucket, sat down, and consumed every last morsel of them. I seemed to be in a constant state of hunger. The only thing that helped me to stop thinking about exactly how hungry I was as I hiked along, was the scenery along this amazing trail. After finishing lunch, I left MTR at one o'clock carrying a heavily food-laden backpack, and gratefully made my way back to the trail.

Seldon Pass was now in my sights, which was another six miles away. Seldon Pass is described as one of the last big passes. Rising to 10,900 feet, the climb was made a bit tougher with the added burden on my back. At around 3:30 p.m. I'd made it about two thirds up the mountain, when I came to Sallie Keyes Lake. There were a couple of hikers setting up camp there, and I was so tempted to remove my heavy burden and pitch my tent there too. Instead, I reminded myself of my self-imposed goal of at least 20 miles for the day, then placed one foot in front of the other and repeated. Once I reached the pass, I was very happy with my decision to continue—the views were well worth the additional effort. The descent down the north side of Seldon Pass went quickly—gravity was my friend—with the last hurdle of the day being Bear Creek. Bear Creek is known as another difficult creek crossing with raging waters in spring and early summer. It has been known to knock hikers right off their feet. But not today. I was easily able to rock-hop Bear Creek and not even get my feet wet. I was definitely hiking the Sierra at the right time of year.

That next day there was an unobstructed moon, and countless stars were still faintly visible in the early morning sky. The brisk, early morning breezes had the aspen tree leaves shaking and shimmering as though they knew what was coming. As the morning continued, the weather started to turn. Dark and ominous clouds circled the mountain tops, causing those cool breezes to turn into frigid gusts of wind. I would often start the morning wearing my down jacket, and eventually have to shed it after I'd built up some body heat from hiking. But not today. Today was a day that required every defense against the harsh weather conditions. My climbs above 10,000 feet meant I had to keep moving just to stay warm. When I made it to Silver Pass, which sat right at 11,000 feet, the wind tried its best to knock me onto my posterior. My only defense was not to stop or linger to take in the views, but to get myself over the pass and down the north side as quickly as possible.

The hike up to Silver Pass wasn't supposed to be all that difficult, but for some reason, it was for me. I was having a tough time making it all work that day. Was I just tired? Or, was it the fifteen additional pounds of food in my pack weighing me down? Whatever it was, it had me working my hardest to get up and over that pass.

One of the highlights of this very difficult day was something that happened when I was about halfway up to Silver Pass. As slowly as I was moving, I was still a bit faster than a woman I happened to come up to on the trail. As hiking etiquette dictated, she stepped aside to allow me to pass. Polite pleasantries were exchanged as I passed her, and then it hit me. I knew this person. I turned back around and asked her name, to which she replied, "Milla." I knew it!

I had first met Milla and her husband, 173, at Big Bear Lake when I was with Scooby hiking the desert of Southern California. I had seen them again just over the Oregon border, but not since. Milla and I then hiked together and caught up with 173. We chatted for a bit about trail news and I told them about The Incident, which they had already heard about through the trail grapevine. As it turned out, like me they had also flipped to Chester early on to skip the snow in the Sierra. So that was where their thru-hike would end. Before we parted, I took a quick photo of them, we hugged one other, and said our goodbyes... possibly for the last time.

173 and Milla

When I finally made it to the top of Silver Pass, I realized I still had another five miles to reach my planned campsite. By this time, I was just dragging myself along. At around four o'clock, I seriously considered stopping to boil water for coffee. The only problem was, it was much too cold to stop hiking. Some days you just aren't feeling it...

When I arrived at my planned campsite of Lake Virginia, I found it too exposed to the high winds and cold temperatures to make camp. I had to keep moving. Somewhere, somehow, I got a second wind—no pun intended—and started to pick it up a bit. I think it was more about self-preservation than anything, but somehow, I gathered the strength to move my legs. Eventually I found a site barely big enough to pitch my tent, and not the most level spot, but that was going to be home, period, end of story. I was just too tired and cold to continue.

My campsite left quite a bit to be desired, but it was actually comical in its own way. Being extremely tired and desperate, I had accepted a site that normally I would have passed up. Prior to setting up my humble abode, I was in the habit of taking my water bottle and laying it on the ground as a bubble level to find the flattest spot. I didn't bother with that today. I already knew the result would only deter me and frustrate this tired hiker. I woke up several times overnight to readjust my sleep pad so as to avoid rolling out of my tent, down the mountain, and into nearby Purple Lake. But I managed to survive.

When I awoke in the morning, I was excited to recall that this was the day I would finally have a shower. I had hiked twelve days since my last shower...which had actually worked in my favor by keeping all wild animals at bay. Laundry was a different story. I was in the habit of faithfully rinsing out my shirt, socks, and underwear in any nearby lake, creek, or stream. No, I don't use any soap, as that would be harmful to the environment. However, I couldn't say for certain whether or not there had been any negative ramifications to fish populations from rinsing my toxic clothing in those lakes, creeks or streams.

As I hiked to the day's destination of Red's Meadow Resort, I had a bit of a chuckle when I realized I was hiking thirteen miles...but I was considering those thirteen miles to be a day off. Which it was, compared to most of my daily miles. I had forgone getting off the trail at Independence and Bishop for the Vermilion Valley Resort, with the intention of stopping at Red's Meadow instead.

I arrived at the resort at eleven fifteen, and was thrilled that they had a cabin available for just sixty dollars. It was just a room with two beds and electricity, the shower and bathroom being in a separate, shared facility, but I didn't care. I was going to sleep in a real bed in my own private cabin. I knew I really should have taken a shower first, but I was in desperate need of a real meal. I made my way to the Mule House Café for a big, fat hamburger, a heaping serving of potato salad, and a bottomless glass of Dr. Pepper. Once done with lunch, I was off to the resort's clean and modern showers and laundry room, then finally back to my cabin to clean and repair my gear. The tips of my trekking poles had long since broken off, leaving me with inadequate safety on rock surfaces. The carbide tips grip the rock, but without them the trekking poles slip dangerously. The Muir Trail Ranch didn't have any tips, and unfortunately, neither did the General Store at Red's Meadow. I checked with the resort manager, and he produced a couple of old trekking poles other hikers had left behind. With borrowed tools, I was able to rob the tips off those poles and, with a bit of ingenuity, retrofit them to my poles.

The day was still young...and the selection of IPAs in the general store cooler caught my undivided attention. I did a taste and quality check, and determined that the Stone Brewery IPA was the clear winner. Finally, it was dinnertime. I decided to repeat what I'd had for lunch, but this time I topped it off with chocolate ice cream. Red's Meadow had a serious problem, which I was happy to assist with. They would be closing for the season in a couple of weeks, and they had too much ice cream left in their freezer. When I asked my waitress if I could have a scoop of chocolate ice cream, Brandy asked, "Would you like chopped up Butterfinger topping?" Well, sure! That was when she explained they had too much ice cream. Seriously, can you really ever have too much ice cream? My one scoop turned into a bowl full of what I would call a healthy hiker portion.

There was cell and data service at Red's Meadow, so I stayed up past midnight uploading my journal entries for the previous ten days. Once finished, it was lights out. I was exceptionally tired and looking forward to sleeping in a real bed.

Way to soon, 6:30 a.m. rolled around. Time for this hiker to get moving. The first thing I did was to call Annie...because I could. Next, I walked over to use the washroom—the one with a real flush toilet...because I could. And finally, I went to the restaurant and ordered coffee and a big hiker breakfast...because I could. These were a few of the simple luxuries that you really miss while living on the trail for months at a time. I definitely had a greater appreciation for these and other luxuries.

After breakfast, I went back to my cabin and finished packing my gear. My stay at Red's Meadow had only been for 21 hours, but had been such a restorative time, exactly what I'd needed to recharge. It seemed funny how I had even picked up a few items from the General Store to top off what I would need for the next four to five days, but my pack felt lighter now. I returned the key, filled a water bottle, and started hiking.

I felt so at peace and relaxed that morning. It wasn't long before I realized I hadn't stopped smiling the whole time. Rest can really help change your attitude, lighten your load, and put some pep in your step.

The trail today took me past Devil's Postpile. This national monument is an incredible geological feature where tall, vertical, natural hexagonal formations of basalt formed millions of years ago as violent lava eruptions slowly cooled. This natural wonder is a national treasure, and too unique to begin to adequately describe. That day I also went over Island Pass, which is a very minor pass at just 10,200 feet. Island Pass was named after the Thousand Island Lake which the trail took me past, and which was absolutely stunning.

Storm clouds over Thousand Island Lake

I made a short day of it and quit at four thirty in the afternoon because it was getting extremely windy and cold, and looked like a storm was brewing. I made camp at the base of the approach to Donohue Pass, which was just a 3.4-mile hike up to an elevation of just over 11,000 feet. That was going to be my warm-up hike the next morning.

When I awoke that following day and gathered the courage to creep out from under my quilt and get my bear canister, there was about half an inch of snow on the ground and it was still coming down. Once safely back in my tent, I made my breakfast and hot cocoa—there had been no coffee in the MTR hiker box or at the Red's Meadow General Store. I put on my rain jacket and pants, packed my backpack, and was breaking down my tent just as it stopped snowing. Mine were the first footsteps going up to Donohue Pass that day. It was a slow and laborious climb because of some difficulty locating the trail, and because there was a sheet of ice under the snow making it slippery at times. I found that I had wandered off the trail a couple times, which no doubt frustrated the hikers who followed my footprints later in the day. I slipped and fell once, with no harm or damage done, thank goodness. When I reached the pass, I was a bit disappointed because the views were not that great. Yes, I was still unfairly comparing to my gold standard of Glen Pass. All that work and nothing to show for it but the miles hiked...which was really okay. It was cold and I needed to keep moving anyway.

While planning the day's hike, I noticed on Guthook that after you hiked down the north side of Donohue Pass, the trail leveled off at 8,500 feet. There would be a stretch of virtually flat trail that ran for about fifteen miles. That motivated me to make this a big miles day. The trail took me through mile upon mile of beautiful open meadows—meadows with creeks running through them and the tall Sierra Nevadas as their backdrop.

At midday, I thought I had chosen the perfect place to have lunch. After lunch, I hiked a bit farther and found a slightly better place. A short time later, I found an even better place. The point being that it was all incredibly perfect. When I started getting close to Tuolumne Meadows, I ran into waves of day hikers. With a road and a large parking lot close by, masses of daytrippers converge here to take full advantage of this beautiful natural resource. I met and spoke with many of them, all very curious about my hike. I lost count of how many times I explained that the trail they were walking on goes all the way from Mexico to Canada. I guess they thought it was just the half mile they walked to and from their car.

Of course, I hiked the very short spur trail to Soda Springs, where carbonated water literally bubbles out of the ground. This geological feature is a mystery to geologists, who cannot explain why the water is carbonated. The water is full of minerals, and is said to be safe to drink but wild animals enjoy it, as well, and can contaminate it, so I skipped tasting it for myself.

While passing Tuolumne Lodge, I came across a hiker who went by trail name Nat-Geo—short for National Geographic. Nat-Geo had recently finished his thru-hike and was taking a few days to give back in the way of trail magic. We chatted for a bit while I enjoyed the magic—a cold beer in the late afternoon with many more miles ahead of me was just the trail magic I needed. The bonus beer that Nat-Geo made me put in my pack for later went very nicely with my dinner.

As the day hikers made their way back to their cars, I continued on, and found myself once again a lone hiker in the wilderness. But then I heard loud banging, and at first wondered if it was the sound of gunshots. As I hiked closer, though, I discovered it was a trail crew building and repairing a portion of the trail. The banging I heard was one of the crew members swinging a sledgehammer, breaking up rock. As I had at each previous encounter with trail crews, I thanked them profusely for their work.

It was just about seven o'clock when I arrived at my planned destination for the day, tired and ready to eat dinner, and anxious to crawl under my quilt. It had been a good day. I'd hiked 30 miles, which meant I was 30 miles closer to going home.

When freezing conditions were expected, an experienced hiker knows to sleep with their water filter. If the filter were to freeze, it would cause damage to the filtering membrane, rendering it virtually useless. I slept with my down jacket on and kept my filter safely tucked in a pocket. When I awoke, there was ice on the ceiling of my tent, so I called up a weather report on my Garmin. The report came back with a temperature reading of 28 degrees. No wonder I was shivering that morning!

Here is the ironic thing about those excessively cold temperatures. About a week earlier, I was speaking with another hiker about the perfect weather conditions we'd been enjoying. Out of the blue, he warned me to beware of September 19th, "Because there is always a weather event on September 19th."

Today was September 19th. That guy should be a meteorologist.

My biggest climb for the day was going to be Benson Pass. At 10,100 feet, Benson wasn't supposed to be too tough, but for some reason, again I really struggled. I wasn't sure what the problem was, but I seemed to be moving in slow motion. It may have been the fact that I had hiked 30 miles the day before, or it could have been the lack of caffeine since I was out of coffee. The views were a little disappointing, as well. I didn't mind working hard to make those big climbs, but a bit of a payoff in the way of a view would have been nice.

On the way down on the north side of Benson Pass was Smedberg Lake. The views changed as the trail took me along the shore of this beautiful lake. I couldn't believe how pristine and pure the lake water was. Not a single contaminant would be found in it. No jet skis or motorboats had ever stirred those waters. Not a drop of oil or fuel had ever contaminated that beautiful lake. When standing at the base of any mountain, it's difficult to imagine the treasures that await you. Exquisite lakes and meadows were hidden from you, only to be revealed after you climb the beast that guards them. That is when the energy spent, the exploding lungs, and the burning leg muscles receive their reward.

The treasures that await you

So, back to the weather. These past few days had had me wondering if I was going to have a rough time for the remaining time I had in the Sierra. It had been windy, freezing cold, and even snowing. But today the sky was back to a cloudless powder-blue with a full sun. The only blemish in the sky were the jet contrails crisscrossing one another, which looked like there had been a lot of near misses, or that they were playing a game of sky tic-tac-toe.

When I got to camp at 6:30 p.m., I set up my tent and opened the flaps in an attempt to dry it out while I prepared dinner. The ice that had been on the ceiling that morning had long since thawed, leaving quite a soggy mess. I should have set it out to dry during my lunch break, but didn't think of it.

I was now just 37 miles from Sonora Pass, which marked the end of the required bear canister carry. Like most other hikers, I would unload this anchor at Kennedy Meadows. Yes, another Kennedy Meadows, but this one goes by Kennedy Meadows North.

What a relief it was when I woke that next morning and the temperature was 37 degrees. I'd guessed that the winter weather conditions these past few days had just been a warning shot across the bow—the Sierra's way of saying, "Hey, move your butt, Whistler, winter is coming. This is your final warning."

Early that next morning, I spoke with two different hikers who had flipped north of the Sierra Nevadas earlier, and were now heading southbound. The first one, who went by the trail name Flawless, told me that she was late finishing her thru-hike because she had broken her foot early in her hike and had been forced to return home to heal. The second hiker, Squeaks, had gotten her trail name because during her first week on the trail she'd come down with bronchitis and her lungs would squeak when she breathed. She, too, had to go home to recouperate for over six weeks before getting back on the trail. Both of these young ladies were prime examples of the perseverance it takes to complete a thru-hike.

My hike now took me over a couple of steep climbs and then a stretch of about twelve miles of gradual ascent, and then finally to

Dorothy Lake. If it hadn't been so early in the day, this lake would have been my choice for a campsite. But I knew another perfect campsite would no doubt reveal itself when the timing was right.

Today I finally hit the anticipated big bubble of SOBO hikers, with a pretty steady flow of them passing by throughout the day. Interestingly, I noticed that as we approached one another, if they were listening to music with earbuds, they would politely remove them when they saw me. It was a signal that they were open to talk. So, we did. We shared simple pleasantries, of course, such as, "Have a great hike," but sometimes more than that. Sometimes they wanted to know what was coming up ahead for them. Sometimes they just wanted to talk because they were lonely. That can happen out here—you can definitely feel lonely at times.

That evening I camped at the base of the approach to Sonora Pass, which I would take on first thing in the morning. Once over the pass, the descent would take me down to California State Route 108, where I would hopefully hitch the nine miles into Kennedy Meadows North. I'd already put together my shopping list for what was likely to be the second-to-last resupply I'd need to complete my 2,650-mile hike. Kennedy Meadows North was also where I would get to mail my bear canister home. That in itself would make it a great day.

Sonora Pass didn't seem like much of an adversary. It was either really easy, or it was the lure of that hamburger lunch waiting for me at Kennedy Meadows North driving me. The climb is up to 10,800 feet, but an overall easygoing hike. I had previously read a few comments in Guthook from hikers back in July who'd still been fighting deep snow and using ice axes to make it through the pass. Which further substantiated that I was definitely hiking the Sierras at the right time of year.

The landscape in this section had taken on an entirely different look. These mountains were virtually devoid of trees or any other flora. The trail was well-graded but the lack of trees meant there was no wind break. The wind was frigid, brisk, cutting, and made numerous forceful attempts to sweep me off my feet. There were no boulder climbs—in fact, there were no boulders or granite slabs as I'd become used to. This mountainous area would leave a hiker completely exposed if the weather made a turn for the worse—no trees or rocks to use for cover. Today there was a bit of fresh new snow on and along the trail. I had heard from several SOBO hikers just a few days ago that they had hiked Sonora Pass during a snowstorm, and the evidence was still present.

No trees also meant no birds, chipmunks, squirrels, or any other animals. Although, I couldn't miss seeing the mountain lion tracks in the remaining snow. My imagination told me that this mountain lion was looking for a nice, juicy hiker to have for breakfast, lunch, or dinner. I found myself checking over my shoulder a couple times to make sure I wasn't on the menu. A bit later, I came across a hunter in full camouflage garb, including an orange hunter's vest. When I asked, he told me he was hunting for bear. Unfortunately, I hadn't happened to pack an orange vest, hat, or any other florescent apparel to alert hunters that I was not a bear. I knew I smelled like one, so I could only hope there weren't any visually impaired hunters who hunted using only their keen sense of smell.

Once I had made it to Hwy 108, I attempted the hitch to Kennedy Meadows. There was very little traffic, with an occasional car passing by every couple of minutes. The drivers all seemed friendly as they waved at me while passing by. I was eventually able to get a ride from two hunters who were on their way home after a fruitless weekend hunting deer—score one for the deer. These two guys were very nice and went way out of their way to deliver me to the front door of the resort at Kennedy Meadows.

I checked in, then made a beeline for the restaurant and ordered a big, fat cheeseburger, fries, and in honor of its namesake, a Sierra

Nevada IPA to wash it all down. While eating, I wrote out a few post-cards for my grandchildren. Next, I researched the particulars on shipping my bear canister, which I mailed to my son Brian in South Carolina. It was around this time that I discovered the only shuttle back to the trail was scheduled to leave at three o'clock, and it was now already 1:30 p.m. I really had to hustle things up. I did the shopping for my resupply, which included an excessive amount of food because, to be honest, I was dead tired of being hungry all the time and losing weight that I couldn't afford to lose. I took my purchases to the hiker tent, where I plugged in my electronics to charge while I sorted and packed everything up. With such limited time I couldn't take a shower or do laundry, so I skipped the shower, but I did wash socks and underwear in the bathroom sink. I shaved with a cheap razor from the general store, and now had just a few minutes to call Annie. The twelve-passenger shuttle van pulled up, and there were ten hikers along with their gear ready to load up and head back to the trail. From what I gathered, the other nine hikers had arrived the day before and stayed in the bunkhouse for the night, taking today off, up till three o'clock. I was the only crazy hiker to spend less than three hours at the resort. But it was perfect for me because I really felt great and was ready to hike some more miles. After we were dropped off, I hiked another seven miles, and quit at just past six o'clock with another 20 miles behind me for the day. Another 20 miles closer to home.

With my food bag stuffed so full that I couldn't even close it, I decided on a bigger than normal breakfast. I started with two packs of oatmeal, a handful of dried apricots, a 600-calorie almond bear claw pastry, a half liter of orange Tang, and hot coffee. I started hiking at exactly 6:30 a.m., and by seven I was already hungry again. I made myself wait till eight o'clock, then had the first of four 250-calorie Cliff Bars I'd alloted for the day. At lunchtime, I had a flour burrito filled with cheese and summer sausage, half a bag of Fritos, and a handful of nuts, which made for a meal that was well over 1,000 calories. Even with my belly full, I was already starting to plan what I would have for dinner. I found myself to be in a constant state of incurable hunger that was impossible to fully satisfy.

When I mailed my bear canister to my son Brian, I had included a few other items that I knew I wouldn't need, to help lighten my backpack weight. My micro spikes, an extra battery bank, and a bottle of Deet were jettisoned. In all, I was able to reduce my pack weight by close to four pounds.

The trail was once again leading me through an area with unimpressive views, which was okay because it allowed me to concentrate on laying down some miles. With the exception of the beautiful view I caught of Noble Lake, there was nothing much to see, so it was nose to the trail pretty much all day. I had told myself that if I didn't see another beautiful view for the remainder of the hike, I wouldn't be disappointed or dissatisfied, because I had seen enough gorgeous views for a lifetime. There may not have been any good views, but the trail was definitely good to me, with limited climbs, fairly good trail conditions, and plenty of water available all day long.

One thing had become apparent, though, fall was in the air. The plants were wilting, drooping, turning yellow and brown, ready to go dormant. I could feel the season was changing, which made me realize that my days on the trail were almost up. It was time to finish up this hike.

Time to go home.

My habit was to spend time in the comfort of my tent each night researching and planning what the following day's hike would bring, looking at things like changes in elevation and upcoming water sources, and I always tried to identify potential campsites. It was looking like for tomorrow night there would be a campsite at 20 miles, and then not another spot for fourteen miles further on. Twenty miles would have been too close to get in the miles I needed. Thirty-four miles was a long distance, and would be my longest mile day so far.

There were three ways to hike more miles. You would start hiking earlier, you could hike faster, or you could keep hiking longer. You could also do any combination of the three, including doing all three. Which was what I did. I started hiking at 5:50 a.m. the next morning by the limited ambient light of a crescent moon, a sky full of stars, and my trusty headlamp. My bonus for the early start was that it positioned me to see a beautiful sunrise. The early morning miles were really good, with a smooth, flat trail and no obstacles, making navigating in the semi-darkness an easy task. I was putting on quick miles...until my approach to Carson Pass. Here the terrain got pretty rough and slowed my forward progress. That was okay, though, because there were some beautiful views. After I got to the pass, it wasn't long before I was crossing California State Route 88, where I had imagined lovely visions of epic trail magic...which never came to fruition. But the next best thing to trail magic did appear there—trash cans. It was always a good day when you could unload the useless weight of the garbage you'd been carrying in your pack. After Carson Pass the trail really opened up, and I was able to make up time and miles. I got to my planned campsite at 6:40 p.m. Just a bit later than typical for me, but with a record 33.8 miles hiked.

I stayed up a bit late to make some additional repairs to my shorts. I had to stitch up a new hole in the pocket where I kept my phone, and to re-stitch the seat, as well. That's what happens when you wear the same clothes every day, month after month. Other equipment fails included a broken buckle on my backpack from when I cinched it too tight—not a major concern. I was also dealing with a small leak in my sleep pad, that so far had just required that I re-blow it up once a night. My fifth pair of shoes, the ones I'd hoped would take me to the finish of the trail, were getting holes in the uppers. I used some duct tape to fix that, but the soles were getting pretty worn too. Everything—including me—only had to make it another 245 miles. It was now just 245 miles to Chester California, the end of my 2,650-mile journey.

That night I enjoyed listening to the gentle breeze and the resulting steady rain of pine needles falling on my tent, until finally giving in to deep sleep. When I awoke in the morning, I completed my routine as usual, and was hiking by 6:30 a.m. The trail was covered with those same pine needles—another warning shot across the bow. Fall really was coming, and winter wouldn't be too far behind.

Immediately after getting to Echo Lake, the trail follows the shoreline, then starts an ascent on a foot-bruising, shoe-wrecking, rocky trail. Summer cottages along the lakeshore that had likely been recent centers of activity, now sat empty and boarded up for the certain approach of winter.

The timing for lunch couldn't have been better. It was close to noon when I found myself at the base of my next big climb, Dicks Pass. Dicks Pass sits at an elevation of 9,400 feet, but at its base was Susie Lake, the perfect shady spot where I would enjoy my lunch in peaceful serenity. After lunch I felt really good, and more than ready to take on Dicks Pass. In fact, I found myself passing eight or nine other day hikers on my way up. It was shortly after I reached the Pass that I hit a wall. All at once I felt worn out, as though the life had been sucked out of me. I started tripping and stumbling as though I had been drugged, and I knew I needed to stop before I hurt myself. I had planned on hiking 30 miles, but that was not going to happen. I checked Guthook for water and nearby campsites, but this section was looking really limited for both. I finally decided to hike to Middle Velma Lake, the only reliable water for miles, where I could filter water to take to the next viable campsite. When I arrived at the lake, I found a spot I would ordinarily have passed up because is was sloped and barely big enough for my tent. In other words, at that moment it was perfect.

It was only 4:45 p.m., but I was done for the day. After setting up my tent, I crawled in and would have gone to sleep, but I made myself write my journal entry first. I was convinced my problem was that I had been hitting the trail ridiculously hard these past weeks, and it had finally caught up with me. Although I'd only managed to hike 23 miles that day, the following morning would bring a brand-new day, and I was sure I would make up some miles. But, for the moment, it was time for lights out.

I got what I needed that night—ten hours of much-needed sleep. When I awoke, I started thinking back to the previous day and my sudden loss of energy. I had a feeling that in addition to being physically exhausted, I might have allowed myself to become dehydrated. It was as I had predicted—it was a new day, and on this new day, I committed to keeping myself hydrated.

Word on the street, or in this case, the trail, was talk of an early winter storm heading our way. Hikers are a really good source of pertinent information, even better about sharing it. Throw in an occasional local day hiker or two, and you can really assemble the data needed to help make good decisions. I was already planning on going into Truckee for my next resupply, so I decided I might as well stay the night to see how the weather played out. The forecast was calling for rain at the lower elevations, but heavy snow above 5000 feet. The storm was forecast to be a high wind event, as well. My strides that morning seemed longer and with greater purpose than usual, almost as though my legs had minds of their own. They just seemed to take over. "Hey Whistler, we'll take it from here and get you home. Just sit back and enjoy the ride."

The trail conditions were excellent, with a smooth trail and no obstacles for miles upon miles. There were times I didn't feel like I was walking as much as rolling along. The views were absolutely beautiful, especially while hiking across a five-mile ridge overlooking the ski slopes of Tahoe and incredible views of Lake Tahoe. The winds on the ridge were pretty intense, so I could just imagine what it would be like during a storm, such as the one that was on its way. The few hikers I met that day all spoke of getting off the trail to avoid the coming bad weather. I was less than 190 miles from Chester and extremely anxious to finish, but common sense dictated getting off the trail and waiting out the storm.

It was slim pickings for breakfast the next morning. So, I prepared one of my specialties, which, if nothing else, filled the huge hole in my stomach—chicken ramen with instant mashed potatoes, better known on the trail as a Ramen Bomb. It would serve its intended purpose—to get me the next twelve miles to Donner Ski Ranch. I was ready to start hiking, but just then I noticed the beautiful sunrise peeking up from the horizon. It was one of those vivid sunrises that you only see when there is a storm brewing. I turned off my headlamp and just waited to behold and be witness to another new and glorious day. It also occurred to me that I had phone and data service, so I FaceTimed Annie and we watched the sun come up together. Once it made its appearance, it was time for me to go to work.

The first couple of miles were easy going, but then I came to Tinker Knob. At 8,949 feet, it was an early morning heart-racing climb. By now, the pre-storm winds had kicked in, and were doing their very best to knock me off my feet. After reaching the peak of Tinker Knob, I followed a ridge that was absolutely amazing. The sun was in perfect alignment to turn one of the many lakes far below in the valley into a giant reflecting pool. As I got closer to Historic U.S. Highway 40 at Donner Pass, the day hikers increased by great numbers. The conversations with everyone I met on the trail quickly turned to the weather. After I arrived at Old Hwy 40, I made an immediate left turn and headed toward the Donner Ski Ranch. While reading and researching comments on Guthook the night before, I couldn't help but notice they have a restaurant, and that thru-hikers can get a free beer by showing their hiking permit. They had me at free beer. The ski ranch was only about half a mile off trail, and so worth what I thought at the time would just be a side trip for lunch. I ordered a cheeseburger with fries and washed it down with that free beer.

I had learned long ago that if you need information, sit at the bar. The bartender was really good at his job and able to multitask with ease. Without having a clue where I might be able to stay that night to weather the storm, I asked the bartender if he had any suggestions. Well, it turned out the ranch has a dormitory for their winter ski season associates, and they book bunks to thru-hikers in the off season for 30 bucks a night, showers and laundry included. That was a great deal because a hotel room in Truckee was over $200 a night, and another ten miles away. My good fortune placed me just a half mile from the trail, providing easy access once the storm had passed.

I still needed to shop for my resupply, so my next challenge was to get a ride to the Safeway supermarket in Truckee. I grabbed my backpack and walked to Old U.S. 40 and stuck out my thumb. The third car pulled over and took me to the front door of the Safeway. Getting back to Donner Ski Ranch ended up being a lot more difficult. For that, I used Uber.

Meanwhile, my next dilemma was whether or not my shoes would make it to Chester. I was just 178 miles from finishing my hike, and pretty convinced those guys would make it. I had worn Altra Timps for the entirety of my hike, but there is actually an issue Altra needs to resolve. There are four lugs on the sole of each shoe that, after about 200 miles, come loose. When I was in a town and able to, I purchased Super Glue and glued the lugs back down so that they wouldn't catch anything on the trail and cause me to trip. With that fix, I was able to get about 500 miles out of each pair. I was now on my fifth and hopefully last pair.

That bunkroom at Donner Ski Ranch ended up being my own private suite. With no one sharing the large seven-bunk room, I spread out and took my time completing my chores. The use of an actual washing machine and dryer got my clothes surprisingly clean compared to my creek and lake washings. I cleaned my cook pot and water filter for what I realized would likely be the last time before I finished my hike. As was now my habit, I purchased more food than would fit in my food bag, but I didn't care. The additional calories would be worth the effort it took to tote it all up the last remaining mountains that lay ahead. As I prepared to shower, I was horrified by the reflection in the mirror. I looked back at a totally unrecognizable person. My legs had taken all the nutrients they needed, but had left little nourishment for the rest of me. From the waist down, I look like I could model men's socks, from the waist up I look like a frail, starving hiker.

While at Safeway the day before, they'd made an announcement they were running a five-dollar special on doughnuts. Hello, that got my attention. I raced across the store to the bakery, prepared to fight some little old lady for the last box. I got my doughnuts, and later regretted having only gotten one box. I picked up two bags of Fritos because they were two for six dollars instead of the regular price of $3.79 each. A bag of Fritos has nine servings at 160 calories per serving. As a starving hiker, I guiltlessly consumed an entire bag of 1,440 calories while I caught up on some emails. I did do the adult thing, though, by purchasing some bananas and a two-pound bag of California's finest green seedless grapes. I binged on those while I binge-watched *The Walking Dead* on Netflix.

With nothing else to do, I took a rare late morning nap. It was 10:30 a.m. when I heard the door open and two hikers, Plugging Along and Boppin entered my private suite, which had all of a sudden become a bunkroom again. This hiking duo was southbound, and planning to take a couple of days off to avoid the storm.

As forecast, the snow started at about two o'clock that afternoon, blowing horizontally and causing visibility for car drivers and hikers alike to have been near zero. While having lunch that afternoon, a hiker from the U.K. told the rest of us that he was heading back to the trail. My first thought was that he was a better man than me. My second thought was that he was out of his blooming mind. It was just before dinner when he returned after hiking up to Tinker Knob. He told us the winds were too strong and visibility was too dangerous to hike in, so he'd returned to the safety and shelter of DSR. I had been hoping to hike out in the morning, but was having second thoughts and booked my bunk for another night.

Seriously? Dungeons and Dragons? Rene, the bartender and permanent year-round resident of the house I was bunking in warned me and my bunkmates that Saturday night was his nerding out night. Rene let us know that he and his friends would be playing Dungeons and Dragons, and that they might stay up late and make a bit of noise. Thanks for the warning Rene, and for that lousy night's sleep! I finally got to sleep around one o'clock in the morning, and unfortunately my trained hiker self woke up at the normal time of 4:30 a.m. When I crawled out of my bunk, Trail-name-withheld-to-protect-his-identity was heading to the bathroom. He came out to the common area and explained that he had no idea how he'd gotten back to the bunkroom from the ranch bar the night before. In fact, as he stood there nearly naked, he shared that he couldn't remember taking his clothes off, where they were, or where his wallet and credit card were. Thankfully, he later found them in his shoe.

Meanwhile, Mr. sensible Whistler had been in his bunk at seven o'clock watching Netflix, then woke up in the morning and enjoyed a fruit smoothie, banana, his last two remaining doughnuts, and coffee for breakfast. My other bunkmate, Plugging Along, couldn't take the filth left in the kitchen by our resident bartending Dungeons and

Dragons-playing housemate and friends, and spent the entire morning cleaning up their mess.

As I looked out over the beautiful winter wonderland that morning, my first thought was, "What will I eat today?" My next thought was that I was seriously disappointed I couldn't hike out, but was still happy with my decision to wait out the storm in safety.

The restaurant opened at eleven, with myself and my bunkmates standing at the door when they did. I ordered a large pepperoni pizza and a Sierra Nevada. I paced myself and was successful in eating only half of my pizza and reserving the other half for dinner. With each bite and sip of beer, I told myself, "Only eat half, only eat half, only eat half." I am truly a man of strong convictions and absolute willpower. With lunch taken care of and dinner all set for later, it was time to take another nap. My muscles and bones appreciated this unscheduled break, but I was going out of my mind and couldn't wait to get back to my purpose. It was past time to finish this.

What happened next wasn't at all what I had expected. I woke up at around two-thirty in the morning to use the bathroom, and took a peek outside. I couldn't believe how much it had snowed. By seven that morning I was out of my bunk, in the kitchen, and making toast with peanut butter and a cup of coffee. With daylight breaking, it was far worse than any of us had expected. Boppin and Plugging Along had already decided to hike over to the Clair Tappaan Lodge which was about a mile and a half away. The benefit being that you can get their hiker deal of $35 for a bunk and $35 for the meal plan of breakfast, lunch, and dinner. Lone Wolf had arrived late the evening before, and was now our newest bunkmate. Lone Wolf and I had been leap-frogging one another since Washington. You may recall, it was Lone Wolf who'd arrived at the northern monument within minutes of me, and was the hiker who, along with her friend, had taken my photo for me before I crossed the Canadian border. She also happened to be finishing her hike in Chester, and after some discussion, we had agreed to hike out together in the morning.

But the heavy new snow quickly changed our minds. I looked at Guthook, and found that we were just 7.4 miles from the Peter Grubb Hut, which remained open to hikers in the off season. Lone Wolf and I both decided we would hike out that afternoon and spend the night in the shelter. The shelter has a fireplace, and according to Guthook, was fully stocked with firewood. This new plan would place us nearly eight miles farther up the trail, and allow for an early start the next morning.

Meanwhile, I received a phone call from Plugging Along, informing me that he and Boppin were on their way back from Clair Tappaan Lodge. He told me they didn't like the vibe of the place. I think that may have been code for there wasn't a bar. I and my bunkmates enjoyed lunch together, and afterward, Lone Wolf and I prepared to make our way back to the bunkroom to pack up and then we hit the trail.

The snow at lower elevations was just about four to five inches deep, but up to eighteen inches at the higher elevations. It wasn't bad hiking at all because the wind had fully subsided. Wet shoes, socks, and subsequently wet feet, were the only discomforts. We arrived at the hut at around 5:30 p.m. and the first thing I did was start a fire in the wood stove. We both took off our wet shoes and socks and hung them close— but not too close—to the fire to dry them out. The hut itself was perfect, much nicer than I had expected. Besides the wood stove and the endless wood supply, the hut was wired with electric lights. The lights were powered by a solar panel and battery system. We were able to get the inside temperature up to 54 degrees, which was far warmer than it was outside. Lone Wolf and I agreed on a departure time of seven the next morning. The weather forecast was calling for sunny skies and temperatures in the forties. I woke up three times that night, climbed down from the upstairs loft, and stoked the wood stove with more firewood. It was worth the effort because we woke up to a warm and cozy cabin.

Erin (Lone Wolf) at the Peter Grubb Hut

It was now the first day of October. As planned, we were on the trail at exactly seven o'clock, and made our way up the snow-covered trail. The higher we climbed, the deeper the snow, and the more difficulty we had following the trail. With soaking-wet and freezing-cold feet, we trudged on. Hiking through the deep snow seriously slowed our forward progress, but we kept slogging on. The elevation changes were minor, and if not for the snow, it could have been a 30-mile day. The snow was up to three feet deep with higher drifts in places, especially above 8000 feet, but we trudged on.

We had gone all day and not met a single other hiker until around five o'clock when I ran into Klondike. Lone Wolf, who had been following me and was a few minutes behind, caught up and joined the conversation with the sole SOBO hiker of the day. We shared hiking data with Klondike and he with us. As we hiked on, I got ahead of Lone Wolf again as I was now following Klondike's footsteps. That ended up being a serious mistake, because his footprints took me off the trail. Once I realized this, I used my GPS to find my way back to the trail by crossing an open, snow-covered field. I made my way to the creek where Lone Wolf and I had earlier agreed to collect water, and then hiked the additional half mile to our agreed-upon campsite at a dirt road that was now deep under snow. It was after six o'clock, and as I set up my tent, I kept expecting for Lone Wolf to come walking out of the woods, but she didn't. My guess was that when I lost the trail earlier by following Klondike's footprints, she had remained on the trail and gotten ahead of me. Not seeing me at the agreed-upon site, she might have continued north. But I walked to the trailhead, and there were no footprints heading north in the fresh snow. Lone Wolf was still somewhere behind me.

This was what could happen when you hike with someone. You feel responsible for them, which is both good and bad. We had earlier in the day agreed how hiking out together in that snow was a good idea. It was now seven o'clock and getting dark, and I was becoming worried like a father waiting for his daughter to come home from a date. Lone Wolf was a 38-year-old woman and had hiked the same 2,500 miles I had, and yet, I was still worried. I knew she had food and shelter, but I was still worried. At eight o'clock, I was in my tent and I saw the light of a headlamp through my tent. "Lone Wolf is that you?" I shouted.

Nope, it was two SOBO hikers, and they wanted to know if I'd seen Klondike.

"She's going to be fine." I told myself over and over. "She's going to be fine."

I woke up at three the next morning with crazy thoughts of Lone Wolf. It was 23 degrees out and I was shivering, while wondering what could have possibly happened to her. I knew she wasn't lost, but then I thought that even a seriously capable hiker like Lone Wolf could still end up injured. Yes, I convinced myself, she must have been hurt. A sprained ankle perhaps? Then I told myself, no, she just got tired and made camp early. Or, perhaps she'd found the perfect campsite and couldn't pass it up. Three o'clock in the morning, and there was no way I could return to sleep. The one thing I knew for certain was that she had a resupply box waiting for her at Sierra City. I decided I would hike there and wait for her. If she didn't show up for her resupply, I would contact the authorities. I ate, broke camp, and with headlamp on, started hiking the fifteen miles to Sierra City.

The hiking on that side of the mountain was a breeze. There was so little snow that I could actually see the trail. When I reached California State Route 49, I got a hitch almost immediately that took me the 1.5 miles to Sierra City. It's a very small town, one way in and one way out, so I'd definitely see her when she arrived. At noon, I decided that I'd eat lunch, and if she wasn't there by one o'clock, I'd call the police. I sat on the front porch of the General Store to eat the hamburger sitting before me, and just then a sheriff's SUV came up the street. I flagged him down and he pulled in, giving me the perfect opportunity to report a possible missing hiker. This whole time I was wondering to myself, was I overreacting? All I knew was, I couldn't hike another mile until I knew she was okay.

I gave the officer every detail, and actually surprised myself. I knew her full name. I never ask a hiker their real name, but for some reason I had asked her what hers was. I knew and described her equipment and clothes in full detail. I told the officer how Donner Ski Ranch would have her registration card with her phone and address information. He had been with me for 30 minutes taking down all this information, when I happened to look up the street and saw Lone Wolf. I didn't run, but I walked swiftly toward her. Her bottom lip quivered as she told me that she thought something had happened to me. We determined that she had misunderstood and had camped at the water source. I had been just half a mile ahead of her. Even with losing the trail as I had, I'd arrived at the creek, gotten water, and hiked to the dirt road before she'd made it to the creek. Meanwhile, the officer was happy with the safe outcome, although perhaps a bit disappointed because he said he enjoyed flying in the search helicopter.

Lone Wolf decided that she was going to take a zero in town, but I wanted to hike some more miles. I gathered my gear, we gave each other a hug, and said our goodbyes. I got a ride back to the trailhead the second I put out my thumb, and was hiking north by 2:30 p.m. I hiked fast and strong for another twelve miles. The entire time I wondered what I could or should have done differently. At the end of the day, what was most important was that everyone was okay, and that a crisis had been averted.

There is something about a cold, brisk morning that makes you just want to get moving. With my fingers nearly frozen, I knew the best antidote was to get my blood pumping. My late climb to and over Sierra Buttes the night before, and subsequent camp at Packsaddle Campground, had left me with just 124 miles to Chester. It was looking like a successful completion of my thru-hike was all but guaranteed. While the snow I'd hiked through yesterday afternoon had been soft, slushy, and slippery, it was now refrozen and crusty, which made for faster hiking. Puddles from the snowmelt were now miniature skating rinks, which required a bit of sidestepping. The name of the game today was: Hike as fast and as far as you can, Whistler. Hiking on the sun-exposed side of the mountain, I was able to make up time and distance. Hiking the northern side was slow going over the snow, especially in the afternoon when it was a slick and slippery mess. The snow was no deeper than my shins, but just deep enough to soak my socks and shoes.

At lunchtime I had just come to a dirt road with a fresh-water spring close by, so I took off my pack and sat in the middle of the road, feeling certain no one would be coming up that mountain pass. Two minutes later, sure enough, three four-wheeled ATVs came by and stopped. "Hunting season!" the first guy yelled to me.

Good God, I hoped so, after seeing all the artillery hanging off their four-wheelers. My first thought was that I'd been out in the woods so long I had missed the news of a Russian invasion. I swear I saw a box of hand grenades on one four-wheeler, and a rocket-launcher on another.

"Seen any deer?" asked the second guy.

"About a couple hundred," I replied.

That got their attention. But I explained about my hike and how I probably had seen a couple hundred deer during the past few months. They asked a lot of questions, the typical questions like, "What do you eat out there?" I politely answered all of their questions, then they fired up their ATVs and took off. It seemed to me that it would be pretty difficult to sneak up on a deer with all that noise. I didn't tell them that. Score another one for the deer.

It was looking like I wouldn't see another hiker, when all of a sudden two SOBO hikers appeared. I never got their names, but one was another northbound hiker who'd flipped to avoid the snow and would finish her hike at Kennedy Meadows South. The other was a true southbound hiker who was heading to the southern terminus. They would both have a rough time in the High Sierras where it was getting really cold and snow was already starting to fly.

I had a couple of climbs that took me to 7000 feet with some beautiful views, but what struck me was how just a few weeks ago, on September 11th, I had been on top of the world on Mount Whitney at14,505 feet, twice my current elevation.

The climbs were smaller and faster now, as I got closer to the end of my hike. As of that evening, I was just 94.4 miles from Chester. Knowing this had me even more motivated to keep moving.

I really don't want to be misunderstood here. I have loved this hike and had a huge appreciation for the opportunity of experiencing it all, but now it was time for me to go home.

I left camp at 6:00 a.m. sharp the next morning, with my headlamp trained on the trail directly in front of me, I was determined to get in some early miles. If that wasn't enough of an indication of wanting to get home, I don't know what would be. I turned off my night guidance system, a.k.a. headlamp, at seven o'clock and checked my distance. I'd hiked 2.7 miles that first hour before the sun had even come up. The trail tread was perfect for fast miles. Mostly rock-free and very little snow. For the early part of the day, it wound through a beautiful forest which offered no views worth mentioning, though that would change later.

It was a bit early for lunch, but at 11:30 I arrived at the Bear Creek bridge and decided that would be where I would enjoy my meal. I sat directly in the middle of the long bridge span with the rushing waters of Bear Creek 20 feet below me. I hadn't seen a hiker at all today, so I doubted I'd be in anyone's way. I took a full 45-minute break, then hopped up, put my pack on my back, and started the six-and-a-half-mile climb. When I had reached the top, I stopped and climbed Lookout Rock. This rock outcropping offered great views and made the big climb worth the effort. I finished the day after putting 30.5 miles behind me.

Six o'clock on the dot the next morning it was boots on the trail. I was on a mission. I had a nineteen-mile hike into the town of Belden for a lunch date with a fat hamburger and an oversized order of fries. I would also take a bit of time to finalize my travel plans. Annie had already researched the local bus and transit system in Chester. I was all set for getting to the Reno Airport, so all I needed to do was purchase my plane ticket. For that reason, I found myself practically running down the trail toward Belden.

I crunched along on the re-frozen snow and the hard-crusted mud with frozen footprints semi-permanently enshrined. The sun had been beckoned to undo the work of the prior night's freezing temperatures. I had just gotten to within two miles of town when I suddenly came upon a young man with a very full pack and a rifle at the ready. I slowed down and eventually came to a complete halt. If he was tracking a deer, I didn't want to be the guy that ruined his shot. He waved me over and pointed to two bucks further down and deep in the woods. It wasn't just hunting season, it was also rutting season, and those two bucks were fighting for that right. I couldn't believe I was fortunate enough to be witnessing this wild animal ritual. Afterward, the young man told me his name was Anders. I looked up at him quickly and with such surprise that I got an equally shocked look from him. You see, with just a couple of days left before I finished my hike, I had just been thinking of all the wonderful people I'd met along my journey. Virtually minutes before coming upon this hunter I was thinking about the young couple from Norway I had met, and was trying to remember their names—Tuva and Anders. But that was a different Anders.

This Anders shared that this was his very first hunt. Then he suddenly got down on one knee and carefully aimed his rifle in the direction of the bucks. It looked like there was going to be a loser in their fight. Anders took careful aim while he and I both held our breath. He was careful and deliberate as he squeezed the trigger. It was loud. My ears rang, and even though I had been expecting the shot, it shook me for a moment. Anders slowly and quietly stood up, and I could tell he was truly excited for getting his very first deer. Or had he...?

I liked Anders; he was soft spoken, and I could tell he was kind. He wasn't riding the backwoods on a four-wheeler ATV chasing deer, he was walking calmly and quietly, tracking the deer with a hunter's sharp senses. He'd heard those bucks and their antlers as they fought, something I would probably never have noticed. There was no bragging from him for what he had done, only a quiet sense of soothing tranquility over his successful hunt. Or had it been...?

As much as I wanted to continue to my destination, I told Anders I would stay with his pack while he climbed down to get the deer. He took his rifle, a large knife, a field saw for butchering, and wild game bags for what would be the final step in this process. I watched him climb down, knowing his heart must be pounding, racing with anticipation and excitement. He disappeared in the direction the buck had gone wounded to bleed out. Or had it...?

Just then Anders yelled up to me that there was no blood trail. He'd missed. I was sad for him, while at the same time elated for the deer. I figured someone was going to take that buck down one day, it just wasn't meant to be that day. Or wasn't it...?

I let Anders know that I would be moving on, and we said our goodbyes. He congratulated me on my hike as I walked away, and I wished him good luck on his hunt. I was probably half a mile farther down the trail when I heard another rifle shot coming from his direction. Did Anders get his buck after all? I'll never know for sure.

Anders preparing for his shot

I made it to Belden, ordered lunch, checked the airlines via my iPhone, and now it was my turn to pull the trigger. I did so, and purchased the plane ticket that would take me home to Nova Scotia in a few days. With that business taken care of, it was time to hike on.

With my brain scattered and running in every direction, I happened across a section hiker named Slash. She didn't seem too dangerous, so we chatted for a bit. Slash was planning on section hiking as far as she could get by the end of the month. When she asked about my hike, I told her I was just completing a thru-hike that would be finished when I made it to Chester. As I was telling her this, I realized I had a huge smile on my face. In fact, I couldn't stop smiling. She congratulated me on my hike, and we went our separate ways.

It was really starting to hit me that I was close to completing my hike. I was so close to achieving my purpose, and completing my hunt. Had I been searching for something? Or had I just been on a long walk...?

Did every question require an answer? Or could some questions be internalized and left unanswered? What I did know was that my journey had been incredibly rewarding and worth every mile. I believed some questions now had answers, while I simultaneously found answers to questions still unasked.

Just 38.6 miles to Chester…

There was no big rush for me to get on the trail the next morning. I only needed to hike 25 or so miles to set myself up for an early finish the following day. The morning climb was steep, and I felt pretty good knowing it would be the last major climb I'd have to do. Once again, I thought to myself how appreciative I was that my legs could make these climbs with relative ease. I came across a couple of hikers early in the day, and stopped to chat with them. They were just starting to pack their gear, and I could tell they weren't in a big rush, either. Their trail names were Shakespeare and Firefly, and they were doing a section hike from Chester to Belden. Shakespeare shared that they had already hiked over 400 miles of the PCT. With that same big smile on my face, I told them I was finishing my thru-hike at Chester. They were genuinely happy for me, and so kind.

This last full day of my hike was a solitary day for personal reflection. Each step I took put the past behind me, while also being a step toward my future. Each step was made with purpose, without hesitation, always knowing that what lay ahead was good...positively good. When I made it to the top of my climb, what did I see again, but Mount Shasta. It was in the far distance, but still regal with its perpetually snow-covered peak.

Later, I came upon three guys riding mountain bikes, carrying all the gear that goes with mountain biking. This was quite interesting because I had hiked over 2,600 miles on the PCT and hadn't found a single illiterate person who couldn't read the posted signs that clearly stated the PCT is a foot and equestrian trail. No mechanical vehicles allowed. In fact, you don't even have to be able to read, because they post pictures of a bike with a big red circle and line through it for those who can't. Hundreds of thousands of man-hours go into the building and maintenance of these trails, and mountain bikes do nothing but tear them up. I could tell by the sheepish looks on their faces that they were fully aware of this. They tried to be polite as they dismounted their bikes to allow me to pass. I kept my negative thoughts of disappointment to myself and hiked on.

I cooked what would be my last dinner on the trail that night, and would prepare my last breakfast the following morning. The only food left in my food bag would be five protein bars. My backpack was so light, I barely noticed its weight on my back. With just over thirteen miles to go, I would arrive at California State Route 36 between ten and eleven on the next and final day of my hike. There would be no fanfare, no marching band, sign, or monument to mark the end of my adventure. I would just be a hiker exiting the deep woods of Northern California looking for a ride eight miles east to a small town called Chester. I'd be a hiker leaving God's glorious wilderness and looking to re-enter society. Would that society be the same as it had been when I left it behind? Would I be the same person who had entered the desert on April 11th, when I exited the Northern California woods on October 7th?

Sleep wasn't in the cards that night. I was up at 3:30 a.m. and anxious to get moving, so I was packed and on the trail by ten after five. It was an hour and a half before sunrise, so I was hiking by starlight and my trusty headlamp. This was it—the final miles of my journey.

At one point I realized how quiet it was. I stopped, stood perfectly still, and turned my headlamp off as I looked to the heavens. The sky was brilliantly lit by millions of stars, seemingly made brighter by the deafening silence. All I could see were the stars and the dark shapes of the tall conifers that surrounded me. I hoped upon hope that I might get one last PCT sunrise, that the trail might take me from the deep woods to an east-facing outcropping to stand upon and watch my final sunrise. What I got instead was a fluorescent orange glow through the forest, which I happily accepted as a pretty good consolation prize.

My thoughts this morning mostly lingered on the solitude and loneliness of the trail during these last days of my hike. Seeing just one or two people a day had been the recent norm, and I actually appreciated that since it allowed for private time to truly reflect. Then of course there was the feeling of success and personal achievement I felt for completing this monumental hike. Next, I pondered, if it were possible, who would I want to see when I reached mile 2,650? Annie would obviously be the very first person on that list. But I'd also like to see all of the people who had supported me on my hike. I'd want to high-five them, hug them, and personally thank them for their help. I couldn't name them all, for the list was ridiculously long. Family, friends, trail angels, readers of my journal, perfect strangers, but all supporting me nonetheless, with everything from simple messages of encouragement to care packages mailed to me along my trek. These selfless acts of kindness drove me, motivated me, and honestly, held me accountable to myself and my goal. I also thought back to The Incident, and to the time I was lying in that Salem, Oregon, hospital, certain my fall had ended my hike. I recalled telling Annie, "I guess my hike is over," and her responding, "No, it's not Bill. Come home, heal, then go back and finish it." I remember looking at my phone and asking myself, "Who is this woman? How could I be so blessed?"

As I hiked and ticked off those last remaining miles, I continued to reflect on the past six months. Finally, as I reached the point where I only had ten miles left, I started a countdown with Annie via text messages. Ten miles...nine miles...eight miles...and so on. When I was a tenth of a mile from Hwy 36, I FaceTimed her, and she joined me live as I took those final steps.

But in reality, she had been with me every step I had taken.

The magic didn't end there. No, my story wasn't quite over yet.

Hike 2,650 miles: check. Get from the trail where it intersects with Hwy 36 to Chester eight miles east: Hmmm... Start walking, Whistler, and stick out that stupidly lucky thumb of yours.

Maybe a tenth of a mile into my eight-mile extended journey, a car heading in the opposite direction passed me, made an abrupt stop, U-turned, and pulled up behind me.

"Hello Whistler! Remember us?"

It was Shakespeare and Firefly back from their section hike, and they just happened to drive by minutes after I completed my thru-hike. Yep, the magic continued.

A HIKER'S PRAYER

With that first step, you can't change your mind,
you will leave your love, leave her behind.
Hike on, my boy, hike on, hike on.
There will be hunger, there will be thirst,
there will be pain that will surely hurt.
Hike on, my boy, hike on, hike on.
Hike each day, that endless trail,
you will not quit; you will not fail.
Hike on, my boy, hike on, hike on.
When you are lost, it is true,
angels will watch over you.
Hike on, my boy, hike on, hike on.
When you take those final steps,
and it is time to no longer roam,
go home, my boy, go home, go home.

The last trail marker I saw before I finished my hike....

Acknowledgments

Well, there you have it, that was my thru-hike. Unique to me, special and different from all who had hiked before me, and from all who will come after. I hope I have given you, my readers, a true perspective of what a thru-hike on the Pacific Crest Trail can look like.

Would I have wanted to do anything differently? Yes, I would have preferred *not* to have taken that fall on my sixtieth birthday. Other than that, no, it was perfect. It was mine and will remain mine forever.

I don't know if it is possible to express how appreciative I am for the help and support I received before and along the way, without which this journey would never had been possible. Annie's unwavering love and support was paramount, and honestly, left me to question how I could possibly be so blessed to have her in my life. The trail angels and perfect strangers who give tirelessly of their time, hearts, and treasure to help us lowly hikers realize our dreams, continues to leave me in a constant state of puzzlement while I ask myself, why? The only answer I have is that people really are good. As an American Canadian, I am so proud of the people I encountered on and off the trail. In an informal survey, I asked numerous thru-hikers from all over the world what had surprised them most about their hike. Without fail, every time, the answer was the same: they were surprised by how giving Americans were. Some shared that when they told friends and family they were going to America to hike the PCT, they had been told, "You better be careful." What they expected was what they see on TV, in newspapers, and what is spread throughout the world by the media as a mostly false narrative. Are Americans perfect? Absolutely not. But then, none of us humans are. Kind and giving trail angels are the epitome of our best ambassadors to the rest of the world.

In this book, I wrote about much of the help I had received along this journey. To those named and unnamed, thank you again. I offer special thanks to friends, new and old, for their support by way of packages sent, text messages, emails of encouragement, and safe refuge in my times of need. Thank you, God, for watching over me and for providing the skilled, knowledgeable, and compassionate medical attention of Dr. Barr, Dr. Conyers and nurses.

And of course, I would be remiss if I did not thank Mark, a.k.a. Scooby, for his support, friendship, and especially for going far out of his way to drive me the 650 miles past the Sierra Nevada to Chester, California.

Finally, what's next? Hmm... I'm taking a serious look at the Continental Divide Trail. There just might be a triple crown in Whistler's future. Please stay tuned!

About the Author

Born in New York and raised in Miami, Bill Monk retired after a successful 31-year career with a large supermarket chain in the United States. Since his retirement, he has lived in Nova Scotia, Canada, with his wife of forty years, Ann Marie. Together they own and operate A Seafaring Maiden Bed and Breakfast, Ann Marie's 140-year-old ancestral home in Granville Ferry, Nova Scotia. An outdoor enthusiast, Bill enjoys hiking, kayaking, snowshoeing, and biking, and his hobbies include furniture restoration, woodworking, and the loving care and maintenance of their historic heritage home.

Bill's first book *Whistler's Walk: The Appalachian Trail in 142 Days* was released in 2018 to rave reviews.